The Study of Criminal Courts: Political Perspectives

The Study of Criminal Courts: Political Perspectives

Peter F. Nardulli, Editor
University of Illinois

Ballinger Publishing Company • Cambridge, Massachusetts
A Subsidiary of Harper & Row, Publishers, Inc.

International Standard Book Number: 0-88410-797-3

Library of Congress Catalog Card Number: 79-14848

Printed in the United States of America

Library of Congress Cataloging in Publication Data
Main entry under title:

The Study of criminal courts.

Includes index.
1. Criminal courts—United States—Addresses, essays, lectures. 2. Criminal justice, Administration of—United States—Addresses, essays, lectures. I. Nardulli, Peter F.
KF9223.A75S89 345′.73′01 79-14848
ISBN 0-88410-797-3

Contents

List of Figures

List of Tables

Preface

This collection of essays is an attempt to catalogue at least some of the significant advances in our understanding of criminal courts that have occurred over the past decade. The idea for it was conceived in the summer of 1977 after a series of telephone conversations with several researchers who were prominent in the study of criminal courts. The consensus of everyone was that while there had been significant conceptual and theoretical developments in a number of different directions, there had been no systematic attempt to "pull together" these efforts. As a first step toward that end a roundtable discussion on "The Study of Criminal Courts" was held at the 1978 Annual Meeting of the American Political Science Association.

The roundtable discussion was based upon earlier versions of the papers by Jacob, Zemans, Gibson, Kritzer, Flemming, and Heumann. The Sarat, Nardulli, and Cook chapters were prepared especially for this volume. The different chapters touch upon one of three topics: criminal courts as dispute processing institutions, theoretical approaches to the study of criminal courts, and innovative approaches to long-standing policy issues. The essays in the first section are primarily concerned, in different ways, with elaborating upon the observation that much of what criminal courts do might be labeled dispute processing. Essays in the second category provide overviews of different theoretical approaches and attempt to identify promising avenues for future research. The third group of essays approach different problem areas (bail, plea bargaining, sentencing) in light of recent developments in our understanding of criminal court phenomena and make original contributions in each area.

I believe that this collection goes a long way toward meeting its objectives. A thorough reading of the various essays will give the reader a good grasp on many of the recent intellectual developments in this area. It should also give researchers and policymakers some aid in constructing future agendas. Whatever the ultimate contribution of this book, it comes as the result of the diligence of a number of people. I want to acknowledge first of all the efforts of the contributors, many of whom had to put up with my overbearing comments through several drafts. The help and encouragement of Carol Franco at Ballinger Publishing Company also facilitated a very difficult task. Anna Merritt's long hours of editing should also be acknowledged and applauded. Her careful attention to detail, precision, and clarity of thought have made this a better collection. Florence Edmison typed most of the final drafts and should be commended for doing such a fine job under difficult circumstances—I have an annoying habit of peering over her shoulder whenever she types a manuscript of particular interest. Velma Sykes, Lorena McClain, and Jean Baker should also be acknowledged for their typing efforts on this work.

Peter F. Nardulli
Urbana, Illinois

Editor's Introduction

While empirically oriented legal scholars have sporadically examined the operations of criminal courts since at least the 1920s, political scientists have only recently begun to focus their research efforts in this direction. Political scientists interested in the relationship between law and politics have traditionally been concerned with such things as the Supreme Court, appellate courts, and constitutional law. With the notable exception of Herbert Jacob, who has been researching and writing in this area since the early 1960s, most political researchers have ignored the question of how trial-level courts distribute justice. This situation is rapidly changing. During the past decade a series of books on criminal courts has appeared: Klonoski and Mendelsohn (1970), Cole (1973), Jacob (1973), Eisenstein (1973), Neubauer (1974), Eisenstein and Jacob (1977), Levin (1977), Heumann (1978), and Nardulli (1978). As a result, the study of criminal courts, and trial-level courts in general, is quickly establishing itself as a distinct subfield within the area of law and politics.

Increased interest in this field of study over the last decade has produced notable intellectual developments. The aim of this collection of original essays is to recount as well as develop some of these recent advances. More specifically, the essays will be concerned with developments in three areas. The first pertains to the rather recent observation that criminal courts are more than agents of social control concerned with norm enforcement. They are also dispute processing institutions. This has implications for studying, understanding, and evaluating criminal courts, as the essays in Part I indicate. The second area to be addressed in this collection concerns theoretical developments relating to the operations of criminal courts. Here there have been significant advances at three levels of analysis: the individual level (applications of role and attitude theory); the contextual level (organizational approaches); and the environmental level (political culture). Essays in Part II provide an overview of the developments in each of these areas, as well as some insights to guide future research. Part III addresses issues that have generated controversy for over fifty years: bail, plea bargaining, and sentencing. Each essay in this section provides fresh insights into each of these areas.

The first essay in Part I, Herbert Jacob's "Related Party Disputes in Criminal Courts," begins by reviewing data on one category of disputes regularly handled by criminal courts, related party cases. What is striking about these data is the frequency with which such cases involve property-related complaints such as burglary and theft; their existence in murder, rape, and assault cases has long been known. While these related party cases are often considered "junk" or "garbage" cases, Jacob contends that it is important to understand their implications for, and impact upon, criminal courts. They cause considerable problems for criminal courtroom personnel and criminal justice policymakers because they seem to defy resolution through normal criminal court procedures. In addition, they keep coming back!

Because of the significance of related party cases, Jacob examines the characteristics of the victims and incidents in such cases and compares them with stranger cases. After speculating as to the likely differences in the two types of cases he examines several hypotheses using data on cases involving assaults, which were collected in the victimization surveys. He compares the two types of cases with regard to the victim's social class and attitudes toward the police and the characteristics of the incident giving rise to the complaint. What is most remarkable about the data analysis is that it shows more similarities than differences in the two types of cases.

In Jacob's view, the fact that the data show related party cases not to fit the stereotype of "unsolved conflicts of poor people who lack alternative resources to resolve problems" creates difficulties for those desiring to understand how courts operate, or how they should operate. As a first step in clarifying these difficulties, Jacob contends that we should recognize that courts really perform two very different kinds of functions. The first, dispute settlement, is the most widely understood. The second is dispute processing. The difference between the two functions is that in the latter cases courtroom officials have no real intention of resolving or settling the case. They merely intercede at one stage of a continuing conflict and process it until the disputants lose interest. This is acceptable, Jacob contends, because the parties have no desire to settle the conflict. One party simply desires to use the court temporarily as an ally in order to establish a new equilibrium in his relationship with the other party. This explains why such cases keep recurring on criminal court dockets even though they are seldom "resolved." Because of the difference between the two types of functions, we should look at different factors to understand how they are performed, and we should use different criteria in evaluating criminal court operations.

Like Jacob, Frances Zemans, in "Dispute Processing: The Medium and the Message of Criminal Justice," contends that one must consider the role played by disputes and dispute processing in the criminal justice system. To fail to do so, she argues, is to ignore important environmental factors which are essential to understanding the operation of the criminal process. After criticizing the traditional view that criminal courts enforce norms while civil courts process disputes, Zemans cites several developments documenting the growing recognition of the role dispute processing plays within the criminal realm. She then introduces a dispute processing model which, she contends, will eventually lead to a single theoretical framework applicable to both the criminal and civil process.

In this essay Zemans develops the model only with respect to the criminal process. She focuses on three stages: the decision to seek formal redress (usually made by one of the initial disputants); the decision to formalize the dispute (usually made by a police officer); and the dispositional decisions (usually made by various courtroom actors). The reason for the broad scope of the model is implicit in Zeman's approach. To understand why courts operate as they do, we need to know more about how the cases which they process got there, a point missed in most analyses of criminal courts.

To focus research on these matters at the various stages, Zemans proposes a three-dimensional model which includes an incident dimension, an interpersonal dimension, and an accessibility dimension. Basic to her analysis is the contention that the model applies to all three stages she discusses, even though they are dominated by different actors. All that is necessary is that the model be adapted somewhat to reflect differences across stages. To support this contention, after discussing the various dimensions of the model and their subcomponents, Zemans elaborates upon the implications of the model for the different stages of the process. She concludes by noting the potential advantages of her model over others.

While Zemans stresses the importance of the role of disputes and dispute processing for understanding criminal courts, Austin Sarat is concerned with various expectations surrounding the operations of criminal courts. In "Doing the Dirty Business of Coping with Crime," Sarat asserts his belief that these expectations are derived from a fundamental misunderstanding of what the courts do. These misconceptions, combined with the increased visibility of criminal courts due to unprecedented levels of empirical inquiry by social scientists, have led to the contemporary "crisis" of American criminal courts. Implicit in his argument is the notion that a better understanding of what criminal courts do, and a corresponding adjustment of the expectations concerning them, will do more to quell this crisis than the implementation of various ambitious programs for criminal court reform.

At the heart of his paper, Sarat outlines and critiques three of the most prominent, but unwarranted, societal demands made upon courts: the demand for strict legality; the demand for social defense; and the demand for social services. The demand for strict legality is an expectation that court processes be in accordance with legal dictates and procedures; it is unjustified because these legalities have so little to do with the day-to-day problems encountered by courtroom personnel. The demand for social defense is a demand for punishment. Sarat believes this expectation is unwarranted because of the controversy surrounding punishment and its consequences. If society cannot determine whether incarceration deters crime or creates criminals, then it should not criticize judges for being indecisive or inconsistent in their sentencing behavior. The demand for social services pertains to the expectation that courts provide individualized treatment to defendants suffering from various problems resulting in maladaptive behavior; it is an unwarranted demand because courtroom personnel have neither the competence nor the facilities to analyze such problems. In addition, courts do not have the technology to administer solutions even if they could be devised.

It should be stressed that Sarat's chapter is not arguing that courts should be free of external demands or expectations. Courts, like any other social organization, should be responsive to external demands. Sarat's point is simply that these demands should be formulated with regard to what criminal courts in fact do. To this end he suggests viewing criminal courts in light of what decision-making theorists call incrementalism. Incrementalism is a method of decision-making based upon the belief that social decisions are tentative and subject to error. It is cautious and accepts the fact that decisions are always based upon inadequate information. Because of these basic attributes, Sarat believes that incrementalism provides the basis for a more appropriate descriptive paradigm of decision-making in criminal courts than do earlier paradigms. Implicit in this assertion, of course, is the recognition that criminal courts are essentially decision-making units (that is, their outputs are decisions) which frequently work under adverse conditions. After describing the relevance of incrementalism to criminal courts more fully, Sarat elaborates upon the more realistic expectations that can be formulated concerning criminal courts from an incrementalist perspective.

James Gibson, in the first essay in Part II, thoroughly reviews one very general, individual-level approach to understanding criminal court operations, role theory. In "A Role Theoretic Model of Criminal Court Decision-making," he contends that while there have been many theoretical approaches to the study of criminal court decision-making, and few attempts to integrate them, role theory provides a promising integrative framework. To outline its potential, he first reviews role theory, particularly as it has been used in judicial research at the appellate level. In his view there have been two main problems with this research. The first concerns the ambiguity over the relationship between different role orientations and behavior; the second concerns the inadequate conceptualization of role constructs. In addition to these general problems, there is also the more specific question of the applicability of role theory to trial-level courts.

To resolve the first two problems, Gibson proposes a reconceptualization of role theory. At the heart of this reconceptualization is the notion that role orientations are judges' beliefs about what kinds of factors should affect a particular decision. The basic implication of this assertion is that for judges who adhere to one orientation various decisional criteria are relevant for a given decision. For judges who adhere to a different role orientation, however, a wholly different set of criteria may be relevant for the same decision. Thus, Gibson's approach not only clarifies some conceptual problems surrounding role theory but also clearly specifies the relationship between role orientations and decisional behavior.

With the notion of role theory and decisional behavior clarified, he moves to the question of the applicability of role theory to trial-level courts. This question arises because of two distinctions between trial-level and appellate-level courts. The first is that while the notion of precedent and adherence to precedent looms large in appellate court decision-making, it has very little to do with most of the critical decisions made in criminal courts. This is important because most applications of role theory in judicial research have focused upon judges' orientation toward precedent. For Gibson, however, this is not a problem. His reconceptualization of role theory is broad enough to incorporate judges' feelings about the legitimacy of a wide variety of factors (for example, defendant attributes, public opinion) relevant to decision-making in criminal courts. All that needs to be done is to reorient role concepts to the distinctive substance of criminal court decisions.

The second problem is more serious and challenging. It concerns differences in the context of decision-making across the two types of courts. At the appellate level, decisions are more the result of individual orientation and preferences than they are at the trial level. In criminal courts, particularly, research has shown that much decision-making is shared and is constrained by a series of established norms and mutual expectations. Thus, one could argue that a focus on individual preferences and orientations would not be extremely helpful in understanding decisional behavior. While not disputing the existence of a these organizational constraints, Gibson disagrees. His basic contention is that the best way to understand the impact of these constraints and expectations is to understand how the individual actors view them. He argues that they can simply be incorporated into the general role model.

At this point he reviews some empirical evidence on the relevance of role theory to criminal court decision-making. This is important because, as previously noted, most court-related empirical research has taken place at the appellate level. He presents evidence using role orientations in conjunction with case attributes, attitudes, and public opinion as decisional criteria. He concludes that the results of these analyses demonstrate the promise of the role theoretic approach. He also outlines some directions for future research.

Peter Nardulli, in "Organizational Analyses of Criminal Courts," provides an overview of one approach to understanding contextual determinants of courtroom behavior, organization theory. It should be noted that treating organizational approaches as contextual approaches does not mean ignoring or excluding individual- or environmental-level factors. Rather, organizational approaches simply stress the primacy of context. After pointing out that studies normally considered within the organizational paradigm constitute a diverse lot, he reviews the development of this body of thought in two areas. The first pertains to thoughts on how the "court organization" operates; the second section pertains to thoughts on why courts operate as administrative bodies.

Nardulli examines the thinking in these areas as it evolved in three phases of development in organizational studies. The first includes the seminal work of Blumberg and Skolnick; the second includes transitional works by Cole, Feeley, and Mileski; and the third includes "second-generation" analyses by Carter, Fleming, Mohr, Eisenstein and Jacob, Heumann, and Nardulli. Across these three phases, according to Nardulli, organizational studies progressed in several respects.

Later works developed more sophisticated and comprehensive theoretical schemes and borrowed more explicitly from the literature on organizations. They also progressed to the stage of hypothesis development and empirical testing. Finally, they moved from a reliance upon the traditional notion of "caseload pressure" to more sophisticated explanations for the prevalence of bureaucratic due process.

Despite the notable progress in this line of thought, it still has severe shortcomings, and these are discussed in the last section of Nardulli's essay. There is not only a lack of continuity in the area and little agreement on several basic issues, but there are also a plethora of different conceptual focuses as well as a good deal of disagreement on the reasons for the prevalence of bureaucratic due process. Despite these problems, there are broad commonalities in second-generation analyses. They include a concern with decisional criteria, as well as with factors affecting how these criteria are reflected in various decisions. The essay concludes with some examples of how an awareness of these commonalities can lead to prospective insights to guide third-generation analyses.

In "Political Cultures, Trial Courts, and Criminal Cases" Herbert Kritzer examines one approach to understanding the relationship between criminal court operations and their environment, a political culture approach. After briefly reviewing the role of this concept in appellate-level judicial research, he outlines an argument for its applicability at the trial level. In Kritzer's view, in order to extend the political culture approach to trial courts it is useful to dichotomize the relationship between these courts and political culture along two dimensions. One must view the external and internal facets of both federal and state courts. External facets are decisions made outside the court system (structure, selection of personnel); the term internal facets refers essentially to decision-making by courtroom personnel.

Before Kritzer discusses the impact of political culture in light of this fourfold categorization, he examines in more detail the concept of political culture, paying particular attention to the work of Elazar, Sharkansky, and Johnson. He then undertakes to construct several measures of the dimensions of political culture relevant to his immediate concerns. Using factor analysis and a series of political culture indicators, he derives three factors: the role of government, the role of politics, and the role of the legal system. Using these three measures as well as relevant prior research, Kritzer examines the impact of political culture in the four areas noted above. He begins with external facets.

Because the structure of federal courts is established by Title 28,

Kritzer says that the impact of local political culture upon the external facets of these courts—beyond personnel recruitment—is limited. He does suggest, however, that the use and formation of federal districts and divisions within states might be related to the value placed upon local control. With regard to the external aspects of state courts, Kritzer uses prior research and his own measures of political culture to examine the relationship between culture and the content of the criminal law, court structure, resource allocation, and the selection process. He finds these very useful, especially his measures of the role of politics and the role of the legal system.

Kritzer argues that local political culture can influence internal decision-making in three ways: directly, indirectly, or in a complex (interactive) manner. In federal criminal cases the impact of local political culture upon decision-making has been examined largely in draft cases. The evidence for direct effects (public opinion) is somewhat mixed but there is a stronger case for indirect effects. Because of the rather limited nature of prior research in this area, Kritzer examines some data in nondraft criminal cases. He uses his three measures of political culture in conjunction with two measures of sentencing severity and some data compiled by Carp in which he codes district court decisions on criminal procedure as liberal or conservative. The results of the analysis, however, are mixed.

In his final main section, Kritzer examines the relationship between political culture and the internal aspects of state courts. Here the literature is much more diversified, including the comparison of disposition rates across jurisdictions by crime survey researchers in the 1920s; Balbus's comparative analysis of the black revolts; Levin's study of sentencing differentials in Pittsburgh and Minneapolis; Eisenstein and Jacob's three-city study; Church's work on delay; and some of Hagan's work on sentencing. These studies examined the role of political culture from a number of different perspectives and concluded that it does play a significant role with regard to internal decision-making. Kritzer also adds some original analyses on sentencing indicators aggregated at the state level which lend some limited support to this view. Kritzer concludes that the impact of local political culture upon internal matters is not as great as in external matters. Moreover its impact upon internal facets is often apt to be indirect and complex.

Part III of this volume contains three essays on questions that have concerned both policymakers and scholars for decades. The first is Roy Flemming's "Punishment before Trial." It presents a model that describes the factors affecting basic policy decisions regarding bail. The model integrates the concepts of risk (uncertainty, threat, vulnerability) and resources with the view of criminal justice officials as satisficers. He views bail policies as reflecting an approximate equilibrium between environmental constraints and detention resources. After discussing the basic components of the model in some detail, Flemming addresses the question of policy change. The usual impetus for change, according to Flemming, is some environmental disturbance. Examples include a significant increase in arrests due to some changes in police policy, a jail riot, or a lawsuit pertaining to jail capacity. These disturbances cause disequilibrium and activate a search for a new equilibrium. The search, according to Flemming, will be very limited initially and will continue only until a satisficing solution is reached. Moreover, it will utilize a risk avoidance criterion. Far-ranging bail reforms are often put off in favor of more limited changes due to the uncertainty they introduce.

After fleshing out his process model with some concrete examples, Flemming applies it to bail policy in Detroit's Recorder's Court between 1968 and 1972. The initial disturbance that upset the existing policy was a very significant increase in the number of felony cases followed by civil litigation that eventually put a limit on the number of prisoners to be housed in the Wayne County jail. This all occurred during a period when private bondsmen were withdrawing somewhat from the criminal market. In response to this situation the recorder's court eventually changed its bail policy. What is important from Flemming's perspective, however, is that the change was only marginal (release-on-recognizance, or ROR, rates were increased from about 33 to 48 percent) and it was not effectuated until several less risky alternatives were implemented. The court's initial response was to increase the pace of dispositions (an approach which has many political dividends), thereby relieving some of the jail stress. They did this by utilizing visiting judges, encouraging guilty pleas, and shifting dispositional priorities (from a "freed first" to a "jailed first" system). It was not until this disposition slack was eliminated and an effective ROR program was established that the court began to increase its ROR rate.

In "Thinking about Plea Bargaining," Milton Heumann identifies, discusses, and integrates three important concepts in the literature on criminal courts: resource constraints, "going rates," and legal culture, broadly defined. His concern is twofold. First, he believes that a further understanding of these concepts could lead to the development of a comparative theory of the plea bargaining process. Second, he contends that they can lead to insights into several important public policy issues, sentencing reform and deterrence.

Heumann urges a return to the concept of resource constraints.

Researchers have recently been attacking the traditional caseload hypotheses, which held that caseload pressure "caused" plea bargaining. While agreeing with these attacks, Heumann suggests that resource constraints can *affect* the rate of plea bargaining, and case disposition specifically, in a given jurisdiction. Regarding the concept of going rates (defined as the standard sentence for a typical criminal convicted of a "normal" crime) Heumann is concerned with their origin, nature, and determinants. He disputes the view that plea bargaining necessarily results in lenient sentences (low going rates). While acknowledging that there is always a difference between going rates and statutory maximums, Heumann contends that these going rates are likely to vary across jurisdictions. As for the third concept, legal culture, Heumann is really concerned with broader environmental phenomena than are normally associated with the concept. He includes such things as public opinion, tradition, and historical accidents. These things are important because they tend to be self-perpetuating and account for otherwise inexplicable differences across courts.

In attempting to integrate these concepts into a theoretical perspective on the plea bargaining process, Heumann begins with the example of a system with no resource constraints (a "pure" system). Such a system will have a core of cases that result in plea bargains. Across pure jurisdictions, however, factors such as legal culture, public opinion, and historical happenstance will affect the size of this core (that is, the guilty plea rate) and the going rate for various crimes. By dropping the assumption of no resource constraints, Heumann introduces additional complexities into the analysis. As these constraints begin to be felt a number of things may happen. The guilty plea rate may, for example, increase; or the going rate may decrease; or the sentencing differential between guilty plea and the trial cases may increase; or the number of dismissals may increase. Having thus fleshed out the implications of his analysis for understanding the plea bargaining process, Heumann turns to a discussion of its policy implications.

Here he is concerned with developing the insights of his analysis for the movement to introduce some form of determinate sentencing as well as efforts to study the deterrent effect of criminal sanctions. He contends that an awareness of some of the points he raises would sensitize sentencing reformers to the problem of merely shifting discretion from the judge to the prosecutor and to the difficulties of eliminating long-established going rates. In addition he suggests that deterrence researchers should note that the inverse relationship between sanction and crime rates may be an artifact of variations in the plea bargaining process.

In "Sentencing Problems and Internal Court Reform," Beverly Cook is concerned with elaborating upon the nature and complexities of the long-standing problem of criminal sentencings and some rather current internal efforts at sentencing reform (training sessions, judicial councils, guidelines). In her view, there are two basic problems with sentencing: one concerns its effectiveness, the other its fairness. To illustrate the nature of these problems and the complexities involved in their resolution, Cook approaches sentencing from a number of different perspectives.

First, to illustrate the rather unique nature of sentencing, Cook approaches it as one of several societal assignment processes. In comparing it to those processes used to assign people involuntarily to other institutions (schools, mental hospitals, armies), a number of distinctive problems are highlighted. While some of these other processes classify people by attributes, sentencing attempts to classify people on the basis of behavior. Moreover, in the sentencing process the assignor is not closely connected to the treatment of the offender, and the responsibility for classification is much more diffuse than in other areas.

Next Cook moves to a brief discussion of the problems caused by the ambiguity of sentencing goals and the inherent contradictions involved in the prevailing set of sentencing goals. These goals work toward different effects, require different types of information, and often lead to conflicting sentences. One cannot move toward a rational sentencing policy under such circumstances. This situation also leads to a state of confusion which permits other factors to influence the sentencing decision.

She considers these "other factors" by introducing a "Political Modeling of Sentencing" which incorporates such varied concepts as "Law and Culture," "Political Inputs" (legislative, executive, bureaucratic, public opinion), and "Decision-maker Inputs." To illustrate the complexities of these forces she discusses each in some detail, with a special emphasis upon reviewing empirical evidence relevant to each.

Having highlighted the nature of sentencing and sentencing problems, Cook then turns to a discussion of internal attempts at sentencing reform and the reasons for their ineffectiveness. In this regard she considers attempts at judicial education, sentencing councils, and sentencing guidelines. She concludes by reconsidering the two problems she began with, fairness and effectiveness, and then outlines several alternatives to traditional sentencing practices.

REFERENCES

Cole, George (1973). *Politics and the Administration of Justice.* Beverly Hills, California: Sage.

Eisenstein, James (1973). *Politics and the Legal Process*. New York: Harper and Row.

_______, and Jacob, Herbert (1976). *Felony Justice: An Organizational Analysis of Criminal Courts*. Boston: Little, Brown.

Heumann, Milton (1978). *Plea Bargaining: Experiences of Prosecutors, Judges, and Defense Counsel.* Chicago: University of Chicago Press.

Jacob, Herbert (1973). *Urban Justice*. Englewood Cliffs, N.J.: Prentice-Hall.

Klonoski, James and Mendelsohn, Robert, eds. (1970). *The Politics of Local Justice*. Boston: Little, Brown.

Levin, Martin (1977). *Urban Politics and Criminal Courts*. Chicago: University of Chicago Press.

Nardulli, Peter F. (1978). *The Courtroom Elite: An Organizational Perspective on Criminal Justice.* Cambridge, Mass.: Ballinger Publishing Company.

Neubauer, David (1974). *Criminal Justice in Middle America*. Morristown, N.J.: General Learning Press.

Part I

Criminal Courts as Dispute Processing Institutions

Chapter One

Related Party Disputes in Criminal Courts: Some Data and Speculations about Alternative Functions, Herbert Jacob

Herbert Jacob

Criminal courts are usually thought of as places where guilt or innocence is established and where legal sanctions are applied against criminals who have been found guilty of violating legal norms. That is what happens in many instances, but it is not the only thing that happens. Our image of the criminal victimizing innocent strangers and then being punished requires many kinds of correctives. Numerous studies have already suggested that a large number of offenders are not punished by the courts because they are never apprehended. In addition, formal sanctions are applied to only a small minority of alleged offenders because the courts dismiss more defendants than they convict. Even dismissed defendants, however, suffer some deprivations; the informal sanctions they endure may involve considerable costs, including the expense of an attorney and bail, time lost from work, the stigma of arrest, the discomfort of temporary detention, and the uncertainty of the eventual outcome.

Yet another corrective is required. Many defendants are charged with violating the rights not of strangers but of acquaintances, friends, and relatives. In such cases the role of the courts may be quite different. The courts' function in these cases may not be to adjudicate but to process disputes. The outcomes may involve sanctions, but of a different nature than in the case of stranger crime. This paper addresses these problems with some data about the frequency of related party crimes, their perception by victims, and some speculation about the meaning of what happens in court.

THE FREQUENCY OF RELATED PARTY CRIME

We have no reliable estimates of related party crime, both the Uniform Crime Reports (UCR) and the victimization surveys are flawed instruments for estimating related party offenses. The UCR reports only those alleged offenses made known to the police. In many instances, police do not record the result of a service call as a crime when they come to a family or neighborhood fight and manage to cool things off without making an arrest. If the police do not perceive the act as criminal, it does not enter the UCR statistics. Further, some acts which the police would record as criminal are not brought to their attention. Victims simply accept the results and go on their way; they avoid further confrontation by not calling the police.

Victimization surveys are flawed in another way. They depend on the victims' recalling incidents that occurred in the past six or twelve months. The way in which they recount the incident determines whether it is perceived by the interviewer as involving a crime; that is often a matter of nuance which easily changes with the passage of time. Further, it appears that, in many instances, known victims are reluctant to recall to surveyors criminal assaults committed by related parties—perhaps because they fear retaliation, because the conflict has receded or been settled in the meantime, or because they no longer believe it to have involved a crime, inasmuch as the case was dismissed against the alleged offender. Consequently, we have no reliable estimates about the frequency of related party offenses for the country as a whole.

A recent study by the Vera Foundation of felony dispositions in New York City, however, provides some valuable estimates of the proportion of cases coming to court that involve related parties (see Table 1-1). The results indicate that such cases are much more frequent than usually presumed. In addition, while it had always been assumed that many assaults and rapes involved people who knew each other, the data reveal that a large proportion of thefts, burglaries, and even robberies also involve related parties. These cases come to court with perhaps greater frequency than warranted by their true incidence. The prior relationship between offender and victim makes arrest relatively easy because the victim is often able to put the police on the trail of the offender. However, the life of many of these cases in court is brief. Most of the nonconvictions shown in Table 1-1 are dismissals and most of the dismissals in related party cases result from refusal by victims to continue their prosecution. They balk at cooperating with the police and prosecutors and they refuse to provide testimony in court.

Table 1-1. Proportion of Cases Involving Related Parties and Their Disposition in New York City

	Percent of Cases Involving Related Parties	*Percent Related Party Cases Not Convicted*	*Percent Stranger Cases Not Convicted*
Assault	69	52	71
Grand larceny	55	45	33
Rape	83	60	0
Robbery	36	63	12
Burglary	39	43	11

Source: Vera (1977), p. 19.

Without victim testimony, prosecution in most of these cases is unfeasible. Even if the state were able to win a conviction, however, most prosecutors do not wish to continue when the victim appears to consider the case as too trivial to pursue.

The principal consequence for the courts is that a large number of cases come to them only to be dismissed. This result is viewed with considerable dismay by prosecutors and judges. They often indicate that such cases are a waste of their time and limited resources; such cases clog dockets even though they will not reach trial. A judge in Connecticut, for instance, is quoted as follows by Heumann (1978, p. 38):

> Well, we're dealing with cases primarily which are not that important. You understand that. Most of the cases . . . I hate to use the word, we use it all the time . . . we call them junk. It means of such minor . . . it was such a minor matter that the most you can say for it is that technically it happens. . . .

A prosecutor in the same court comments, "Most of the stuff that comes through the court is garbage . . . a husband gets into an argument with his wife, they call a cop . . . that kind of thing. Two neighbors get into a sort of back-fence thing . . ." (Heumann, 1978, p. 38).

At the same time, court personnel, sensitive to the human needs of victims and offenders, often feel that the courts are unable to provide the services which such cases demand. They see wifebeatings, husband assaults, child abuse, the breakup of friendships. All of these seem to demand psychotherapy. While offenders and victims appear to need an understanding ear and help in meeting financial problems, all the courts can offer are legal deprivations. A recent LEAA report (Galvin, 1977, p. 49) notes:

> A substantial proportion of criminal complaints are related to family and neighborhood quarrels and petty neighborhood crime. The persons involved ordinarily are known to each other. Often they are involved in a relationship which is likely to continue despite an isolated (or chronic) eruption involving assaults, property damage, threats, thefts, or other behavior within the scope of criminal law. Traditional criminal justice procedures and sanctions are impersonal, often clumsy, slow, and costly. They are not well designed to resolve crises, settle personal disagreements or bring about adjustments in the relationships and behavior of people at the family or neighborhood level. . . . Some of the personal problems contributing to [these disputes] can be identified and resolved through social, economic, health, or other services.

CHARACTERISTICS OF RELATED PARTY VICTIMS

Despite these speculations about the effects of judicial intervention in related party disputes, little is known about the disputes, the victims, or the aftermath of official intervention. Related party victims drift in and out of court almost as maligned as the offenders they accuse. Whether pitied or scorned by court officials, they rarely are closely questioned about the consequences of judicial action or inaction. There is simply an operating assumption that related party cases are different. It is presumed that victims of related party assaults are predominantly lower class because the middle class resolves its disputes in a less violent manner or, when violence occurs, is less likely to call the police.

Furthermore, one might speculate that related party disputes should leave some residue among those involved. On the one hand, being a related party victim might make an assault less disturbing because it is not entirely unanticipated. The victim usually contributes substantially to the incident and therefore is prepared for it to some degree (Luckenbill, 1977; Block, 1977). The familiar presumably terrorizes less than the unknown. Many of the incidents may not be perceived as criminal. Fights among friends usually take place in familiar surroundings; they are qualitatively different from assaults by strangers. Consequently, we would expect related party victims to be no more concerned about crime than any other victim. In fact, related party victims should be less concerned about being out alone at night, for instance, because their victimization comes at home in the company of others. They should be less concerned about crime in the neighborhood since their victimization is not so much the consequence of general social conditions of a neighborhood as of the particulars of their own living arrangements. Related party victims should also be less likely to report that they are afraid to leave their homes than the victims of strangers would be.

On the other hand, since the relationship between a related party victim and offender must often persist after the incident, matters may be made worse by outside intervention. Thus related party victims may be much more ambivalent about police effectiveness than others. The police usually are able to arrest the culprit, since that person is known to the victim and can be located readily. But whatever action police and courts take will be viewed as ineffective, since either incarceration or release may have damaging consequences for the victim. Putting the offender in jail may deprive the family of its breadwinner; releasing him may make it vulnerable to his vengeance.

SURVEY FINDINGS

Some evidence to test these hypotheses is available from the victimization surveys conducted by the Census Bureau for LEAA since 1972. Several surveys exist: A continuing national sample as well as distinct samples of selected cities surveyed between 1972 and 1975. Only the city samples included attitude items. In each city approximately 10,000 households, or 22,000 individuals, were interviewed. The attitude items were administered to a random half of persons sixteen years old or older in this sample. The present study uses the results of the surveys taken in 1973 in the five largest cities (New York, Los Angeles, Chicago, Philadelphia, and Detroit) combined into a single file.[a] We examine only respondents who reported some kind of assault; property crimes and all household victimizations are omitted. After weighting to account for differences in sampling ratios, we have 2,073 incidents available for analysis.

The data set has some important limitations. We know from pilot studies that some related party victims fail to report their experience to surveyors (LEAA, 1974). This may be because they do not perceive the incident as involving a crime, because they do not wish to revive a conflict which may have become dormant, because the assailant is listening to the interview, or for some other reasons. Whatever the cause, the fact of underreporting makes it impossible to estimate reliably the frequency of related party assaults. We can only speak about the characteristics of those assaults which have been revealed in the interviews. For stranger assaults we do not suspect a similar bias;

[a]I am grateful to Wesley Skogan for making this data file available to me and for his assistance in interpreting it.

they appear to yield more reliable estimates of the true incidence of such events.

In addition, the census files are organized according to incidents rather than persons. Some people report several incidents, and their attitudes would therefore be counted as many times as they reported incidents. Thus, a woman with a single rape would have her attitude counted once, but a battered wife who reported three assaults would have her attitudes counted three times. I have segregated these multiple responses, thereby reducing the number of persons in the file to 1,796.

Characteristics of Reporting Related Party Victims and Stranger Victims

As one would expect from accepted stereotypes of lower class life and middle class solutions to familial conflict, more of the reported related party victims of assault have low incomes, moderate education, and are black than is true for victims of stranger assaults (see Table 1-2). While these differences are in the expected directions, the surprising feature is that the differences between related party victims and stranger victims are small. This is not simply a function of there being few low-income, grade-school respondents in this sample. When we look only at these groups, 55 percent of the low-income victims and 58 percent of the victims with a grade-school education were victims of stranger rather than related party assaults. What Table 1-2 indicates is that, among those who admit a related party victimization, a slight tendency exists for related party victims to be lower class more often than is the case for stranger victims.

Table 1-2. Income, Education, and Race of Related Party and Stranger Victims of Assaults in Five Largest Cities, 1973

		Related	*Stranger*
Income:	<$5,000	31.1%	24.3%
	$5,000-14,999	51.6	50.7
	⩾$15,000	17.3	25.0
		N = 574	*N* = 1,023
Education:	⩽ 8th Grade	7.2%	9.5%
	9-12	66.2	54.9
	>12 yrs.	25.1	34.3
		N = 623	*N* = 1,114
Race:	White	62.1%	71.1%
	Black	37.2[a]	28.4[a]
		N = 623	*N* = 1,116

[a]Remainder are other.

The data also suggest only slight socioeconomic differences between those related party victims who called the police and those who did not. Moreover, these differences are in the opposite direction from that which our presumption predicted. Middle-income related party victims were the most likely to call the police; white were more likely to call the police than blacks. However, those with little education were more likely to call the police than were the well educated. It is, of course, possible that the police screen out the middle class victims and prefer charges only for lower class related party victims. It is equally likely, however, that a significant number of related party victims in court come from more substantial backgrounds than is generally assumed.

Incident Characteristics

There are few differences in the kinds of assaults that related parties and strangers fall victim to, as Table 1-3 indicates. About one-fifth of both are victims of major assaults, which include rape and serious assaults that may involve a weapon or theft. Attempted major assaults occur slightly more frequently among related party victims, while less major assaults (attempted rape, minor assaults without a weapon but with possible theft) involve strangers slightly more often than related parties. Attempted minor assaults occur with the same frequency for both kinds of victims. There is one important difference, however. As Table 1-4 shows, related party assaults occurred much more frequently in the home or in some other quasi-private place. Stranger assaults took place much more frequently on the street or in public places.

Consequently, the principal difference for these two categories of victimizations is that of place. The behavior itself is very much the same. The related party victim knows his offender and is abused in familiar surroundings; such a victim is likely to know where to expect danger. The stranger victim does not know his assailant and is attacked in a public place that is perhaps less familiar to the victim than home; the victim is more likely to be surprised by the attack. Another important difference may be that the stranger victim is symbolically tied to the rest of the community. An attack on a stranger is an attack on all of us, for anyone of us might have been the victim. The related party victim, on the other hand, may be perceived by the general public as sharing fault, because the victim chose to associate with the assailant. Thus there may be larger differences in public perceptions of these two kinds of victims than is justified by the circumstances in which each finds himself.

Table 1-3. Types of Assaults Reported by Victims in Five Largest Cities, 1973[a]

Type of Assault	*Related*	*Stranger*
Most serious (rape; serious assault with or without weapon or theft)	21.8%	23.6%
Attempted serious assault	27.5	22.2
Less serious (attempted rape; minor assault without weapon, with or without theft)	16.5	20.8
Attempted minor assault (without weapon or theft)	34.1	32.4
	N = 705	*N* = 1,248

[a]This table includes both single and multiple incidents.

Attitudes toward Crime and the Police

Our original speculation about related party and stranger victims led us to expect that related party victims would feel safer about going out on the street alone at night than victims of stranger assaults. This is because the related party victims were assaulted more often at home in a quasi-public place in the company of relatives, friends, or acquaintances. Being alone, even in the dark, should hold no special terror for them. But that is not the case. There is no difference between related party victims and stranger victims as to their feeling of safety at night alone in the neighborhood. The survey results show that, in each instance, about half indicated that they felt very or reasonably safe. The same is true for feelings of safety during the day. An exception to the latter is that in both instances approximately six-sevenths felt safe being out alone in the neighborhood during the day, in contrast to only one-half feeling safe at night.

Table 1-4. Places of Assaults Reported by Victims in Five Largest Cities, 1973

Place of Assault	*Related*	*Stranger*
At home	29.3%	5.8%
Near own home	13.8	8.7
At or in vacation home	1.1	0
Inside commercial building	7.1	14.3
Inside office	3.9	1.3
Inside school	4.6	3.0
On street	28.2	62.7
Other	11.9	4.1
	N = 614	*N* = 1,342

Another of our expectations was that related party victims would view the crime problem more in terms of their personal social surroundings and less as a societal problem. The data provide only slight support for that hypothesis. A few more related party victims thought that crime was caused by people in the neighborhood than did stranger victims, who associated crime more frequently with outsiders. Very slightly more stranger victims thought crime had risen in the United States over the past year or two than did related party victims; a few more stranger victims thought that their chances of being attacked or robbed had gone up during the past few years than was true for related party victims (see Table 1-5). The differences between the two sets of victims, however, are quite insubstantial; the two sets are more alike than they are different.

Another difference we expected was that related party victims would much less frequently indicate that they stayed home because of crime. Indeed, home was where their crime took place. Again, there is a very small difference between the two groups in the expected direction, but too small to be either statistically or substantively significant.

Finally, we hypothesized that related party victims would be more ambivalent toward the police than victims of stranger crimes. This was because while the police were more likely to make an arrest, the consequences of an arrest fall almost equally on victim and assailant. The data in Table 1-6 do not show more related party victims to be ambivalent; rather, more of them are negative. Related party victims are divided into almost equal thirds displaying a wide variety of attitudes toward police effectiveness.

These results suggest that related party victims are not distinguished by their attitudes toward crime. Their experiences as

Table 1-5. Perceptions of Crime by Assault Victims in Five Largest Cities, 1973

	Related	*Stranger*
Source of danger:		
People in neighborhood	39.1%	33.7%
Outsiders	35.6[a]	39.9[a]
	N = 619	*N* = 1,106
Has crime increased in US in past year or two: yes	80.0%[a]	82.9%[a]
	N = 620	*N* = 1,108
Stay home because of crime	7.1%	9.6%[a]
	N = 623	*N* = 1,116

[a]Remainder in other categories.

Table 1-6. Perceptions of Police by Assault Victims in Five Largest Cities, 1973

	Related	Stranger
Local police do good job	30.6%	35.8%
average job	36.4	35.7
poor job	31.4	25.5
DK	1.6	3.1
	N = 622	*N* = 1,109

victims and in some cases as complaining witnesses do not produce the distinctive set of perceptions we expected. Their perceptions of crime closely resemble those of stranger victims.

COURT PROCESSING OF RELATED PARTY CASES

The varied background of related party victims, their propensity to call the police, and the variety of attitudes they display about crime and about the police suggest that related party victims are anything but a homogeneous group. This variety makes them a highly complicated phenomenon for the courts to deal with. They do not simply represent the unsolved conflicts of poor people who lack alternative resources to resolve problems. Some fit that description, to be sure, but others do not. To understand their place on court dockets, we need to be self-conscious about the functions which criminal courts perform.

The criminal court function that is most widely understood is dispute settlement. It may be accomplished by formal means through adjudication proceedings or informally through negotiations that take place in and out of court. Disputes are settled in both instances. When a case is adjudicated, the court imposes its judgment directly on the defendant and indirectly on the complainant, who is formally represented by the state. An acquittal means that the complainant has no claim to retribution; a conviction together with an official sentence determines how the culprit will be punished and what, if any, compensation shall be paid to the complainant. Negotiations[b] produce other kinds of settlements. The complainant and offender agree to a formula which leads the complainant to drop the formal case in court. Usually the agreement involves some kind of compensation or commitment to

[b] I do not include plea bargaining in this set of negotiated settlements because the complainant is usually not a party to the settlement and because a formal adjudication accompanies the plea. It results in a formal conviction and adjudication, albeit based on negotiation rather than on a trial.

desist from future unlawful acts. Both adjudicated and negotiated settlements are in some sense "final." They close a chapter of the dispute and end the claim of the complainant on the resources of the court with respect to that particular incident.

A second function of the courts is to process disputes. Disputes are not finalized or settled; rather they are simply entered on the docket and made eligible for negotiation and adjudication. Before they reach this stage, however, they drop out, not as the result of some negotiated settlement but from simple disinterest. Complainants in these disputes do not wish a settlement. Perhaps they cannot conceive of one. They simply desire to use the threat of court sanctions against the offender to establish a new equilibrium in their ongoing relationship. In many of these cases, the relationship is inherently conflictual. Resolving the conflict would involve dissolving the relationship.

When courts process disputes, they participate in but one stage of the dispute's life. Many disputes of this nature come to court with long histories; they may also have considerable futures. Fights between spouses or lovers, for instance, are likely to have their origin in many months of bickering; they are likely to linger for many months more. Such a state of affairs does not indicate an unstable relationship in every instance. It is naive to presume that the normal state of all relationships is a peaceful one. Some relationships apparently thrive on conflict and continue to be conflictual for their entire duration. Such conflicts are just as likely to come to court as those in which disputants conciliate. But, in these durable conflicts, settlement is neither desired nor attained. Calling the police and going to court is simply a tactic likely to be used by the weaker party to reestablish an equilibrium in the relationship. As a tactic, it uses the judicial process as a threat; it engages the court as an unwitting ally. It imposes the discomfort of being detained and jailed for a few hours, the inconvenience of making a court appearance, the annoyance of having strangers interfere in personal affairs, and the expense of even a brief court engagement. Having mobilized the court as an ally, the "victim" may be in a position to continue the relationship. The dispute which brought the parties to court has not been resolved, but the relationship can continue at its new conflict level.

The presence of dispute processing in related party cases in criminal courts may explain the persistence of such cases despite the apparent failure to resolve the conflicts through court action. Many observers of these cases have despaired about the inappropriateness of court intervention; because the courts do not have appropriate social or psychological resources, it appears as if nothing useful is being done for related party victims or offenders. If that were really true, it would seem likely that victims would also become aware of the futility of seeking court intervention, and such cases would become infrequent. That does not appear to be happening. Rather, a substantial number of victims go to court, some repeatedly. Such action makes more sense if they seek the kind of dispute processing I have described rather than the dispute settlement conventionally presumed.

If dispute processing is one of several functions that criminal courts play in handling related party cases, some of the criticisms of court procedures must be viewed with caution. The absence of social workers, psychologists, and helping resources becomes less critical, since they are not needed for dispute processing. The dismissal of cases even without reconciliation or compensatory payment ought not to be automatically categorized as a failure or a waste of court resources. Judges and prosecutors are not necessarily wasting their time and the public money in accepting and then dismissing such cases. In these instances, the adjudicatory process serves as an important adjunct to another process which allows people to continue their lives and relationships in a relatively stable fashion. The relationship is not one recommended by most marriage manuals, but it is one from which some people gain satisfaction.

I would hasten to add that the dispute processing function I have described has not been documented; it is hinted at by the data I have presented and by my observations of criminal courtrooms. Unfortunately, we have almost no direct descriptions of the travails of related party case participants. Scorned as the junk and garbage of the criminal courts, related party cases have not been the object of empirical research. Not untypically, solutions to the problem of related party cases are sometimes offered without good evidence about the scope of the problem. We need to learn much more about these cases and the alternative effects police and court intervention have on them. Perhaps it will help spur research to recognize, as our evidence suggests, that related party cases are not a monopoly of the very poor but are shared by the middle class. By conventional middle-class norms, they involve a social pathology that is spread widely, if thinly, throughout the population. If their consequences are to be understood, they must first be reliably described.

REFERENCES

Block, Richard (1977). *Violent Crime*. Lexington, Mass.: Lexington Books.

Galvin, John J. (1977). *Instead of Jail: Pre- and Post-Trial Alternatives to Jail Incarceration*. Washington, D.C.: Law Enforcement Assistance Administration.

Heumann, Milton (1978). *Plea Bargaining.* Chicago: University of Chicago Press.

Law Enforcement Assistance Administration (1974). *Crimes and Victims: A Report on the Dayton-San Jose Pilot Study of Victimization.* Washington, D.C.: Government Printing Office.

Luckenbill, David F. (1977). "Criminal Homicide as a Situated Transaction," *Social Problems*, 25.

Vera Institute (1977). *Felony Arrests: Their Prosecution and Disposition in New York City's Courts.* New York: Vera Institute of Justice.

Chapter Two

Dispute Processing: The Medium and the Message of Criminal Justice

Frances Kahn Zemans

In contrast to traditional concerns with the development of legal doctrine, social science interest in the law has focused upon the administration of justice in both its norm enforcment and dispute resolution capacities. These two roles have generally been treated as if they are clearly reflected in the dichotomization of the formal law betweeen criminal and civil justice, respectively. The criminal system is defined as a means of social control; law, as a mechanism for enforcing the norms established by the political regime. In contrast, the civil system is typically described as a forum for the settlement of private disputes; law, as a mechanism of dispute resolution. Actually the two functions are neither inherently nor empirically distinct. Both fit Pound's definition of social control as "the process of determining causes and controversies according to authoritative guides" (Pound, 1942, p. 40).

In fact, both the civil and criminal justice systems include norms intended to control the behavior of the populace. In addition both also provide opportunities for individuals to use public power for issues and in ways delineated by legislatures and courts.[1] Indeed, for most criminal offenses, the victim has the option of suing the assailant in civil court under tort law quite separate and apart from any proceedings in the criminal arena. The limited exercise of this option, due in large part to the costs far exceeding the potential benefits, should not be interpreted as an inherent inability of the civil process to deal with "criminal" matters.

The very limited theoretical development generated in studies of the criminal courts has been constrained by the division of the research effort coincident with the dichotomization of the formal law, implying the necessity of a minimum of two separate theoretical models. Indeed, with the exception of the application of an economic model to the legal system, none of the proposed theories or even quasi theories has been applied beyond the legal sphere within which they were developed.[2]

Recent attention to the role of the criminal courts in dispute resolution, traditionally considered within the sphere of civil law, suggests that a single theoretical model might be developed for the trial courts in general, particularly since the mode of operation is essentially the same in the administration of both the criminal and civil systems. This chapter will argue that the dispute processing format of the courts provides the appropriate basis for such an explanatory model. After outlining the trend toward increased recognition of the role of the criminal courts in dispute processing and resolution, a model of the criminal justice system will be presented. This model emphasizes the centrality of dispute processing in criminal court operations and argues that for reasonable explanatory power the variables affecting the entry of cases into the criminal courts bear considerable attention. The model will then be compared to other proposed models of the criminal courts and supported by some reflections on the empirical research done in criminal justice.

DISPUTE PROCESSING AND THE CRIMINAL COURTS

Dispute resolution has traditionally been recognized as one of the functions performed by the courts. Recent anthropological research has taught us that "dispute processing" may be more accurate terminology because it includes both disputes which are settled as well as those which are not, including particularly those never intended by the participants to be resolved in a courtroom setting. Indeed, the zero-sum nature of the adjudicative format makes it inappropriate for the resolution of many disputes, particularly among individuals who wish to maintain a continuing relationship with each other.

There has probably always been a large proportion of court cases that do not continue to actual resolution, though it is difficult to tell from available data how many of the dismissals are due to a decision by the complainant not to pursue the case and how many are due to some outside settlement encouraged and perhaps facilitated by courtroom actors. Reports of courtroom observations and interviews with relevant actors indicate that the latter have accounted for many dispositions.

Dispute Processing Programs

Increasing official recognition of the dispute processing function of the courts is reflected in the development of programs designed to deal specifically with cases for which adjudication seems inappropriate. This is somewhat paradoxical, for the adjudicative mode is designed precisely to deal with disputes. The explanation for this seeming paradox can be found in the requisite narrowing of issues in dispute to fit procedural requirements. By so constraining a dispute to fit a statutorily defined offense, and by severely limiting the evidence which can be presented, the basic dispute may be left untapped. The failure to get at the underlying dispute is exacerbated by placing blame in the narrowed context of the case at hand. With the basic issues left unsettled, the conflict is likely to erupt again in another incident subject to intervention by the criminal justice system.

The first official recognition of this reality, as well as the development of formal mechanisms to attempt to deal with it, was probably in the area of domestic relations, where it was clear to all concerned that the event which brought the parties to the criminal courts was only symptomatic of an underlying problem. Many court systems have consequently developed specialized courts to deal with disputes arising within family groups. A variety of techniques have been employed, but the avoidance of adjudication has been a common theme. In some cities the courts simply acquiesce to the wishes of the victim-complainant, who often prefers dismissal once tempers are cooled. In other cities quasi-judicial programs with informal procedures are begun by the police before the courts become involved. Still others encouraged pretrial interviews in an attempt to divert the cases from the criminal courts.[3] When the courts are forced to adjudicate such disputes, sentences are extremely light, sometimes to the point of being nonsentences like Chicago's peace bond, by which the defendant promises to behave.

One of the first programs that extended beyond family disputes to include neighborhood quarrels as well was the Columbus, Ohio, Night Prosecutor Program. Appropriate cases are referred for mediation which proceeds without regard to rules of evidence, burdens of proof, or normal courtroom procedures. The Law Enforcement Assistance Administration pamphlet publicizing the program emphasizes that it "seeks to maximize communication between the disputing parties and minimize attention on the guilt or innocence of the respondent. *The emphasis is on a lasting solution to an interpersonal problem rather than a judgment of right or wrong.*"

Perhaps the ultimate in established recognition of the need for dispute processing mechanisms was the recent National Conference on

Minor Disputes Resolution which was convened by the American Bar Association. The report of that conference (Sander, 1978) includes a compilation of alternative dispute mechanisms both inside and outside of court systems, some relying on lay personnel, some on legal professionals.

While recognizing dispute processing and dispute settlement functions for the courts, nearly all of these developments place these functions near the periphery of the criminal courts' role in society. They are regarded as less important functions since the emphasis is upon the settlement of cases involving minor disputes that would translate into misdemeanors.[4] The hope is to divert such cases from the court system or to devise some special mechanism to deal with them. In fact, part of the pressure behind this trend stems from the high caseload burden on scarce court resources. This has resulted in efforts to divert the less essential work of the criminal courts to other forums, thus leaving more time and resources for them to deal with their core function, the enforcment of societal norms. Curiously enough, active efforts to accommodate the dispute processing role performed by the criminal courts with either special programs within the structure of the courts or by diversion to other forms have not been accompanied by recognition that dispute processing is the modus operandi of the judicial system.

Dispute Processing as the Medium of Courts

Although criminal courts are a mechanism of social control employed by the state to enforce its norms, as required by the judicial article of the United States Constitution and followed by state jurisdictions, virtually all cases which come before courts do so in the form of disputes. Dispute processing is the medium through which courts operate. The criminal system is structured so that the processing of cases assumes the existence of a dispute. The denotation of criminal cases as *The People of the State of* ________ *v. Defendant* is consistent with the view that criminal courts deal in public disputes, in efforts of the state to enforce its normative standards. Yet, with the exception of murder and victimless crimes where the state substitutes itself as complainant, the overwhelming majority of cases depend upon a citizen complainant. Indeed, the unexpected but abysmal failure of the law to deal with victimless crimes simply reflects a deficiency in the recognition of criminal justice as a dispute processing system. For the system to function, there must be actual disputants. Without them, as in victimless crimes, cases simply do not come before the courts and the norms are only rarely enforced.[5] Complainants thus serve society in its norm enforcement effort. As a case in point, a Chicago study found that approximately 95 percent of the criminal incidents known to police came to their attention through citizen initiative (Reiss, 1971). Subsequent victimization surveys have confirmed the basically reactive role of the police.

While complainants are required for effective social control, their incentive for participation is basically the pursuit of their own individual disputes with defendants. Indeed, recognition of this very point is reflected in recently developed programs designed specifically to increase incentives to victims to bring and pursue their cases in the criminal courts. These have taken the form of both victim compensation and witness assistance programs.[6] Most of the statutes covering these programs include cooperation with the police as an eligibility requirement. That is, they provide a direct incentive to the complainant to maintain the original dispute with the suspect. Some programs have focused specifically upon assistance to witnesses and are thus not limited to victims. These include monetary remuneration for time lost, as well as easing participation by providing transportation to court and keeping witnesses informed so as to avoid unnecessary trips to the courthouse.[7]

What the criminal law provides is simply a framework within which complainants can pursue their disputes to their own benefit with the assistance of the criminal justice apparatus. Indeed, the definition of criminal behavior may create disputes in the sense of affecting the perception of the participants involved in an incident. That is to say, disputes are largely in the eye of the beholder. In addition to providing a forum for the pursuit of a dispute, the criminal justice system also affects the way actors perceive behavior. In that sense the criminal justice system not only provides a means of processing and possibly resolving one's dispute, but also plays a part in determining what will be defined as a dispute.

The reference to disputes as chronologically preceding the invocation of the criminal justice system is not merely for the purpose of describing procedures as being concerned with issues in the form of disputes. It is also meant to demonstrate that any attempt to develop a model of the criminal court operations must consider the factors that influence the decision to bring a dispute into the public judicial arena. Without it, the courts tend to be evaluated as closed systems. Indeed many, if not most, studies of the criminal courts imply as much by concentrating on plea bargaining, judging, sentencing, and the like. Only casual reference is made to the disputants, or for that matter to the more general environment in which the courts operate. Where the latter is recognized, it tends to be related back exclusively to the incidence of plea bargaining (Eisenstein and Jacob, 1977) and to the severity and distribution of sentences (Levin, 1977). It is a basic thesis of this paper that any explanatory model of the criminal courts must necessarily include the factors that affect the flow of cases into the court's sphere of influence. The dispute processing model to be elaborated upon applies to both the precourt and intracourt stages in the administration of criminal justice.

DISPUTE PROCESSING MODEL OF CRIMINAL COURTS

As noted earlier, an explanatory model of criminal courts requires consideration of the place of the courts within the context of the administration of criminal justice and must recognize the reactive nature of the legal machinery. The proposed model takes such advice. Early in this century Roscoe Pound, in an oft-quoted discussion of "The Limits of Effective Legal Action," alluded to the importance of the initiator of legal action for the implementation of legal rules. He advised the lawmaker who wished to ensure the enforcement of the law that "last and most of all he must study how to insure that someone will have a motive for invoking the machinery of law to enforce his rule in the face of opposing interests of others in infringing it" (Pound, 1917, p. 167). An inquiry into the functioning of the criminal court must similarly consider the factors influencing the decision to initiate the process that will determine the form and substance of its workload.

This section will attempt to integrate these considerations into a dispute processing model of criminal courts. To do so, however, we must first take cognizance of the stepwise nature of the criminal process illustrated in Figure 2-1. It is clear that different actors dominate different stages of the process. For example, the disputants (victim and offender) are the most important actors in the first three stages, while the police officer along with the complainant is critical in the next stage. Various courtroom actors dominate the final stage. Nonetheless, the basic argument here is that similar factors affect the process at these different stages. However, because the different stages are dominated by different actors, the analysis must be adjusted accordingly. Before elaborating this point, it is first necessary to outline and discuss the basic components of the dispute processing model.

Variables Relevant to Dispute Processing

The model contains three sets of variables which together affect the various stages of the process depicted in Figure 2-1. The variables concern the nature of the incident; the relationship among relevant actors;

Incident→Perception of Wrong→Some Action to Be Taken→Activate Criminal Justice Mechanism→Pursue Case to Disposition

Figure 2-1. Stages of the Dispute Process

and the accessibility of the criminal courts. The dimensions of each variable appear in Figure 2-2. Although analytically separable, these dimensions are not necessarily mutually exclusive empirically. For example, the greater the anticipated dollar loss, the greater may be the intensity of feelings about the incident. In discussing the degree or direction of the influence of each facet of these variables, all other facets and relevant external factors will be assumed to remain constant.

Before discussing the model further, it should also be noted that there is no presumption that all individuals respond identically to any of the dimensions. It is only argued that the various dimensions do influence behavior (that is, the invoking of the power and authority of the criminal courts) in the same direction. One individual may be more

Incident Dimensions	*Interpersonal Dimensions*
Salience	Salience
Intensity	Intensity
Duration	Duration/Frequency
Frequency (where noncontinuous)	Affinity
Periodicity (where noncontinuous)	Role Relationship
Loss (actual and anticipated)	Social Distance

Accessibility of Criminal Justice

Perceived as Relevant to Case

Perceived Chances of Success

Benefit Worth the Time and Costs

Experience with the Process, Personal and Vicarious

Availability of Alternative Mechanisms (including civil court)

Figure 2-2. Dispute Processing Model

or less likely than another to act similarly given the same variables operating in the same degree and direction. Personality differences alone may dictate the extent to which an individual actively responds to a perceived wrong. It is also presumed that one learns both the definition of wrongs and the appropriate response to being wronged through lifelong socialization. A combination of familial, cultural, and legal factors influences an individual's decision to act, and to what degree. Thus we speak of litigious or aggressive individuals, or cultures that value harmony versus those that value the assertion of rights.

These phenomena play an important part in the decision-making process with which we are concerned, and the individual differences they represent are central to the argument presented here. For an ideal norm-enforcement process to operate, all individuals similarly situated with respect to victimization in a criminal offense would similarly have to invoke the authority of the criminal justice system. But victimization surveys have confirmed what was generally known before, that individuals similarly situated respond quite differently to incidents defined as criminal by the formal law. Furthermore, the likelihood and nature of the response under similar circumstances is most predictable if the process is evaluated in light of a dispute processing model. Initially each incident can best be interpreted if conceptualized as a dispute between victim and alleged perpetrator, with an evaluation of the incident and the interpersonal variable providing the basis for predicting the extent and nature of victim response. The decision actually to invoke the authority of the criminal courts is additionally dependent upon the facets of accessibility delineated in Figure 2-2.

Incident dimensions. While studies of criminal courts have always acknowledged that the nature of the incident is important to predicting how a case will be handled, "seriousness of the offense" is typically the only incident variable evaluated. Whether referring to notification of the police or the prosecutor's decision to pursue a case, the seriousness of the offense is presumed to be critical to the decision-making process. Indeed, there is evidence that this is in fact so (Black, 1971; Block, 1974; Eisenstein and Jacob, 1977). Yet, seriousness as defined by the formal law is really only a surrogate for a number of aspects of an incident which influence a victim's perception and decision to initiate the criminal process, the police officer's decision to make an arrest, and the prosecutor's decision to charge and pursue a case to disposition.

The formal law, of course, plays a part in socializing the public to abjure behavior deemed socially unacceptable, as well as informing them that the criminal justice system is available for the redress of the denoted wrong. Changes in perception of social acceptability may in fact be generated by new statutes, which define a heretofore legal action as criminal, or by a shift in public attention to previously little recognized problems for which statutes had been available. Victims increasingly receive support for defining themselves as victims and encouragement, sometimes even the means, to bring the matter before the criminal courts. Indeed, one of the most interesting phenomena in criminal justice is the influence of changing social norms on the workload of the courts.

Increased attention upon child abuse and wife beating provides recent examples. Although there is no evidence that either offense has been increasing, and though appropriate statutes have been on the books for years, recent public attention has influenced both the likelihood that such incidents will be conceptualized as criminal (that is, subject to consideration by the criminal justice system), that the police will be notified, that an arrest will be made, that the complainant will pursue the case in court, *and* that the prosecutor and defense counsel will take the case seriously.

While this does relate to the perceived seriousness of the offense, both our understanding of the decision-making process as well as predictability of the action to be taken is substantially enhanced if the incidents are evaluated for each of the dimensions illustrated in Figure 2-2. Duration, frequency, periodicity, and loss are all aspects of "seriousness." In addition, salience and intensity relate to the feelings which the incident generates in the individual victim; they are by their very nature person-specific. Such variables may seem inappropriate to a norm-enforcement mechanism; they are, however, peculiarly relevant to a criminal justice system that is organized in a dispute processing format and the activation of which is dependent upon stimuli from persons outside the system. The salience of an incident and the intensity of feelings about it vary for different individuals and may be personality-connected. As noted above, they are also related to the society and subgroups with which the decision-maker identifies. As will be discussed subsequently, the public actors in the process additionally, if not primarily, evaluate these incident dimensions based on their perceptions of the perspectives of the initial disputants. Although some of these dimensions are clearly more difficult to operationalize than others, we need to recognize that they all play a part in the definition of an incident as criminal, in the decision to seek redress in the criminal courts, and in the pursuit of the case to disposition.

Interpersonal dimensions. Recent studies of the criminal justice system have begun to take cognizance of the importance of the interpersonal relationship between victim and perpetrator in the decision to invoke the criminal law and to pursue a case to court disposition. The most obvious example is the marital dispute. Police have known for years that there is often no desire on the part of the victim (assuming easy identification of the appropriate person to whom to affix that label) to have the criminal law invoked against the perpetrator-spouse by an arrest. Even where an actual arrest is sought, it is typically for the purpose of immediate separation and control rather than to seek the full potential of the criminal law sanction. One need only observe the flow of cases growing out of marital disputes for which no complaining witness appears in court to press charges. Such cases are almost invariably dismissed.

More recently anthropologists studying other cultures have noted that public authority is frequently invoked to settle matters without pursuing one's "rights," that the goal is often a return to harmony. While they have concentrated upon cultural traits that orient courts toward balance and harmony versus the establishment of rights, there has been increasing recognition in studies of our own legal system that very often litigants simply wish to settle the matter at hand and are only faintly concerned with legal rights and duties. It is this growing awareness that is exemplified in the emergence of the dispute settlement programs discussed above. In these programs, as well as in the anthropological inquiries, much emphasis is given to the desire of the parties to maintain continuing relationships with each other, and the difficulty of doing so in the context of the zero-sum game format of the adjudicative process.

The interpersonal dimensions in this model recognize the importance of continuing relationships to the perception of victimization and to the decision to invoke the criminal justice machinery, as well as within the court system itself. Like the incident variable, however, there are a number of distinct dimensions to the interpersonal relationship between relevant actors, and they are not necessarily mutually exclusive. Where a personal relationship exists, the importance of maintaining it can be analyzed along five dimensions: salience, intensity, duration, affinity, and role relationship. Salience, intensity, and affinity are, of course, difficult items to operationalize, yet that makes them no less important to the perception of an incident as a crime rather than a personal matter, and to the decision to seek assistance in the criminal courts. These dimensions are particularly appropriate to incidents involving persons with some prior relationship, where there is some potential for continuation. While that certainly applies to many matters which have the potential to become cases in the criminal courts, there are others where the victim and perpetrator are total strangers. For the latter, social distance provides a surrogate measure of relationship. It is this dimension, along with role relationship, that accounts for the variability in the reporting and pursuing of offenses according to the race and income of the participants. While most studies which consider such variables concentrate upon the social status of the victim (Block, 1974) or the social status of the alleged offender (Eisenstein and Jacob, 1977), this model hypothesizes that it is the magnitude and direction of the discrepancy in status between victim and offender which explains the variability found.

The two-person incident and relevant bilateral relationship used for illustrative purposes are not requisite to the model. They are, however, the simplest and possibly most frequent situations. When more participants are added, the resultant multilateral relationships must be considered. In fact a multiplicity of relationships is always relevant, for the disputants' behavior will vary in accordance with their perceptions of the effects which their actions will have on their relationships with the larger audience. They may consider the impact of their behavior on future disputes for which this one may set a precedent, or simply the effect on their general reputation in the relevant community.

The relevance of the interpersonal dimensions is not limited to the relationship between victim and offender. The dependence of the adversary system upon the representation of interests by specialized advocates requires consideration of the complainant-prosecutor and defendant-defense counsel interpersonal relationships, as well as that between the advocates themselves. For each of these, the same dimensions can be evaluated to determine the importance of the relationship, the perceived need to maintain it, and the impact it will have on decision-making in the criminal courts.

Accessibility of the criminal justice system. The decision to "do something" about an incident does not necessarily inexorably lead one to the criminal justice system. In most situations there are a number of alternatives which do not involve seeking the intervention of a third party. The decision to invoke the criminal justice machinery is further tied to the accessibility of that system to the victim-complainant and the perceived likelihood of success therein. The dimensions of accessibility that will influence the bringing of cases into the public arena are illustrated in Figure 2-2.

At one level of analysis it would be sufficient simply to say that the criminal justice authority will be invoked by the victim-complainant if the perceived benefits outweigh the perceived costs, with the risks of losing included on the cost side of the equation. While surely correct, such a formulation does little to elucidate the issues to be considered in seeking entry to the criminal process. Both the perceived relevance of the criminal law to the case at hand and the calculation of likely success are related to one's understanding of the criminal law, and presumably to the statutes themselves. The greater these are, the more likely the victim-complainant will be to seek assistance from the criminal courts. These of course will be balanced against the time and dollar costs attendant to pursuing the case in the criminal courts. Experience with the legal system, both personal and vicarious, will increase the accessibility of the criminal courts for appropriate cases. Such experience should increase success in using the courts, both because of more accurate knowledge of the issues of which the criminal law takes cognizance, and because of greater expertise in using the institutional network (Carlin and Howard, 1965).

The final dimension of accessibility of the criminal courts predicts that the greater the perceived availability of alternative mechanisms to handle the dispute, including civil court as an option, the less likely the victim-complainant will be to invoke the criminal law. Such availability is itself dependent upon the shared identities between victim and offender. For example, family decision-making structures, parish priests, school disciplinary mechanisms, gang hierarchies, and so on, may all offer alternatives to the criminal courts.[8]

There are also alternatives open to the public actors in the criminal courts. Adult diversion programs have become increasingly popular as mechanisms to "solve problems" rather than prosecute offenders.[9] Additionally, in economic crimes prosecutors often act as mediators generating restitutive settlements even though the law clearly calls for criminal penalties.[10] Both of these in effect constitute available alternatives that filter cases out of the criminal court workload.

Dispute Processing Variables and Decision-making in the Criminal Process

With different actors assuming the major decision-making position at different stages in the stepwise criminal justice process, the dispute processing variables discussed above need to be evaluated accordingly. Although the victim-complainants are critical to initiating the processing of cases in the criminal courts, other participants become equally or more central once the criminal justice system has been invoked. In particular the police, the prosecutor, and the defense counsel become the decision-makers appropriate as objects of study. This section describes the applicability of the dispute processing model to initial disputants and the decision to seek redress; the police and the decision to formalize the dispute; and prosecutors, defense counsel, and dispositional decisions.

Initial disputants and the decision to seek redress. Illustrations of incidents with the legal potential to become part of the workload of the criminal courts will serve to elucidate the efficacy of the model with respect to initial disputes. Take the situation of a shopkeeper who observes a customer stealing an item from a display counter.[11] The shopkeeper clearly has the option of calling the police to report the incident, for theft is a violation of the criminal law in every state. Yet, will that be likely to occur? To determine that, we need to evaluate the shopkeeper's views on the perceived incident, the interpersonal relationship between victim and perpetrator, and the accessibility of the criminal courts. How salient is shoplifting, or theft, to the shopkeeper? Has this been a frequent problem? How often, and for how long? Have the incidents involved the same person or persons, or have the perpetrations appeared to be unrelated? What has been the dollar value of the stolen goods? What is that value in proportion to anticipated profits? How strongly does the shopkeeper feel about this matter in relation to the other concerns of a retail business? Does he perceive the criminal law to be relevant to the case, and how does he evaluate his chances of success against the costs involved in initiating action in the criminal courts? How experienced is the shopkeeper with the legal process, and what alternatives are available? A number of hypotheses can be derived from this scenario to predict the likely response of the shopkeeper. In each case the victim has opted against avoidance as a means of dealing with the incident.[12]

1. The more salient shoplifting is as an issue, the more likely the victim is to proceed toward using the criminal justice system.
2. The more frequently shoplifting has occurred, the more likely the victim is to proceed toward initiating the criminal justice system.
3. The greater the value of the stolen goods, both absolutely and in proportion to income, the more likely the victim is to initiate the criminal justice system.
4. The more intensely the victim feels about the issue in general and the incident in particular, the more likely he is to initiate the criminal justice system.

Although in this case it may appear that the criminality of the act is obvious, and not subject to definition by the victim, that may not be the case. In this particular example, the potential for variability even in the definition of the incident may become clearer by the formulation of hypotheses based upon the interpersonal dimensions important to the initiation of disputes in the criminal justice system.

1. The greater the shopkeeper's affinity for the perpetrator, the less likely he is to initiate action.
2. The longer the shopkeeper has known the perpetrator (with positive affinity), the less likely he is to initiate action. (With negative affinity, an increase in the duration dimension will have the opposite effect.)
3. The more intense the shopkeeper's feelings toward the perpetrator (with positive affinity), the less likely he is to initiate action. (With negative affinity, an increase in the intensity dimension will have the opposite effect.)
4. The more salient the shopkeeper's relationship with the perpetrator (with positive affinity), the less he is likely to initiate action. (With negative affinity, an increase in the salience dimension will have the opposite effect.)

Further hypotheses relate to the dimensions of accessibility of the criminal courts and the likelihood that this public authority will be invoked by the victim.

1. The greater the perception by the shopkeeper that the criminal law is relevant to the incident, the more likely the legal authority will be invoked.
2. The greater the shopkeeper's perceptions of success in the courts, the more likely the legal authority will be invoked.
3. The greater the costs in initiating the legal process, the less likely the legal authority will be invoked.
4. The greater the shopkeeper's experience with the legal process, the more likely the legal authority will be invoked.
5. The greater the availability of alternative mechanisms for handling the shoplifting, the less likely the public legal authority will be invoked.

Translating this conceptual framework into a hypothetical description may help to elucidate the hypotheses. Shoplifting would be particularly likely to be a salient issue for a shopkeeper losing a substantial amount of gross income to theft. As a result he would be likely to conceptualize the event as a crime and seek assistance from the police. The decision to do so, however, will depend upon the expected benefits as compared to the perceived costs. This evaluation will itself be influenced by previous experience with the criminal courts, particularly as a victim of shoplifting. Yet, if he discovered that the perpetrator in the particular incident was an old friend, who had frequented the store for years, he would be much more likely to handle the event differently. Perhaps letting the individual know on the next visit to the store that he or she would be watched much more closely, perhaps making a comment to allow the perpetrator to "discover" having "forgotten" to pay for the item. A myriad of variations on these same themes could be recited. In each case, however, the same dimensions illustrated in Figure 2-2 would bear evaluating.

Another example might be a situation in which a child was punched to the ground by another youngster. Such an incident might be conceptualized as a case of "boys will be boys," or as a criminal assault. The choice will again depend upon the various dimensions of the incident and the victim's relationship to the perpetrator. How often has this happened; did injuries result? Was it the boy next door who is so kind in other ways, from a nice family, and so on, or the one down the street who's a no-good? Or is it someone we've never seen before who doesn't "belong" in the neighborhood? Each of these will be relevant considerations not only to the definition of the incident but—importantly for our concerns here—to the decision to seek outside assistance. Here again the invocation of the public legal authority will depend upon the perceived accessibility of the criminal justice system. Precisely the same dimensions, and in the same direction as in the previous example, will be important in the determination of the appropriate action to be taken.

Support for the model need not be confined to hypothetical examples, for there is empirical evidence regarding notification of the police which, although conceptualized differently, is consistent with a dispute-processing model. The decision to notify police is, of course, essential if the criminal courts are to take cognizance of a criminal offense. If the victim chooses to invoke the criminal law, notification of the police is generally the appropriate response.[13] Victimization surveys have documented the substantial gap between self-reported victimization and self-reported notification of the police, as well as verifying the discrepancy between self-reported victimization and police knowledge of offenses. There are many reasons why individuals choose not to report a crime to the police. It is argued here that those reasons can be predicted and best explained by a dispute-processing model. That is, the victim's evaluation of the incident and interpersonal dimensions of the event, as well as the perceived accessibility and benefits of the criminal justice system, will determine whether the victim will respond to the offense by invoking the power of the public courts.

In an early victimization study commissioned by the President's Commission on Law Enforcement and the Administration of Justice, a national random sample was asked: "Were you or anyone in the household in a fist fight or attacked in any way by another person—including another household member—within the last twelve months?" Notification of the police for such incidents was shown to be directly dependent upon the relationship between victim and offender and the seriousness of bodily injury as indicated by extent of medical care required. The precise indicator values for the relationship variable were "stranger," "known," and "relative." As predicted, the proportion of victims notifying police declines as the perpetrator denotation moves from "stranger," to "known," to "relative." Sixty-six percent, 51 percent, and 44 percent of the victims reported the incident to the police, respectively (Block, 1974). Those figures surely support the conclusion that the closer the victim-offender relationship, the less likely the police will be notified. Indeed, the dispute processing model proposed here would predict a similar result. The difference lies in the explanatory variable. The dispute processing model implies that while the "stranger-known-relative" continuum "works" in terms of prediction, it actually serves as a substitute for the underlying explanatory variables which constitute the interpersonal dimensions in the model. While in general it is reasonable to expect that the salience, intensity, duration, and affinity of a relationship might increase from "stranger" to "known" to "relative," use of the latter suppresses differences that surely exist, for example the relatives who detest one another and are thus more likely to notify the police than if the incident were between strangers.

A similar argument can be made with respect to the seriousness of the bodily injury variable in the same study. The values employed were (1) no injury; (2) injury, but no medical attention; (3) medical attention, but no hospitalization; and (4) hospitalization. The proportion of victims notifying police under each of these circumstances was 46 percent, 54 percent, 69 percent, and 69 percent, respectively (Block 1974). This measure of "seriousness" of the injury could again be interpreted as a substitute for a number of the incident dimensions illustrated in Figure 2-2, particularly salience, intensity, and loss.

A review of the reasons victimization study respondents did not notify police of assaults indicates the relevance of the accessibility dimensions to the decision to invoke the power of the criminal justice system. Except for decisions based upon the private nature of the incident (that is, interpersonal dimensions), the reasons cited for not notifying the police reflect the following dimensions of accessibility: perceived chances of success, 41 percent ("offender would not be punished," "police would not bother," "police could do nothing," and "offender would be caught"); time and costs, 15 percent ("afraid of reprisal," and "time lost"); and experience, 8 percent ("did not know how to notify," and "too confused to notify"). These data, while limited, reflect the results emerging from victimization surveys. In each case they support the relevance of the dispute processing model to the initiation of the criminal process.

Police and the decision to formalize the dispute. Notification of the police does not necessarily mean that a case will eventually find its way into the criminal courts. Once called, the police officer becomes the critical decision-maker, screening out a substantial proportion of the potential workload of the courts. The police response to a citizen call varies according to a number of factors. It follows from this model that the decision by the police to make an arrest is dependent upon the officer's view of the event as a dispute between victim and alleged perpetrator. Some examples from the literature will clarify the relationship. Goldstein, in his critical discussion of police discretion not to invoke the law (a practice he would like to see severely limited), notes that the police choose not to enforce the felonious assault laws against an assailant whose victim does not sign a complaint (Goldstein, 1960, p. 545). Felonious assault is not a minor dispute; it can be an extremely serious offense. Yet, without a willing complainant, the criminal statute involved is left unenforced. Were social control the modus operandi of the criminal justice system, surely an arrest would need to be made, even if the lack of a supportive complainant would result in the case's being dismissed in court. Actually, from a purely social control perspective, it could be argued that the immediacy of the arrest itself and short-term incarceration pending the making of bail (longer term if bond is not raised) would in itself act as a sanction upon the criminal offender. In fact, however, no sanction is imposed, and the police defer to the wishes of the complainant.

This view of police behavior has been documented by Donald Black and Albert Reiss in a four-city study of police behavior. In an effort to determine the factors which are most influential in the decisions of police officers to make an arrest in citizen-initiated encounters with suspects, Black concludes that "arrest practices sharply reflect the preferences of citizen complainants far more than they serve an organized community" (Black, 1971, p. 1105). Although that finding is quite understandable in terms of a dispute processing model (that is, as a dispute between victim and suspect), Black and others continue to attempt to constrain their findings within a social control model of the legal system. To add further support to a dispute processing view,

Black also finds that "the greater the relational distance between a complainant and a suspect, the greater is the likelihood of arrest" (Black, 1971, p. 1107).

In evaluating police encounters with juveniles, Black and Reiss (1970) report a similar finding. Most police encounters with juveniles occur at the behest of a citizen complainant, and the probability of an arrest reflects the wishes of the complainant. The wishes of the complainant so predominate the encounter that they explain the observed difference in arrest rates between black and white suspects.

That particular finding brings to mind reported and alleged variability in enforcement of the same laws among different communities by the same police department. The phrase "overpatrolled and under protected" frequently used to describe police behavior in urban ghettos may in part be a reflection of both the police perceptions of the wishes of the complainants as well as their actual preferences. If the perception is correct, it may of course be due to the belief by complainants that the criminal justice system does not offer them the likelihood of success were they to wish to pursue the case to judicial decision. The point is, however, that at the time of the encounter the indication to the police may be that there is no longer a dispute to be pursued. Thus a mechanism designed to process disputes no longer has a role to play.

Police perceptions of the nature of an interpersonal dispute and the desires of the complainant may of course be more a reflection of how such disputes are generally perceived rather than an incident-specific evaluation.[14] But the available data strongly point to the complainants' wishes in the context of the particular incident as providing the best prediction to the formalization of the dispute in the criminal justice system. Those wishes are in turn directly related to the variables of a dispute processing model.

Prosecutors, defense counsel, and dispositional decisions. The decision to make an arrest allows a case to enter the criminal justice system, but once made, counsel become the critical actors.[15] Indeed the focus of much of the criminal justice literature has been upon the behavior of lawyers. The adversarial nature of the adjudicative process creates a multiplicity of relationships for counsel within the criminal courts that makes their role rather complex. Criminal courts (and civil courts as well) are formally organized to place counsel in the position of representatives of the parties to a case; they are to become advocates for the interests of others. The interests of counsel are presumed to be perfectly consonant with those they represent and to be case-specific. In reality, of course, attorneys have their own interests, and in evaluating the efficacy of a dispute processing model the prosecutor and defense counsel must be considersd the surrogate disputants that they become in court. The notion that the adversarial system has broken down in criminal courts is based on the faulty assumption that counsel ever were ideal-type advocates. In requiring that the attorneys become surrogate disputants, the process naturally becomes primarily an interaction between these actors. The relevant variables, both incident and interpersonal dimensions, must therefore be evaluated with respect to the lawyers once the case enters the criminal courts.

At one level, prosecutors—like the police—evaluate each incident/offense from the perspective of the complainant and the victim-offender relationship. Part of this is due to the prosecutor's role as advocate for the state and only indirectly for the complainant's interest. Part is a matter of strategy, since the prosecutor's case is typically dependent upon the complaining witness's willingness to pursue the case in court. For example, the Vera Institute of Justice study of felony arrests (1977) found that 87 percent of the cases in which the defendant and victim had a prior relationship were dismissed by the prosecution because of the victim-complainant's failure to pursue the case.

The prosecutor also must evaluate the incident. This model argues that the same incident dimensions relevant to the victim's conceptualization of the act as criminal and decision to notify the police are relevant to the prosecutor. As with the victim-offender relationship, at one level the prosecutor merely evaluates the incident from the perspective of the complainant as a means of determining the likelihood of pressing for actual prosecution. At another level, however, prosecutors evaluate incidents with respect to their own feelings about the nature of the event.[16] No doubt the salience and intensity of the matter to the prosecutor are influenced by the perceived social view of the offense in general, and the media coverage of the actual event in particular. Such influences upon prosecutorial decisions simply reflect the political role of the office.

Figure 2-3 illustrates the multiplicity of intracourt relationships which bear consideration and to which this model speaks. The victim-offender relationship has already been discussed as critical to the decision to invoke the authority of the criminal courts. The victim-prosecutor and offender-defense counsel relationships reflect the advocacy role of each of the lawyers and their professional obligations.[17] However, in contrast to the formal obligation of lawyers to "exercise independent professional judgment on behalf of a client," and to "represent a client zealously within the bounds of the law,"[18] a dispute processing model predicts that the nature of the relationship between

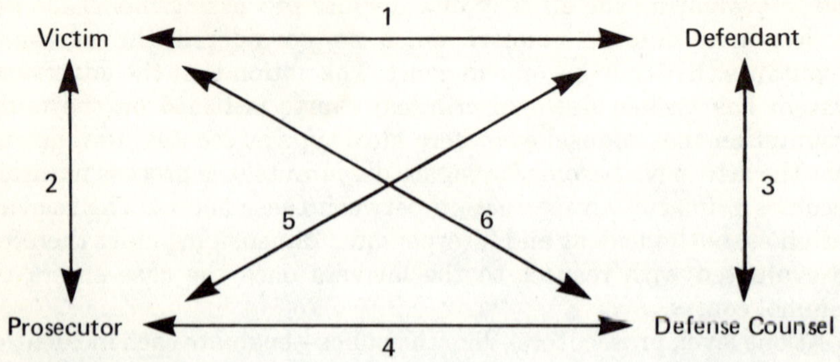

Figure 2-3. Interpersonal Relationships in Criminal Court

defendant and counsel (#3 in Figure 2-3) and between prosecutor and victim-complainant (#2 in Figure 2-3) (for example, duration, frequency, saliency, and so on) will affect the actions of the lawyers in the court. For example, private counsel who represent prominent clients or are frequently called to represent the same individual will, because of the development of a valuable relationship, more nearly meet the ideal-type representation than the case-specific advocacy of many private counsel and virtually all public defenders.[19] In addition, as illustrated in Figure 2-3, the model takes cognizance of the relationships between defendant and prosecutor (#5 in Figure 2-3), and between victim and defense counsel (#6 in Figure 2-3). The former may particularly occur in cases of prominent defendants, where the media and political influence may affect prosecutorial decision-making, or where the defendant may provide information or testimony for the prosecution of other cases. The latter has been known to facilitate mutually agreeable arrangements without regard for the interests of the defendant. Such relationships, however, must be evaluated in conjunction with the more important relationship among the surrogate disputants, the prosecutor, and the defense counsel (#4 in Figure 2-3). Indeed, it is their relationship to which much of the criminal justice research has been addressed. This has been due in part to the attention given to plea bargaining that typically involves interaction between the prosecutor and defense counsel, with actual participation by either the judge or the original disputants quite rare.[20]

The interpersonal dimension shown in Figure 2-1 can easily be applied to the relationship between prosecutor and defense counsel. Although the importance of that relationship to the processing of criminal cases has been stated often (Skolnick, 1967; Blumberg, 1967;

Eisenstein and Jacob, 1977), little if anything has been done actually to develop measures to evaluate it. Rather, a dichotomization is typically drawn between those who work together on a continuing basis, thereby necessarily developing a working relationship, and those who have only occasional interaction and are thus unlikely to develop such a relationship. Prosecutors and public defenders clearly fall into the former category. Among private defense counsel, the typical dichotomization is between "courthouse regulars" and those attorneys who appear in the criminal courts only infrequently.

The development of a collaborative relationship among persons working together on a continuing basis is not peculiar to the criminal courts. Indeed, one need not be a social scientist to recognize such a likelihood. One criminal defendant articulated precisely the same point:

> Mr. Watkins the prosecutor runs his office and Mr. Stankowski, the head public defender, he runs his office, but no one can't tell me that they're not on good terms or even friends. If not friends, they're . . . they've got a nice working arrangement. They've been knowing each other for over ten years. They got to have respect for each other, so forth and so on. Now, I guess when they sit down and go over a bunch of cases, they say, well, look at this guy, what are we going to do about him? You know he's guilty, but he's got this little technicality here, and its true. I think the public defender sacrifice him and in his opinion he justifies it by asking a favor to maybe a kid that he's guilty but he's not pleading guilty. He's going to cause a lot of stink, and he's . . . say, because he's young, let's give him a break. They could go through the trouble of convicting him if they want. Just . . . always, I think, in a sense, one hand washes the other. (Casper, 1971, p. 6)

A somewhat more eloquent, but no more precise, statement of the same point is that "when members are familiar with one another, negotiations are facilitated. When they are not, adversary proceedings are more likely" (Eisenstein and Jacob, p. 37). Or "the desire to reduce uncertainty leads to the development of several norms designed to make behavior predictable. One is 'stick by your work and never mislead deliberately.' Attorneys who violate this norm find they are punished. Another is 'no surprises.' It is often illegal to call surprise witnesses or to introduce evidence that the opposing counsel is unaware of; it is almost always regarded as a dirty trick" (Eisenstein and Jacob, p. 28). While I have no quarrel with any of this, it seems to be another way of speaking about the interpersonal relationships that develop among the surrogate disputants. Indeed, it seems to differ very little, if at all, from the relationships which develop among civil attorneys, particularly in personal injury work where continuing working relationships often exist between defense and plaintiff's counsel.

Although observations of working relationships between prosecutors and defense counsel are plentiful, there is little relevant data. Indeed, distinctions are sometimes made between cooperative and noncooperative regular defense attorneys. That is, not all regular defense attorneys are observed to subscribe to the informal norms that are said to be established in the courtroom (Eisenstein and Jacob, p. 120). Such distinctions among individual "regulars" call for an analysis of the kind provided by a dispute processing model that focuses upon individual interactions and would predict a continuum of relationships rather than a dichotomization.

One study has in fact shown that the frequency of participation (number of cases) by private counsel in the court relates both to plea bargaining rates and to the severity of sentences negotiated. The greater the amount of participation by counsel, the more likely plea bargaining is to occur, and the higher the sentences bargained (Nardulli, 1978). Such findings are consistent with a dispute processing model, for it uses the duration/frequency facet of the interpersonal dimensions as an independent variable. The model would predict that the greater than dimension, the more likely counsel would be to promote the interests of that relationship rather than the formal relationship with the client. In this case it would mean more negotiated pleas, and less adversarial bargaining that would result in more severe sentences for the same offense.

A dispute processing model would further predict that a defense counsel who had previously served as a prosecutor in the same courts would be likely to have a different kind of relationship, and therefore different pattern of negotiating and processing cases, than another regular defense counsel without such prior experience. It would also be expected that prosecutors and public defenders who anticipate long-term careers in the criminal courts, and therefore more highly value their relationships with other counsel in that milieu, would be expected to behave rather differently from those who are there for shorter duration. "Participants develop a stake in maintaining the basic outlines of their ongoing system" (Clynch and Neubauer, 1977). But why? And do all participants develop the same stake? What are the variables which help explain the variability? Ultimately, such questions can only be answered by further research.

THE MERITS OF A DISPUTE PROCESSING MODEL

Models in social science are analytic constructs intended to elucidate parsimoniously the phenomenon under examination. Although predictive capability may be desirable, it is the level of explanatory power by which models are evaluated. With respect to the criminal courts, model-building has only recently begun to develop. In part this is due to the need first to gather descriptive data. What has most prominently emerged can best be denoted as an administrative-bureaucratic-organizational model purported to describe and clarify the criminal courts in operation (Blumberg, 1967; Skolnick, 1967; Feeley, 1972; Mohr, 1976; Eisenstein and Jacob, 1977; Clynch and Neubauer, 1977, Nardulli, 1978).[21]

Beginning with Abraham Blumber's work, *Criminal Justice* (1967), this view in its many variations has attracted an increasing number of proponents. I use all three terms because they are all used in the literature to describe perspectives that are very closely related. Yet I hesitate to denote them identically to avoid imposing a uniformity which does not exist. In some variations the bureaucratic model itself veers from description and analysis to polemic, with attendant charges of assembly-line justice. This series of models is in one important dimension closely related to Packer's crime control model (1968). Where Packer calls for uniformity and predictability, Blumberg provides empirical evidence that those goals are often achieved in practice. It is somewhat paradoxical, however, that the goal of crime control seems no closer. Blumberg notes that the system he examined may actually work to the advantage of the guilty. Actually, the various empirical studies which draw upon these administrative-organizational-bureaucratic perspectives differ considerably in their degree of predictability. Thus, as an example, Blumberg (1967) describes extensive uniformity and regularity; Eisenstein and Jacob (1977), while taking an organizational perspective, find a great deal of individuation in the processing of cases.

The other central variable in the organizational framework is the commonality of goals which develops among regular actors. Each and every participant is viewed as self-interested in the perpetuation of the organization. The traditional view focuses upon the need for measurable results, with the effort to establish the efficacy of the organization often having the effect of distorting organizational goals. This distortion is particularly likely when the essential goals are not easily quantified. More measurable substitute goals then begin to take precedence. In the criminal courts, where the goal of the administration of justice is impervious to clear definition, let alone measurement, the expeditious processing of cases is often substituted as an internal goal. Thus court personnel and court critics focus on caseloads and backlogs as indicators of performance.[22] The adversarial structure dictated by the formal law is doomed to failure under such circumstances. The empirical referent for exposition of this perspective is the extent to which plea bargaining has replaced the trying of fact in the disposition of criminal cases.

As noted above, not all proponents of the organization model take as strict a view as a traditional model would imply. Eisenstein and Jacob (1977) dismiss the formal bureaucratic model as inapplicable to criminal court processes. Instead, they focus upon informal workgroups which, although they develop their own operating rules, tend to vary by individual courtroom. Until now, however, the workgroup concept has been used more as a postanalysis perspective than as a basis for designing research for testing.

The dispute processing model proposed here does not contradict the empirical finds of studies of the criminal courts to date. Indeed, much of it would be predictable from such a model. However, there are several benefits of the dispute processing model over the administrative-bureaucratic-organizational models which have gained prominence in the recent literature. First, as indicated in a number of examples discussed above, many of the variables employed in those models can best be viewed as surrogates for the variables in the dispute processing model. As such, they lead to similar but presumably less precise predictions. Second, models should aim not only for parsimony, but for clarity. The dispute processing model has a number of advantages in explanatory power. It includes variables that predict the documented variance among individual courtrooms and between different individual actors. While concentrating on individual decision-makers, it takes cognizance of the complexity of relationships and incident variables relevant to the handling of cases in the criminal courts. In addition, it broadens the relevant exploratory map, placing criminal courts in the context of dispute processing institutions in general, and makes clear that more research is needed to understand the circumstances surrounding the decisions to invoke the public authority of the criminal justice system.

CONCLUSION

American criminal courts are structured to deal with cases in the form of controversies; dispute processing is the medium of operation. The centrality of that medium to the courts has a strong message that has not been heeded in attempts to understand the criminal courts and the part they play in the system of justice. While empirical research necessitate a narrow focus for detailed analysis, the neglect of the broader context, particularly the relationship of the items under study to other parts of the legal environment, is unwarranted.[23] Curiously the limited attempts to connect the criminal courts to the larger political environment (Balbus, 1973; Levin, 1977) have not explicated the connection; rather, they have moved from the very broad nature of politics and distribution of power in a given jurisdiction to the output of the criminal courts defined as dispositions, most particularly severity of sentence. The dispute processing model attempts to explain a continuous process, albeit with discrete decision points, from the occurrence of incidents which the formal law describes as criminal to and through the criminal courts. In particular, it takes cognizance of the American legal system's reliance upon the initiatives of private citizens, most of whose experience with the criminal justice apparatus is too irregular to involve them in any working relationships so essential to the organizational stance.

In the aggregate, the cases which enter the criminal courts make criminal justice policy. They provide the basis for future decisions to bring cases to the attention of the criminal courts, and often for legislative change affecting access to this governmental power. As noted above, Pound recognized long ago that the efficacy of legislative change was dependent upon the initiation of cases to use the public power thus granted to the advantage of the litigant. The formal law establishes norms in the form of providing opportunities for certain individuals and issues to use public power. But the determination of who uses the criminal justice system, how it is used, and for what ends is dependent upon the variables appropriate to a dispute processing model. Much of the well-documented failure of the criminal justice system is attributable to unrealistic expectations which rest on the assumption that it is basically a system of norm enforcement. A dispute processing model forces recognition that the mode of operation of the criminal courts is such that the cases they process, the manner in which they are processed, and their outcomes are dependent upon the preferences of initial disputants, later decision-makers' perceptions of those preferences, and the interests of the surrogate disputants in court. Additionally, each stage allows for, in fact dictates, consideration of the broader social norms with respect to the acts in question.

Although the dispute processing model does not reject the findings of empirical research on the criminal courts, it does suggest that future research needs to be designed actually to test the efficacy of the organizational models prominent today. The model presented here argues, however, that the indicators be substantially refined and specified, and that the relevant circle of inquiry be expanded to include most particularly the original initiators of the basically reactive criminal courts. Only then will we begin to understand the actual and potential political role that the criminal courts play in the society.

NOTES

1. I have noted elsewhere that the decision to establish and enforce norms in the criminal or the civil sphere is essentially a political-administrative decision made by lawmakers (Zemans, 1977).

2. Although no further references will be made to the economic analysis of the law, I think that both the "costs" and "benefits" of initiating a civil or criminal action in the public legal system have been insufficiently identified and explicated in most of the work in that genre.

3. See Parnas (1970) for a description of the handling of family disputes in a number of cities.

4. The sole exception among the alternative dispute processing programs covered in the ABA Conference Report is the Institute for Mediation and Conflict Resolution's Brooklyn Dispute Center, which handles primarily felony cases. Felony assaults, burglary, robbery, larceny, and statutory rape cases deemed suitable for mediation account for 80 percent of its caseload.

5. Efforts to force fit such cases into a system designed to process disputes have resulted in distortions of the basic structure. In particular, vice squads and the use of informers have proliferated with the rise in legislation prohibiting behavior without an identifiable victim. For a critical discussion of such practices see Goldstein (1960).

6. By 1976 twelve states had instituted victim compensation programs, with a number of others developing them. There have also been federal efforts in this direction, as well as similar programs in Canada, New Zealand, the United Kingdom, and Australia. For a discussion of the various roles of the victim as participant in the criminal justice system, see selected chapters in McDonald (1976). For a brief history and discussion of the experience of state programs see Edelhertz and Geis (1974) and Geis in McDonald (1976). Information on programs in other countries is contained in Linden (1968).

7. For a listing of these programs see "Help for Victims and Witnesses, Annual Report from National District Attorneys Association Commission on Victim Witness Assistance," National District Attorneys Association, Chicago, Illinois.

8. It could be hypothesized that disputes tend to be processed by the dispute resolution machinery of the most intimate social unit with which all disputants are associated. Where there is no "community" (as is often the case in conflicts among strangers in urban America) then invoking the public legal system may be the only option. Indeed, increased litigation may be a symptom of a breakdown of community. The availability of alternative dispute processing mechanisms may also be related to the social distance between the disputants. The more socially separated may be more likely to seek out and proceed with formal adjudication due to less agreement on the basics necessary for unenforceable negotiated and mediated settlements.

9. Diversion was mentioned in the report of the President's Commission on Law Enforcement and the Administration of Justice in 1967, and by 1973 was part of a model criminal justice system proposed by the National Advisory Commission on Criminal Justice Standards and Goals. The latter defined this often imprecisely used term as the kind of alternative included among the dispute processing model's dimensions of accessibility:

> "Diversion" refers to formally acknowledged . . . efforts to utilize alternatives to . . . the justice system. To qualify as diversion such efforts must be under-

taken prior to adjudication and after a legally proscribed action has occurred. . . . Diversion implies halting or suspending formal criminal or juvenile justice proceedings against a person who has violated a statute, in favor of processing through a noncriminal disposition (*Corrections Task Force Report*, National Commission on Criminal Justice Standards and Goals, 1973, p. 50).

10. For an example of this see Zemans (1977).

11. This example is atypical, since the victim rarely observes the perpetrator. Most victimizations, even those reported to police, provide little if any information upon which the criminal justice machinery could proceed. Indeed, such cases do not become part of the workload of the criminal courts.

12. See Felstiner (1975) for a discussion of avoidance as a means of dealing with disputes, particularly in technologically complex, rich societies such as our own.

13. Some criminal complaints are made directly to the prosecutor's office. They generally involve property loss rather than personal damage cases and do not occur at the time of the offense.

14. A contemporary example of this problem is reflected in the recent settlement of a suit brought on behalf of battered wives. Domestic disputes have traditionally been handled as interpersonal incidents rather than as matters of crime control. The role of the police officer has been one of order maintenance, intervention to control ongoing violence. In such cases the police often play the role of mediator to settle the matter on the spot. Recently there have been complaints that the police have not taken the appropriate stance toward such cases, and that their behavior has resulted in further injuries to victims. In a recent settlement of a lawsuit on this issue (*Bruno* v. *McGuire*, Case #21946/76, State Supreme Court of New York County) the New York City police agreed to alter acknowledged department policy including controlling their reluctance to make arrests, declining to act as mediators, and remaining at the scene both to insure the victim's safety and assist in seeking medical help. See *New York Law Journal*, June 27, 1978, for a description of the settlement.

15. The overwhelming evidence in the literature on the criminal courts is that the judge plays nowhere near the central role in the disposition of cases that can be inferred from the formal law. It could, however, be argued that judicial consideration of the incident and interpersonal dimensions from the perspective of the original disputants is obvious. Sentencing is the one part of the criminal justice process where even the formal law recognizes the appropriateness, indeed dictates consideration, of the circumstances surrounding an incident, including presumably the relationship between victim and offender. Partly based on an independent sentencing report, it is the judge's role to evaluate these factors.

16. Prosecutors, of course, also evaluate cases according to the availability and quality of the evidence, as well as statutory constraints limiting the time which can elapse before trial (for example, Speedy Trial Act, 120 day rule).

17. The formal obligation of the prosecutor to the victim is not actually analogous to that of the defense counsel to the defendant, for the prosecutor is the state's attorney. With respect to interactions in the courtroom process,

however, the model predicts that the relationship between the victim and the prosecutor may affect the disposition.

18. Canons 5 and 7 of the Code of Professional Responsibility.

19. The development of even a minimal relationship between defendant and counsel is proscribed in courts where sequential representation is the standard manner of providing counsel for indigent defendants. With a succession of public defenders participating in the same case at different points in time, the defendant has virtually no opportunity to develop a relationship with counsel that might influence the processing of his or her case. See Gilboy and Schmidt (1979).

20. A field experiment in Dade County, Florida, conducted by the Center for Studies in Criminal Justice of the University of Chicago Law School provided for judicial, victim, defendant, and police participation in pretrial settlement conferences for negotiating pleas. Designed specifically to determine whether such participation would alter the rate or results of plea negotiations, the lay participation was far from overwhelming. While defendants attended two-thirds of the conferences, victims attended only one-third. Many, however, claimed that they had not received notification of the conference. See Kerstetter and Heinz (1978).

21. The due process and crime control models explicated by Herbert Packer (1968) are prescriptive rather than descriptive; they are ideals toward which to advocates of each would want the system in operation to aspire. Indeed, Packer gives a great deal of attention to the values underlying each model to elucidate the normative conflict inherent in the criminal justice system.

22. In much the same way prosecutors are evaluated on the basis of conviction rates and police by clearance rates.

23. It should be noted that Eisenstein and Jacob (1977) acknowledge the relevance of environmental factors. Yet they seem implicitly to diminish their importance by focusing upon the internal workgroup as the object of study.

REFERENCES

Balbus, Isaac (1973). *The Dialectics of Legal Repression*. New York: Russell Sage Foundation.

Black, Donald J. (1971). "The Social Organization of Arrest." *Stanford Law Review* 23:6 (June), 1087-1111.

________, and Reiss, Albert J., Jr. (1970). "Police Control of Juveniles." *American Sociological Review* 23:1 (February).

Block, Richard (1974). "Why Notify the Police, The Victim's Decision to Notify the Police of an Assault." 11 *Criminology* 555.

Blumberg, Abraham S. (1967). *Criminal Justice*. Chicago: Quadrangle Books.

Carlin, Jerome, and Howard, Jan (1965). "Legal Representation and Class Justice." 12 *UCLA Law Review* 381.

Casper, Jonathan (1971). "Did You Have a Lawyer When You Went to Court? No, I Had a Public Defender." *Yale Review of Law and Social Action* 1 (Spring), 4-9.

Clynch, Edward, and Neubauer, David (1977). "Trial Courts as Organizations: A Critique and Synthesis." Revision of a paper delivered at the 1977 Annual Meeting of the Midwest Political Science Association, Chicago.

Danzig, Richard, and Lowy, Michael J. (1975). "Everyday Disputes and Mediation in the United States: A Reply to Professor Felstiner." *Law & Society Review* 9:4 (Summer), 675-94.

Edelhertz, Herbert, and Geis, Gilbert (1974). *Public Compensation to Victims of Crime*. New York: Praeger.

Eisenstein, James, and Jacob, Herbert (1977). *Felony Justice*. Boston: Little, Brown and Company.

Feeley, Malcolm (1975). "The Effects of Heavy Caseloads." Paper presented at the 1975 Annual Meeting of the American Political Science Association, September 2-3.

Felstiner, William L.F. (1975). "Avoidance as Dispute Processing." *Law and Society Review* 9:4 (Summer).

Geis, Gilbert (1976). "Crime Victims and Victim Compensation Programs." In William F. McDonald, ed. *Criminal Justice and the Victim*, 237-59. Beverly Hills, Calif.: Sage.

Gilboy, Janet A., and Schmidt, John R. (1979). "Replacing Lawyers: A Case Study of the Sequential Representation of Criminal Defendants." 70:1 *Journal of Criminal Law and Criminology*, 1-26.

Goldstein, Joseph (1960). "Police Discretion Not to Invoke the Criminal Process: Low Visibility Decisions in the Administration of Justice," 69 *Yale Law Journal*, 543-94.

Heumann, Milton (1975). "A Note on Plea Bargaining and Case Pressure." 9 *Law & Society Review, 515-28.*

Kerstetter, Wayne A., and Heinz, Anne M. (1978). "Pretrial Settlement Conference." Chicago: Center for Studies in Criminal Justice, University of Chicago.

Levin, Martin (1977). *Urban Politics and Criminal Courts*. Chicago: University of Chicago Press.

Linden, Allen (1968). The Report of the Osgoode Hall Study on *Compensation for Victims of Crime*. Toronto: Osgoode Hall Law School.

McDonald, William, F., ed. (1976). "Criminal Justice and the Victim." Beverly Hills, Calif.: Sage.

Mohr, Lawrence (1976). "Organizations, Decisions and Courts." 10 Law & *Society Review*, 621-42.

Nardulli, Peter F. (1978). *The Courtroom Elite: An Organizational Perspective on Criminal Justice*. Cambridge, Mass.: Ballinger Publishing Company.

________ (with Kathleen Proch) (1979). "The Caseload Controversy and the Study of Criminal Courts." 70:1 *Journal of Criminal Law and Criminology*, 89-101.

National District Attorneys Association Commission on Victim Witness Assistance. "Help for Victims and Witnesses." Annual Report, Chicago, Illinois.

Packer, Herbert L. (1968). "Two Models of the Criminal Process." In *The Limits of the Criminal Sanction*, pp. 149-73. Palo Alto, Calif.: Stanford University Press.

Parnas, Raymond I. (1970). "Judicial Response to Intra-Family Violence." *Minnesota Law Review* 54:5 (January).

Pound, Roscoe (1917). "The Limits of Effective Legal Action." *International Journal of Ethics* 27 (January).

_______ (1942). *Social Control through Law*. New Haven, Conn.: Yale University Press.

Reiss, Albert (1971). *The Police and the Public*. New Haven, Conn.: Yale University Press.

Robin, Gerald D. (1967). "The Corporate and Judicial Disposition of Employee Thieves." *Wisconsin Law Review* 685.

Sander, Frank (1978). "Report on the National Conference on Minor Disputes Resolution." American Bar Association.

Schneider, Anne L.; Burcart, Janie M.; and Wilson, L.A., II (1976). The Role of Attitudes in the Decision to Report Crimes to the Police." In William F. McDonald, ed. *Criminal Justice and the Victim*, pp. 89-113. Beverly Hills, Calif.: Sage.

Skolnick, Jerome H. (1967). "Social Control in the Adversary System." 11 *Journal of Conflict Resolution* 52-70.

Vera Institute of Justice (1977). *Felony Arrests: Their Prosecution and Disposition in New York City's Courts*. New York: Vera Institute.

Zemans, Frances K. (1977). "Civil or Criminal Litigation of Disputes: A Rose by Any Other Name. . . ." Paper presented at the 1977 Annual Meeting of the Midwest Political Science Association, Chicago, Illinois.

Chapter Three

Doing the Dirty Business of Coping with Crime: The Contemporary "Crisis" of American Criminal Courts,

Austin Sarat

The focus of this chapter is only indirectly on criminal courts in America. Its major concern is with the different ways in which social scientists and others think about criminal courts, the ways in which they describe them and analyze their operations. However, to say that I am concerned primarily with the styles of thought, description, and analysis that are employed in studying criminal courts is not to say that I am concerned only with the sociology of knowledge. Those styles have had an important influence on the way criminal courts actually operate and an important role in generating public and political pressures for reform. The explosion, in the last few years, of empirical research on criminal courts has made those courts more visible than in the past. It has revealed and documented what criminal justice practitioners have always known and what outsiders have either suspected or tacitly accepted.

The business of criminal courts is nasty business. It requires constant interaction with nasty people and constant attention to social troubles. To say this is not to advance the state of our knowledge of criminal courts. However, as obvious as it may be as a descriptive statement, it is one whose implications for criminal courts—as well as for the way in which we think about, describe, and analyze them—are seldom thought through. The fact that criminal courts are nasty places must be taken seriously as we develop expectations about how those courts should operate and as we develop strategies for reform.

The problem of developing such expectations and strategies is a serious one. Social science scholarship has been quick to point to failings in criminal courts and to elaborate normative standards for measuring their performance. At the same time, the "due process revolution" of the 1960s placed new and important demands on the courts, demands which were often quite at odds with the methods and procedures which had, over a long period of time, been employed in dealing with the problems of crime. This revolution clarified the distinction between factual and legal guilt and laid down rules to ensure that the legal rights of the accused were fully protected (Packer, 1968). That distinction and those rules, which struck and continue to strike many as counterintuitive (Fleming, 1978), seemed, at least at first, to make more difficult the "order maintenance" responsibilities of criminal justice officials.

Social science scholarship and appellate court decisions combined to suggest to those who participate in the criminal justice process and to a wider public audience that there was, and is, something wrong in criminal courts and that there were, and are, serious defects in criminal procedure. The result, which contributed to the oft-noted "crisis" afflicting criminal courts, was the widespread belief that criminal courts are neither fully legitimate nor minimally effective in dealing with problems of crime. This awakened sense of crisis reflects no dramatic changes in courts; there is, indeed, little new in the way they operate. It reflects, instead, dramatic changes in the way courts are perceived and evaluated.

My purpose in this chapter is to review the major paradigms used to describe and evaluate criminal courts and to suggest how each of those paradigms is, in its own way, foreign to the constraints and limits which are an inevitable aspect of criminal courts. Each ignores the nature of the tasks confronting those courts. It is the complexity and difficulty of those tasks which goes far in determining what happens in criminal courts. It is unrealistic to expect radical change or dramatic improvement unless or until we change, or limit, the social tasks which are performed in criminal courts.

Due to such deficiencies, it is both necessary and appropriate to develop new paradigms for describing and evaluating criminal courts, paradigms which are closer to what those courts in fact do and which would be recognizable to those who are involved in processing criminals as well as to those who study such behavior (Sarat, 1978). Such paradigms must reflect the fact that criminal courts are not autonomous. They are part of the dispute processing networks which, in every community, deal with social problems and social troubles (Sarat and Grossman, 1975; Neubauer, 1974). Criminal courts interact with other dispute processing institutions and are in turn influenced by these interactions (Eisenstein and Jacob, 1977). There is, however, a division of labor within the network of institutions that process disputes. Some dispute processors—for example, appellate courts—are relatively well insulated and deal with trouble only after it has been thoroughly screened by others or with particular segments of social trouble. Other dispute processors deal only with particular types of people. This is true, for example, of the internal mechanisms of professional or trade associations. Still others deal only with interesting intellectual issues removed from the particular contexts and the particular people whose trouble give rise to those issues (see, for instance, Kagan, 1978).

The normative standards employed to evaluate the operation of criminal courts must reflect, or at least be attuned to, the constraints implicit in the social tasks that criminal courts perform. Dispute processing institutions that are insulated, those that deal with persons of high status, and those that deal primarily with intellectual issues are likely to differ sharply from those that are faced on a daily basis with "bad" people and "messy" problems. Thus, one should not expect criminal courts ever to be as orderly or efficient as, for example, their appellate counterparts. We know, in addition, from studies of the legal profession (Blumberg, 1967) that criminal lawyers are tainted by their association with criminal types. The same is true of criminal courts.

To evaluate criminal courts, it is necessary to examine closely their functions and to think about what it is that they are asked to do in the social order. In this regard, we can talk about the responsibilities of criminal courts in processing deviants or coping with the problems of social disintegration. Or, we can speak more plainly and point out criminal courts do the "dirty business" of dealing with undesirable people and undesirable behavior on a day-to-day basis. Criminal courts do the cleanup work that is inevitable in any complex society and is becoming increasingly necessary as the chaos in other social institutions increases in scope (Nisbet, 1975). Criminal courts will, as a result, always stand at the outer limits of respectability. The good criminal court will always be the "invisible" court.

DESCRIPTIVE PARADIGMS AND SOCIETAL EXPECTATIONS

Academic observers have failed to recognize the functional imperatives that govern the operation of criminal courts. Justice has, throughout American history, either been too fast to satisfy those concerned with the perfection of procedure or too slow to satisfy those who equate slow justice with no justice. Criminal courts have never been models of civility and efficiency (Hydebrand, 1976). They are noisy, disorganized, and at the edge of chaos because there is no ready way to treat in an antiseptic fashion people whose lives are disorganized and chaotic. Courts adapt to their clientele. The behavior of lawyers, judges, prosecutors, and other participants is attributable, in large part, to the nature of the people and problems they encounter. To them the now fashionable crisis which afflicts our criminal justice system has been and continues to be the "stuff" of their professional lives. For them there is no crisis in any meaningful sense of that term; given the nature of the demands placed on criminal courts, crisis is normal (Baar, 1974). The demands are embedded in descriptive paradigms employed in academic studies and attract varying public audiences. Three of these demands seem to be at the forefront of the discussion about the perceived contemporary crisis in our criminal courts.

The first is the demand for "strict legality," perhaps best articulated in Herbert Packer's (1968) "due process" model. The second is a demand that criminal courts contribute to the reduction of crime. It is generally manifested in calls for swift and certain punishment. This set of exceptions is described, in part, in Packer's "crime control" model. It has widespread popular appeal (Yankelovich, Skelly, and White, 1978). The third demand is recurrent and persistent in all institutions that deal with social problems such as crime. It is a demand that criminal courts contribute to the eradication of the causes of crime, that they provide social services within a community context. These three demands—for strict legality, social defense, and social service—are by no means mutually exclusive. Each in its own way, however, reflects an inaccurate understanding of the nature and operation of criminal courts and ignores the problems and pressures involved in conducting the kind of dirty business done by them.

The Demand for Strict Legality

As institutions embodied in a constitutional legal order, criminal courts are expected to enforce criminal law without violating the spirit or meaning of the Constitution. Even a brief reading of the Constitution and the Bill of Rights reveals the importance attached to the guarantees of criminal procedure in those documents. Those guarantees are intended to govern and restrict the way in which the state makes judgments of guilt or innocence and the way punishments are imposed. Legalists demand strict adherence to such guarantees. They see the problems of criminal courts as, in effect, problems of law-abidingness (Davis, 1969; Goldstein, 1969).

The demand for strict legality is based upon a deep-seated suspicion of the state's power. The legalists' response to the problems of criminal courts lies in an elaboration of detailed rules, rules designed to guarantee a fair and equal contest between the state and the accused. Each of those problems is seen as an aspect of the broader problem of discretion within legal institutions (Davis, 1969). Criminal courts are expected to function with a minimum of discretion and a maximum of procedural regularity, according to the legalists.

Current debate over sentencing exemplifies the legalist demands for rules and rule following. Starting with Marvin Frankel's (1972) highly influential book, the problem of sentencing has been pictured as a problem of judicial discretion. The rehabilitative ideal is criticized for giving to judges too little formal guidance (Von Hirsch, 1976); the response is to limit discretion and, at the same time, ensure more uniform treatment of offenders through detailed sentencing guidelines. Major decisions of the Warren Court in the area of criminal procedure exemplify the same tendency to treat the operation of criminal courts as susceptible to control and reform through the imposition of rules.

Viewed somewhat differently, the demand for strict legality is a demand for "perfect justice" (Fleming, 1974). Proponents suggest that any imperfection in the way criminal cases are processed should be sufficient to doom the prosecution. Strict legality further requires that courts and court procedures recognize and respect the distinction between factual and legal guilt. Courts must ensure that all defendants have the opportunity to contest the allegations made against them and that that opportunity is meaningful. This, in turn, means that police, prosecutors, and other officials must restrain their inclination to dispose of criminal cases expeditiously. It requires criminal court proceedings to be genuinely adversarial, that cooperation between prosecutor and defense be minimal.

According to Packer's (1968) due process model, the primary concern of courts is the protection of liberty. The model is very skeptical about the ability of any person to determine with certainty the truth of any factual event. From this skepticism flows an emphasis on adversariness and multiple review, both of which are seen as necessary in providing a check against error. Truth is less important than the procedure through which judgments about truth are made.

The due process model suggests that the main issue in criminal cases is arriving at a decision about whether an accused is legally innocent or legally guilty. It pictures the criminal process as separable into distinct stages—pretrial and trial—and emphasizes that the trial is the proper forum in which that decision can be made. Any departure from strict adversariness is regarded with suspicion and as a threat to the rules of the game and the legitimacy of criminal courts. The due process model generates a demand for the investment of substantial resources in the prosecution and defense of each case. Both sides are expected to treat each case as if the fate of constitutional government were at stake. The contest between the state and the accused is to be played out before a judge and jury, each entity dedicated to upholding the law and impartial as to the particulars of the cases being considered.

The problem with the demand for strict legality and the due process model is that both are far removed from what criminal courts actually do. Each of the participants in criminal courts possesses, as has been shown repeatedly, a greater interest in the establishment and maintenance of working relations than in the outcome of any one case. Cases come and go but police, prosecutors, judges, and defense lawyers interact on a continuing basis. It is unrealistic to expect them to treat each case as the opportunity to have a fight; it is unrealistic to expect that they could coexist in an environment of intense hostility. Cooperative relations must and do develop (Eisenstein and Jacob, 1977; Blumberg, 1967; Mather, 1979; and Feeley, 1973). It is equally unrealistic to expect that in an environment in which the resources available to the court are scarce and in which the pressures of heavy caseloads are substantial that any case could be allowed to consume an inordinate amount of time or energy. Strict legality must give way in the face of such pressures.

Moreover, the task structure of criminal courts derives from the nature of crime, not the nature of law. Criminal courts do not exist to protect innocent citizens; they exist to cope with the guilty. Social science research has taught us that questions of guilt or innocence are rarely at the heart of criminal processes. More often, what concerns criminal courts is the question of how to deal with individuals obviously guilty of a breach of the criminal law, individuals who themselves are rarely interested in contesting guilt (Feeley, 1979).

When viewed in this light, the demand for strict legality seems, at least to some, to require that participants in criminal courts give defendants more than they deserve. It seems to demand forebearance in the face of even the clearest cases of factual guilt and to require that criminal processes operate on the bases of an elaborate set of fictions, fictions that deny the obvious and accord respect to actions that do not merit such respect (Forer, 1975). The demand for strict legality transforms criminal court processes into "games." It focuses attention on how those processes are conducted rather than on their results. As in all games, the game itself and its rules are more important than the outcome of any single contest (Leff, 1978). The success of a criminal court, according to this view, is measured, therefore, by its devotion to those rules.

The reality of criminal courts is that they are not very pleasant places to be for either those accused of crime or for those doing the accusing. The unpleasantness which is associated with and a necessary part of the process of dealing with criminals eventually hardens participants in criminal courts in the same way that the unpleasantness of surgical procedures hardens surgeons. Can one realistically expect that individuals who in their day-to-day professional lives continuously confront the nastiness of social life will be responsive to a system of control which instructs them to presume the innocence of those who they feel certain are guilty? Furthermore, a high rate of guilty pleas need not be interpreted as resulting from unfair pressures applied on the helpless perpetrators of crime through trickery of malevolent prosecutors and judges. The high rate of guilty pleas may well indicate the factual culpability of most, indeed the vast majority, of those caught in the web of criminal justice. In such a setting the guarantees of the Bill of Rights and the pronouncements of the Supreme Court may appear to be no more than legal fictions, fictions which bear little relation to the daily work of criminal courts and which are, at worst, overly generous to the undeserving (Skolnick, 1966).

The Demand for Social Defense

The problem of crime is a major one and is deeply troubling to most Americans. To those concerned with it, the demand for strict legality is seen not only as overly generous to the undeserving but also as standing in the way of effective law enforcement. These individuals articulate a wholly different set of expectations concerning criminal court operations. This set of expectations can be viewed as a demand for social defense, a demand that courts do something about the crime problem. It is a demand that those who commit crime be apprehended and removed from society (Wilson, 1975; Von den Haag, 1975); that adjudication be integrated into the process of law enforcement; and that courts deal strictly and severely with criminals. Its focus is on the crime rate and on the role of courts in reducing it.

Social defense proponents are impatient with formality and the details of criminal procedures. Both are seen as protecting the guilty and exposing innocent citizens to the risk of criminal victimization. The problem of crime is seen largely, although not exclusively, as a problem relating to a well-defined group of habitual criminals. To deal with these people it is necessary regularly to employ punishment, incarceration in particular.

The first obligation of a society, according to those concerned with social defense, is the maintenance of order. Punishment that is swift, certain, and severe is a necessary tool in achieving this goal and is regarded as an effective general deterrent. For every criminal sent to jail, some unknown, but presumed to be substantial, number of others are, at least temporarily, discouraged from committing crime. The social defense perspective suggests that criminal courts all too rarely impose punishment, that the punishment which is imposed is neither swift nor severe enough, and is, as a result, ineffective.

In addition to its focus on the court's role in the war against crime, this perspective differs from the strict legality perspective in several other fundamental ways. First, the social defense perspective and the "crime control" model of which it is a part suggest that criminal courts operate on the presumption that those arrested for and charged with a crime are, in fact, guilty and that the determination of guilt is not a separable and distinct process. The social defense perspective and crime control model describe a process in which all of the participants believe that the truth of criminal events can be known and that the vehicle for ascertaining truth is investigation, not adversariness. Thus, they place a good deal of emphasis upon having an efficacious investigatory process. In their view, police and prosecutors should be given substantial discretion in enforcing the law. Thus, while proponents of strict legality fear an overzealous administration of criminal justice, advocates of social defense fear timidity. The latter look to police and prosecutors to determine the facts of criminal allegations and expect the rest of the criminal justice process to accommodate their findings.

The social defense perspective also differs from the strict legality perspective on epistemological grounds. While the legalists are epistemological skeptics, adherents of the crime control model are epistemological positivists. In their view the facts of criminal events are ascertained early in the criminal justice process. Little is left to doubt. Caution is replaced by certainty. Adversariness is an unnecessary luxury and, at worst, an impediment to truth (Strick, 1977). Thus to social defense adherents the primary work of the criminal court is to convince those accused of crime to acknowledge what everyone knows and to give in to the inevitable triumph of facts (Blumberg, 1967).

Once this is accomplished—and it is, in most cases—then attention is turned to the problem of determining appropriate sanctions, sanctions geared to serving society's interest in deterring criminal behavior. With regard to sentence it should not be surprising that social defense advocates view imprisonment as the most appropriate sanction in the vast majority of felony cases. These advocates also contend that courts do not deal with defendants in an adequately punitive way. Moreover, there is a good deal of research to support their view that courts do not, in fact, mete out severe sentences. The title of a recent book on criminal justice, *The Process Is the Punishment* (Feeley,

1979), accurately captures the reality of criminal court operation. In addition, research by Eisenstein and Jacob (1977) indicates that in the three cities they analyzed only a fraction of all defendants were convicted and no more than two-thirds of those convicted of criminal violations received jail time. In fact, in Detroit, barely one-third received such a sentence. In each city most of those who are convicted of crime but who are not incarcerated are given probation or a suspended sentence. The Vera study of New York City also reveals that in less than one-half of felony cases resulting in convictions were individuals sent to jail (Vera Institute, 1977).

The demand for social defense is, for a number of reasons, as unrealistic and foreign to the operation of criminal courts as is the demand for strict legality. First, while advocates of social defense expect that courts will be both informal in their operations and severe in the punishments imposed on criminals, informality and severity do not easily coexist. The more severe the results of a process, the greater the tendency for that process to become formal, the greater the tendency of participants to invest resources and demand protections. Courts, like all institutions, must choose informality or severity; they cannot have both. A second reason arises from the fact that there are almost always more people who are eligible to go to prison than there are prison facilities to accommodate them. The excess of demand over supply results in an increase in the threshold that must be crossed before incarceration is imposed. Third, there is a widespread suspicion that punishment is effective neither in rehabilitating criminals nor in deterring criminal behavior. This suspicion leads judges to be reluctant to impose jail time. When they do, it is often because they feel that they have no other choice. Jail time is a clear signal that the court has given up on a defendant. It is, thus, an unusual response. This last point is of particular importance.

While many of those who embrace the social defense perspective criticize criminal courts for their failure to administer punishment more regularly and more severely than they do, others have begun to call into question the utility of punishment, especially imprisonment, as a social defense mechanism. Take, for example, rehabilitation as a justification for imprisonment. One view of rehabilitation is that it serves to help the criminal himself live a socially acceptable life. Another view, the view implicit in Wilson's work (1975), is that it is a way of reducing crime by eliminating recidivism. A recent study by Robert Martinson, entitled "What Works," provides a survey of evaluations of a wide variety of programs explicitly designed for their rehabilitative effect. What Martinson found was that "the rehabilitative efforts that have been recorded so far have had no appreciable effects on recidivism" (cited by Wilson, 1975, p. 169). Martinson's findings confirm what many police, prosecutors, and judges have long suspected. Indeed, far from achieving rehabilitative purposes, prisons seem to serve as schools for criminality.

But, even if rehabilitation is ineffective as a tool of social defense, perhaps the application of punishment through the criminal process can serve social defense purposes by deterring others from committing crimes. Social defense advocates stress the utility of the threat of punishment as a deterrent to crime (Von den Haag, 1975). The problem, according to the social defense perspective, is that since criminal courts do not regularly and uniformly impose severe penal sanctions, it is unlikely that punishment can achieve such an effect. It is not clear, however, even to those who endorse the social defense perspective, that imprisonment or any other form of punishment can deter crime. What they claim as the most relevant rationale for punishment is simply incapacitation, namely, that imprisonment reduces the likelihood or incidence of crime by restricting the liberty, preferably for long periods of time, of those who regularly violate the law (Wilson, 1975).

Thus criticisms of punishment are at one and the same time criticisms of the courts for not imposing greater punishments and criticisms of its ineffectiveness. As suggested earlier, such criticisms may, in part, be responsible for the very phenomena of which they are critical. Social science evidence calling into question the effectiveness of the criminal sanction has had an effect on criminal courts. As Wilson (1975) speculates, judges and other participants may be experiencing the kind of futility which comes from ever-rising caseloads, limited resources, and an erosion of conventional justifications for the imposition of punishment. Without a clear sense of purpose, doing society's dirty work becomes all the more difficult, and may result in an attitude of "why bother?"

The Demand for Social Service

To truly understand the demand for social services one must know something about the basic tenets of liberal criminology. Liberal criminology, borrowing a social welfare perspective, regards the problem of crime as symptomtic of basic problems of social or individual pathology (Silberman, 1978). Crime is regarded as maladaptive behavior or as an abnormal response to difficult social situations (Menninger, 1963; Ryerson, 1978). The appropriate response to a criminal incident is neither contest nor punishment. It is, instead, an expression of concern, a desire to understand, and an attempt to help. The administration of criminal justice is regarded as part of the community's social service apparatus. Its function is to help cure the causes of crime, not simply to cope with its aftermath. It should, according to this perspective, provide individualized treatment based on the needs of each individual criminal. The defendant is to be helped. Every effort must be made to reintegrate him into the community and into normal social relations.

Thus the demand for social service is, like the demand for social defense, a demand for informality. It seeks, however, to be neither efficient nor strict. Adherence to legal procedure would limit the flexibility needed to deal with the personal problems resulting in criminality. Criminal courts are expected to get beneath episodes of crime. Informality is appropriate because there is no opposition of interest between the state and the accused. Both desire to find what is assumed to be the best way to cure the criminal. Those who demand social service from the courts are confident that cures can be found and that criminals can be helped. Pleas of guilty are encouraged, but guilt is not assumed to be a matter of personal responsibility. The successful criminal court is one in which justice is individualized and in which decisions are made in the best interest of each defendant.

Like juvenile courts, adult criminal courts are expected to move from each criminal incident to an analysis of the whole person. Courts should, according to the social service perspective, seek to identify the nature of the underlying trouble and establish with the defendant a mutually agreed upon course of treatment. Whereas both due process and crime control seek to limit the focus of adjudication, the social service orientation broadens it. Courts legislate for each defendant. Discretion is not in itself problematic, since there is genuine sympathy for the accused.

The problems created by this view for criminal court practitioners are perhaps best illustrated by the complexities suggested in a recent study conducted by the Vera Institute (1977). It showed that there was a high "rate of attrition" in felony cases, that is, a large number of arrests for felonies ultimately resulted in dismissed charges. A partial explanation for this, the authors argue, lies in the nature of the cases that are brought to criminal courts. The data demonstrate that substantial numbers of felony cases arise out of preexisting situations and/or continuing relations between defendant and victim:

> In half of all the felony arrests for crimes against the person, the victim had a prior relationship with the defendant. Prior relationship cases were frequent in cases of homicide and assault . . . as well as in cases of robbery. . . . Even in property crimes, prior relationships figured in over a third of the cases. This unanticipated level of prior relationships proves significant to the outcome of cases. (Vera Institute, 1977: xiv)

The high incidence and frequently recurring nature of related party cases is taken by some as evidence that criminal courts are failing to provide necessary social services. They fault criminal court personnel for viewing domestic quarrels and other related party problems as "garbage cases" and thus not responding to the needs of the parties involved (see Jacob, 1979). Advocates of the social service perspective suggest that these cases are manifestations of important kinds of social disruption. Furthermore, they believe that criminal courts in dealing with such cases ought to try to reintegrate the disrupted relationship; courts ought to provide a kind of therapeutic intervention. Filing a criminal complaint, or simply calling the police to intervene against an abusive spouse, may be a call for "help" rather than a call for legal judgment. Thus in this view the criminal court is provided an opportunity to intervene actively in troublesome social situations and to forestall later eruptions which might result in serious interpersonal violence. However, instead of taking this opportunity, social service adherents contend that criminal courts are too quick simply to dismiss such cases.

While the Vera data tend to support this argument for felony cases it should be also noted that misdemeanor courts may react differently. According to Feeley (1979), there is much more of a social work orientation in misdemeanor courts than there is in felony courts, where the daily fare is more likely to include serious threats to persons or property. His description of the kinds of cases that come into misdemeanor court in New Haven suggests that many, even those not directly involving related parties, arise from incidents of social disruption rather than serious criminality. As a result, the orientation of personnel in misdemeanor courts is less toward legal judgment than it is toward reaching some sense of what each case is worth. What this means is that personnel in misdemeanor courts attempt, on a regular basis, to see through the legal case to the real nature of the social trouble from which it arose and to deal with that trouble.

In contrast, the Vera data on felony courts reveal that the disposition process in related party cases in which serious harm does occur resembles the disposition process in nonrelated party cases, suggesting that felony courts are equipped to respond to the result of social disruption rather than its causes. Given the problem of "overcriminalization" (Kadish, 1978) and scarce resources, felony courts are able to handle only the most serious cases, with the seriousness of the case being determined by the visible damage or harm done, not by the social distress it may signal (Sudnow, 1965).

To correct this situation, social services adherents have put forth several suggestions. One of the most recent deals with the creation of community-based courts into which related party cases or other similar types of social work problems might be funneled. Such proposals—the Justice Department's Neighborhood Justice Center program is one (McGillis and Mullin, 1977)—are often seen as simply another vehicle for pretrial diversion, whose advocates, like the advocates of community courts, suggest that many violations of the law are really symptoms of illness. However, unlike the pretrial diversion response in which professionals are the primary providers of services, the community court response is indicative of a romantic vision of community participation in the resolution of community problems (Cratsley, 1978).

The community court movement rejects both the epistemological skepticism of the strict legality adherents and the positivism of the social defense proponents. Advocates of community courts criticize adjudication in criminal cases for its inability to deal with the real problems which cause crime (Griffiths, 1970). They claim that the truth of the events involved in a criminal dispute can only be determined by a balanced discussion that provides all parties involved an opportunity to tell their story and in so doing recognize their shared grievances. Criminal courts—operating as they do through investigation and/or adversariness—create situations of stress in which the real problem is often obscured rather than illuminated.

Community courts are also viewed by some as devices for increasing community participation in local affairs (Danzig and Lowry, 1975). The assumption here is that criminal court adjudication serves to discourage such participation by taking community problems and transforming them into legal problems. The community-based court movement presumes that it is meaningful to talk about the existence and/or the possibility of creating social environments in which people contribute to the resolution of interpersonal problems. The social service and community control perspective seeks to make criminal courts responsive to the real needs of people with whom they deal and the communities they serve; short of that, it hopes to move cases out of the courts in which there are perceptible problems of personal maladjustment or in which the community has a substantial stake.

The demand for social service is both therapeutic and romantic. It is therapeutic because it demands that criminal courts act to cure social problems and adapt themselves to that task. It is romantic in the twin sense that it reflects a nostalgia for some—real or imagined—lost or fading sense of community and a belief that community can be created or re-created in contemporary circumstances.

The expectations embodied in the demand for social service are, I believe, unrealistic. Courts have neither the time nor the technology nor the expertise to get at the underlying causes of crime. To expect them to do so is to expect that the causes of crime can indeed be known and understood, and that the interactions surrounding the prosecution of a criminal case provide an appropriate circumstance for an open-ended inquiry into the details of personal histories and the needs of particular personalities. To expect courts to deal with the underlying causes of crime is to expect that training in law can equip judges and lawyers to recognize and treat illness.

A NEW PARADIGM: INCREMENTALISM IN CRIMINAL COURTS

Unrealistic expectations—expectations that are not attuned to the realities of criminal courts—create a sense of crisis that in turn creates problems for criminal courts. What is needed is a clearer sense of what those realities are, a clearer descriptive paradigm for courts. Once such a paradigm is presented, it will be possible to generate expectations and demands appropriate to the nature of courts as dispute processing institutions and to the particular tasks they perform.

Criminal courts deal directly with individuals who, for the most part, are factually guilty. Factual guilt is, however, not as clearcut as, for example, the crime control model suggests. It is quite possible to argue that those who become criminal defendants are generally guilty without arguing at the same time that the precise nature, extent, or form of their guilt is easily or readily known. The task for criminal courts is to find an appropriate means of dealing with the dirty people and messy problems brought to those courts. A major problem for participants in the courts is that they must proceed with a minimum of information and under a good deal of time pressure. A better understanding of how they deal with their tasks may be gained by turning to what in decision theory is called "the strategy of disjointed incrementalism" (Braybrooke and Lindblom, 1963). Moreover, an understanding of this strategy may well suggest the basis for a new descriptive paradigm for criminal courts.

Disjointed incrementalism is a strategy for evaluating information and making decisions in situations in which needed information is difficult to obtain or interpret; it is a strategy that emphasizes compromise and adjustment. Incremental decision-making is cautious, tentative, and premised upon the belief that social decisions are always subject to error. It is understood that any action is as likely to produce unintended consequences as it is to achieve calculable results. Given this understanding, decision-making must allow room for maneuver; it must be open, flexible, and adaptive. Incrementalism seeks to cope with the inevitability that information will always be inadequate at the moment when decisions must be made by limiting the scope of those decisions. Small advances leave little room for big mistakes.

Decision-making in an incremental fashion is based upon a deep skepticism about the possibility of finding right answers to questions of public policy or individual choice. Decision-making activities are, as a result, not designed to reach final, certain conclusions. Incremental decisions match available information with imaginable choices and test the fit. As Braybrooke and Lindblom describe it (1963, p. 73), such decision-making "... proceeds through a sequence of approximations. A policy is directed at a problem; it is tried, altered, tried in its altered form, altered again and so forth." This style of decision-making rarely produces optimum results. Instead, it proceeds in a loose way to produce results that appear workable and satisfy many interests without fully satisfying any. Incrementalism, as a style of decision-making, is uniquely fitted to occasions or situations in which there are many parties, each with a legitimate claim to participate in the decision. It allows for checks and balances among parties with different interests and values.

The Need for Information

Incrementalism, as suggested earlier, is a way of coping with the exigencies of limited information and/or a limited capacity to comprehend information relevant to the problem at hand. The scope and variety of information that is needed and becomes available are almost endless.

Decisions about social problems require an understanding of the particular contexts in which problems occur, an understanding which is generally quite difficult to obtain. By breaking down any decision into several parts and by focusing on the details of particular cases rather than being concerned with end values, incrementalism tailors decisions to informational inadequacies that surround most public problems. Incrementalism further adapts decision-making to those inadequacies by inviting each participant in a decision-making process to contribute some part of what will eventually become a common understanding of a problem. What is important is less that a problem be accurately understood than that those who have to deal with it be able to agree on a mutually acceptable construction of the problem.

Incremental decision-making is retrospective, that is, it is oriented toward "finding elements in the new problems like those of older problems already solved" (Braybrooke and Lindblom, 1963, p. 115). Once a common understanding is reached, the new problem can be fit into an appropriate descriptive category with other similar problems, and past decisions can be used as a guide for the present. Thus incrementalism, in the name of caution, produces some semblance of equity. Incrementalism, as a descriptive paradigm for criminal courts, emphasizes the difficulties of understanding criminal events and directs close attention to each particular case, the closeness of which is determined by questions of resources and the necessity of reaching a common understanding among people with different values and interests. Truth, for the incrementalist, is less important than agreement; solutions are less important than adjustments.

The task of dealing with dirty people and messy problems is first of all an informational one. In criminal courts, knowledge is always scarce. Even simple crimes have complications (Rossett and Cressey, 1976). Everyone involved has a version, a story to tell. No story is necessarily any more reliable than any other and often no two stories are exactly the same (Buckle and Buckle, 1977). The first and continuing problem for all participants is to gain access to information necessary to provide some minimum of understanding of the crime and the criminal and to develop an interpretation of both that allows each of the participants to agree upon a single construction of reality. It is only after that construction has been completed and agreed upon that attention is turned to other tasks, namely, the tasks of finding an appropriate process for dealing with each case and an appropriate disposition for each.

The Need for Compromise

The tasks of information gathering, processing, and disposing of criminal cases are carried out through a complex and ongoing series of negotiations and bargains (Heumann, 1977). Justice is produced through the cooperative interactions of participants in criminal courts. One finds in criminal courts a culture of accommodation, exchange, and cooperation; yet this culture is continuously framed by an awareness of due process norms and the potential for intense conflict.

Bargaining and mutual accommodation are not only continuous, they are also cumulative (Buckle and Buckle, 1977). One cannot understand how any one aspect of the criminal court process works without understanding the process in its entirety. Cases are transformed as they pass from one stage in that process to another and as various interested participants interact and exchange information and impressions. Thus cases are created as they are processed (Feeley, 1979; Sudnow, 1965).

Open, detailed discussion of events occurs continuously. Each participant—police, prosecutor, defense counsel, and defendant—plays a part in this discussion. It is widely recognized that everyone with a legitimate stake in a case should have his say in order that the understanding of the crime and the criminal will not only be consensual but also lead to an appropriate and fair disposition of the case. The accumulation of impressions and assessments which occurs in criminal courts will lead, therefore, to what seems like a natural result.

Incrementalism, Criminal Courts, and Expectations

Criminal courts are neither battle grounds nor assembly lines. The state is by no means as monolithic in its interest as the due process model would imply, nor as confident in its judgments as the crime control model suggests. Each of the participants in courts has something special to contribute and has interests which are different from those of other participants. None of the participants has an incentive to close out the bargaining process at an early stage. There seems to be an internal logic to it which works itself out. Premature closure is likely to lead to surprise either in the form of unexpected information or in the emergence of a previously unrecognized interest.

All of this raises important questions about the extent to which the distinction between negotiation and adversariness is either useful or accurate in portraying criminal courts. There appears to be a rather extensive interpenetration of adversarial and negotiated elements in the operation of criminal courts. Adversariness is not an all or nothing proposition. To the extent that the "due process revolution" has had substantial impact, it has not been made solely or even primarily manifest in the number or conduct of criminal trials. The extension of due process rights has provided new resources and new constraints in the bargaining process. Violations of procedural rights can be used to alter understandings of what cases are about. Those rights give defendants currencies which can be exchanged as those understandings are developed. In many ways the bargaining process in criminal courts resembles the coexistence of nations in the nuclear age. Each party has available to it advantages of which every other party is aware. Success requires that decisions be reached in a manner that does not require any party to employ those advantages. What the due process revolution has done is to ensure the defendant a more secure place in the balance of power. It has also given to each of the parties a greater incentive to work cooperatively. Brinksmanship is avoided in the name of a mutual interest in the continued existence of a viable court culture.

Given that criminal courts operate incrementally and that they deal on a regular basis with social troubles, what can one reasonably expect of or demand from them in the way of performance? First, formal legality must be recognized to be but one aspect of the criminal justice process. The entire purpose of that process is to produce a result which will not necessitate the invocation of rights or the resort to formal procedures. Second, the court should be cautious in its judgments. Punishment is not an inevitable or appropriate result in every case. What is done in each case is tailored to the seriousness of the underlying incident and the extent and nature of the defendant's involvement in it (Feeley, 1979). In most cases, by the time the incident and offender are understood, officials believe that incarceration would be a disproportionately severe penalty. Third, while individualized treatment is the basis of court operations, such treatment is not geared toward understanding causes and prescribing cures. Participants have enough difficulty understanding the symptoms of crime so that, given the time available to them, a curative orientation is well beyond their capacity.

Individualized treatment, however, should and often does produce substantive justice, that is, it produces results which fit the nature of the incident and the involvement of the offender. Justice is situational; procedures are and should be flexible. The impulse to do what seems fair in particular cases draws officials away from formal, legal norms which, in a constitutional sense, define justice. Feeley (1979) cites the Weberian distinction between rational and irrational justice in explaining the operation of criminal courts. The former mandates rule following; the latter is unconcerned with general rules and is case specific. The failure of rational justice is rigidity; the failure of irrational justice is arbitrariness. To demand of criminal courts that substantive justice be done is not, according to some critics (for example, Fuller, 1964), to provide any standards at all. Substantive justice is inevitably subjective. What appears fair to any one person may not appear fair to others. This does not mean, however, that there are no standards implicit in the operation of criminal courts. Quite to the contrary it indicates that the participants in court are sensitive to and aspire to reach fair and right decisions, decisions which could, in theory, withstand outside scrutiny.

What substantive justice requires is a system of checks and balances in which competing ideas of fairness are voiced and are accommodated. Thus, we are led back to process for standards that can be realistically employed to evaluate criminal courts. What is necessary is openness and respect for the interests of all participants, including those of defendants. Process and results cannot, however, be divorced. An open, accommodative process that produces punishments which are not at all proportionate to offenses would not be honored. The standards of legality can properly be brought into that process as resources for each of the participants. Doing justice does not mean that no external constraints can or should be imposed on criminal courts. What is necessary, however, is a willingness to accept that such standards will be absorbed and adapted. They will not and cannot fully govern criminal processes. At the same time, they will not and cannot be ignored.

CONCLUSION

Behind the expectations about, and demands on, criminal courts there is a growing body of social science data. These data show that criminal courts are not meeting the most visible of the demands made upon them. It is doubtful, however, that there was ever a time when criminal courts were more faithful to the law or more effective in providing social defense or more able to provide social services. The explosion of social science interest in the courts has, by itself, served to generate concern about this performance gap, thereby creating a new problem for the courts. One wonders whether criminal courts as we know them will survive the onslaught of social science.

Every society needs people and institutions to deal with its problems. Those who deal with such problems are rarely praised by the society which they serve. They see themselves as unappreciated and misunderstood. They see themselves as subject to conflicting demands, most of which appear quite unrealistic. They have limited resources and limited remedies available to them and yet they are expected to adhere to the high standards of legality, effectiveness, and community service. They are inevitably tainted by their association with nasty people and nasty problems. The problem for social science research and for reform efforts is to find some balance between our highest expectations and the built-in limitations and problems of criminal courts.

This will require close attention to what actually happens in criminal courts and a willingness to see them through the eyes of those who do criminal justice. This does not mean that all external constraints or expectations are either illegitimate or inappropriate. It does mean, however, that those expectations must reflect an accurate picture of what courts do and of the motives and interests of the actors in them. The operation of criminal courts is tailored to allow competing ideas of what is right to surface and to provide an acceptable framework for accommodation and compromise. The result is generally neither strict nor punitive nor penetrating. However, it is, more often than not, appropriate, given the offense, the offender, and the limits of information and time with which criminal courts must cope.

REFERENCES

Barr, Carl (1974). "Will Urban Trial Courts Survive The War on Crime." In Herbert Jacob, ed. *The Potential for Reform of Criminal Justice*. Beverly Hills, Calif.: Sage.

Balbus, Isaac (1973). *The Dialectics of Legal Repression*. New York: Russell Sage Foundation.

Blumberg, Abraham (1967). *Criminal Justice*. Chicago: Quadrangle Books.

Braybrooke, David, and Lindblom, Charles (1963). *The Strategy of Decision*. New York: The Free Press.

Buckle, Suzann and Buckle, Leonard (1977). *Bargaining for Justice*. New York: Praeger.

Resolution within the Judicial System." 3 *Vermont Law Review* 1.

Danzig, Richard (1973). "Toward the Creation of a Complementary, Decentralized System of Criminal Justice." 26 *Standard Law Review* 1.

_______ and Michael Lowy (1975). "Everyday Disputes and Mediation in the United States." 9 *Law & Society Review* 675.

Davis, Kenneth Culp (1969). *Discretionary Justice*. Baton Rouge: Louisiana State University Press.

Eisenstein, James, and Jacob, Herbert (1977). *Felony Justice*. Boston: Little, Brown.

Feeley, Malcolm (1973). "Two Models of the Criminal Justice System." 7 *Law & Society Review* 407.

_______ (1979). *The Process Is the Punishment*. New York: Russell Sage Foundation.

Fleming, Macklin (1978). *Of Crime and Rights*. New York: Basic Books.

_______ (1967). *The Price of Perfect Justice*. New York: Basic Books.

Forer, Lois (1975). *The Death of Law*. New York: David McKay.

Frankel, Marvin (1972). *Criminal Sentences*. New York: Hill and Wang.

Fuller, Lon (1964). *The Morality of Law*. New Haven: Yale University Press.

Goldstein, Joseph (1960). "Police Discretion Not to Invoke the Criminal Process." 69 *Yale Law Journal* 543.

Griffiths, John (1970). "Ideology in Criminal Procedure or a Third "Model" of the Criminal Process." 79 *Yale Law Journal*.

Heumann, Milton (1977). *Plea Bargaining*. Chicago: University of Chicago Press.

Hyderbrand, Wolf (1976). "The Technocratic Administration of Justice." Paper presented at the Annual Meeting of the American Political Science Association.

Jacob, Herbert (1979). "Related Party Disputes in Criminal Courts." In Peter F. Nardulli, ed. *The Study of Criminal Courts: Political Perspectives*. Cambridge, Mass.: Ballinger Publishing Company.

Kadish, Sanford (1968). "The Crisis of Over-Criminalization." 17 *American Criminal Law Quarterly*.

Kagan, Robert (1978). *Regulatory Justice*. New York: Russell Sage Foundation.

Leff, Arthur (1978). "Law And." 87 *Yale Law Journal* 989.

Mather, Lynn (1979). *Plea Bargaining or Trial.* Lexington, Mass.: Lexington Books.

McGillis, Daniel, and Mullin, Joan (1977). *Neighborhood Justice Centers: An Analysis of Potential Models.* Washington, D.C.: National Institute of Law Enforcement and Criminal Justice.

Menninger, Karl (1968). *The Crime of Punishment.* New York: Viking Press.

Neubauer, David (1974). *Criminal Justice in Middle America.* Morristown, N.J.: General Learning Press.

Nisbet, Robert (1975). *The Twilight of Authority.* New York: Oxford University Press.

Packer, Herbert (1968). *The Limits of the Criminal Sanction.* Stanford: Stanford University Press.

Quinney, Richard (1974). *Critique of the Legal Order.* Boston: Little, Brown.

Rossett, Arthur, and Cressey, Donald (1976). *Justice by Consent.* New York: Lippincott.

Ryerson, Ellen (1978). *The Best Laid Plans.* New York: Hill and Wang.

Sarat, Austin (1978). "Understanding Trial Courts: A Critique of Social Science Approaches." 61 *Judicature* 318.

———, and Grossman, Joel B. (1975). "Courts and Conflict Resolution." 69 *American Political Science Review* 1200.

Silberman, Charles (1978). *Criminal Violence, Criminal Justice.* New York: Random House.

Skolnick, Jerome (1966). *Justice without Trial.* New York: Wiley & Sons.

Strick, Ann (1977). *Injustice for All.* New York: Penguin Books.

Sudnow, David (1965). "Normal Crimes." 12 *Social Problems* 255.

Vera Institute of Justice (1977). *Felony Arrests.* New York: Vera Institute.

Von den Haag, Ernst (1975). *Punishing Criminals.* New York: Basic Books.

Von Hirsch, Andrew (1976). *Doing Justice.* New York: Hill and Wang.

Wilson, James Q. (1975). *Thinking about Crime.* New York: Basic Books.

Part II

Theoretical Approaches to the Study of Criminal Courts

Chapter Four

A Role Theoretic Model of Criminal Court Decision-making

James L. Gibson

The decision-making process in criminal courts is unquestionably complex and not very well understood. It is, therefore, not suprising that many different theories have been advanced to explain the process, including attitude theory (for example, Gibson, 1978a; Hogarth, 1971); role theory (for example, Jaros and Mendelsohn, 1967; Gibson, 1977); organizational theory (for example, Eisenstein and Jacob, 1977; Nardulli, 1978); theories of representation and recruitment (for example, Levin, 1972); "fact" pattern theory (for example, Ebbesen and Konecni, 1975); and so on. Yet there has been little effort to explain, or even acknowledge, competing perspectives; even less effort has been expended to integrate the different theoretical approaches. Attitude theorists tend to ignore organizational factors, and vice versa, and role theory rarely considers the impact on decisions of facts, attitudes, or any of the other factors normally thought to be relevant to the decision process. Research on criminal court decision-making is currently characterized by a significant degree of balkanization.

Despite the general insensitivity to building an integrated, comprehensive theory of decisions for the dispositional process, many of these different approaches can be fit into the context of a single theoretical framework: role theory. Because role theory can incorporate its competitors, it provides a quite general and powerful explanation of the decision-making process. In this chapter I will attempt to demonstrate the integrative and explanatory utility of a role

[a]I would like to acknowledge the extremely helpful comments of the editor of this volume on earlier versions of this chapter.

theoretic understanding of the decisional process in criminal courts. First, role theory is reviewed and extant conceptualizations of the major role concepts in judicial research are critiqued, leading to the conclusion that there is a serious need for reconceptualization in this area. Next, an effort at such a reconceptualization is undertaken, resulting in a model of the process through which role characteristics affect decision-making. After addressing several problems in applying role theory to the criminal court context, the results from different studies of the criminal justice process are reviewed in order further to explicate the model. The final section identifies several significant unanswered questions that role research should address.

ROLE THEORY AND DECISION-MAKING

Few theories have claimed greater potential for understanding political behaviors than role theory. In the first major application of role theory to politics (Wahlke and others, 1962), a truly comprehensive theory for the analysis of political decision-making was set forth.[1] The comprehensiveness of role theory was so great that it caught the interest of scholars working in many different substantive areas. It was attractive because of the thoroughness with which the behavior of elites in political institutions could be explained: not only personality and attitudinal variables, but organizational, public opinion, and socialization variables could all be included within a single role framework.

Role Concepts

To explicate the role model (and because conceptual labels have been used in a variety of ways) it is first necessary to understand the significance of the individual in the decision process. To role theorists the most salient characteristic of decision-making within institutions is the constraint imposed on individual decision-makers by the institutional context. Unlike voters, for instance, institutional decision-makers must contend with a variety of constraints on their choices. Such constraints limit, but do not eliminate, discretion in the interest of advancing organizational objectives. Few organizations exist that do not try to circumscribe the alternatives available to their decision-makers.

Role theory asserts that the way individuals accommodate themselves to institutional imperatives strongly influences the decisional process. Several role concepts are of particular importance for understanding the process: (1) The individuals who hold positions within an institution are referred to as *role occupants* or role incumbents. The position occupied receives its content or substance from the formal definition of the institution itself. (2) In addition, however, role occupants are subject to *role expectations*. These are beliefs about how a role occupant ought to behave. They are normative beliefs, supplementing the formal characteristics of the position. (3) Role expectations emanate from *role alters*, a very broad group of individuals, encompassing those within and external to the institution, who interact with the role occupant. (4) Each role occupant must synthesize the expectations, accepting some, rejecting others, to form a *role orientation*. This is the body of the decision-maker's beliefs about the nature of proper decision-making behavior. (5) Finally, role relevant activity is known as *role behavior*.

Judicial Role Research

It is not at all surprising that judicial scholars were so quickly attracted to role theory, for it seems particularly suited to understanding decision-making behavior in judicial institutions. Actors in the judicial system are subject to a greater number of, and possibly more rigidly defined, role expectations than any other institutional political elites. Indeed, the role orientation of "judicial restraint" is often used to justify the elitest character of judicial institutions and to turn back demands for greater political accountability (Wasby, 1978).

In role theory the behavior of judges is posited as a function (to some extent, at least) of the role orientation of the role occupant. This conceptualization of the decision-making process has been widely applied to appellate judges; a few efforts to extend the framework to the trial court level have also been undertaken.[2] While the question of the applicability of appellate court models to the trial court level no doubt requires consideration (see below), role concepts have been invested with meaning primarily through work at the appellate level, so it is useful to examine briefly this body of literature.

Within the appellate context, role orientations vary to the degree that judges feel obliged to adhere to precedents, constitutions, and statutes in making decisions. In this context, adherence included following precedents, strict construction of constitutions, and deference to legislative intent. Thus this role orientation involves the legitimacy of discretion in decision-making—the degree to which legitimate opportunities for decisional creativity are perceived to exist. Much of the role research on courts has focused upon the development of typologies based on this concept. The earliest role studies used open-ended measures that asked judges to characterize the nature of their decisional process (for example, Vines, 1969; Wold, 1974; Howard, 1977), an approach that is a direct extrapolation of the work of Wahlke and associates. While different researchers label the categories somewhat differently, two pure role types have been discovered—the lawmaker and the law interpreter. There is also a mixed role orientation, sometimes referenced as a "pragmatist," which is some unspecified combination of the pure types. Judges of several different state and federal courts have been interviewed and categorized on the basis of this typology.

This conceptualization of role orientations is actually little different from the traditional activist-restraintist distinction. Judges with a strong precedent orientation (law interpreters; restraintists) apparently place a high value upon continuity and consistency in the law, rule by popularly elected, responsive officials, and decisions influenced only by strictly legal criteria; consequently, they attempt to neutralize the impact of their own values in rendering decisions. Activists, on the other hand, seek "justice" in their decisions and are more willing to reject or modify legal rules that appear incompatible with that concept of justice. Appellate court judges, then, are thought to differ in their degree of activism, and this results in different styles of decision-making. These differences reflect the institutional context, or role expectations, that are perceived to impinge upon their decisional behavior.[3]

There are several problems with this role research, however. First, it has been too concerned with typology building and not enough with using role orientations to predict behavior.[4] While typology building is certainly a useful enterprise, it is not an end in itself; to be useful, the typology must tell us something about how and why decisions are made. Perhaps one reason that so little effort has been directed toward explaining behavior is that the linkage between role orientations and role behavior has not been adequately specified at the conceptual level. As a consequence, the few attempts at relating role orientations to role behavior have generated disappointing results. Finally—and this question is of greatest concern in this chapter—even if role theory is useful for understanding appellate court behavior, the problem of applicability to trial courts has not been adequately addressed or resolved. What is needed is a reconceptualization of role orientations, one sufficiently general to apply to every level of the judicial hierarchy and which clearly specifies the interrelationships between key role concepts. When these difficulties are resolved, we will have an extremely powerful theory of decision-making relevant to criminal trial courts. It is to these tasks that we now turn.

A RECONCEPTUALIZATION OF ROLE ORIENTATIONS

The position of judge is incredibly complex.[5] Consequently, judge's beliefs about what is and is not proper behavior for the position are also complex. In no other aspect of the judge's job is this more apparent than in decision-making. Highly simplistic notions of role orientations, such as the lawmaker—law interpreter distinction and orientation toward precedent, are unlikely to be of much help in understanding judges' role orientations or behavior. What is necessary is a reconceptualization of role orientations and how they relate to role behavior.

Judges' role orientations are their beliefs about the kind of behavior that is proper for a judge. In the case of decisional role orientations, the beliefs concern proper decision behavior. "Proper" does not, however, refer as much to the policy content of the behavior as it does to the *process* of decision-making and, in particular, to the kinds of stimuli that influence decisions. A decisional role orientation identifies for the judge the criteria that are legitimate for proper decision-making. Thus, differences among judges in role orientations stem from different evaluations of decisional stimuli. Some judges may believe it proper to be influenced by a particular stimulus while other judges regard it as improper.

This conceptualization of role orientations is compatible with the traditional norms for judging in that a central expectation of judicial and legal traditions concerns the decision-making criteria employed by judges. For instance, equality before the law is not an empirical statement; it does not assert that individual litigants are in fact equal. Rather, the phrase is an exhortation to ignore variables (stimuli), such as power, on which litigants are unequal and render decisions only on variables that provide for equality. It is also generally regarded as illegitimate to discriminate on the basis of social class in sentencing decisions. Class is not viewed as a proper decisional criterion. Similarly, even such concepts as the presumption of innocence in criminal cases are merely expectations that court officials will not allow empirical stimuli relating to the factual guilt of the defendant to influence their pretrial decisions (for example, bail). The presumption of innocence is a norm that defines some criteria of decision-making as proper and others as improper (see Packer, 1968).

Thus the basic function of decisional role orientations is to specify what variables can legitimately be allowed to influence decision-making and, in the case of conflict, what priorities to assign to different decision-making criteria. Role orientations are conceptualized as normative weights attached by each judge to different decisional stimuli. A stimulus viewed as illegitimate, therefore, would receive a weight of zero.

While this conceptualization is a more general and theoretical notion of role orientations, it is not entirely incompatible with the lawmaking-law interpretation and precedent approaches. Lawmakers, for instance, might possibly rely on more and different criteria for decision-making than law interpreters. Lawmakers might consider social injustice as a legitimate criterion upon which to base decisions. Law interpreters probably view social injustice as a less relevant, and possibly even illegitimate, basis for decision-making. The law interpreter would surely assign greater weight to precedents, statutes, and constitutions. Generally lawmakers would rely on extralegal decisional criteria while law interpreters would rely on strictly legal criteria as much as possible. Although this notion of role orientations is compatible with lawmaking-law interpreting and precedent approaches, it also has the advantage of being more general, since any criterion—not just precedents, statutes, and constitutions, which potentially influence decisions—can be evaluated in terms of legitimacy. It also provides a more theoretical basis for developing expectations about how role orientations influence role behavior.

Thus role orientations, in this view, represent a continuum of perceived legitimate discretion in decision-making that ranges from strict adherence to strictly legal criteria to reliance on a variety of extralegal criteria. As such, role orientations may be, and most likely are, multidimensional, but it is still not clear exactly how these orientations influence decisional behavior.

ROLE ORIENTATIONS AND DECISIONAL BEHAVIOR

The major utility of viewing role orientations as a continuum is that it provides a means for predicting decisional behavior. This is not true of the lawmaking-law interpreting and precedent approaches to role orientations. For an example of the difficulties with these earlier approaches we can turn to Vines's (1969) research and the assertion that lawmakers are politically liberal in their decisions while law interpreters are politically conservative. This assertion is based on the notion that

> the law interpreter position, particularly when implemented with support of strict separation of powers and judicial restraint, argues for a more conservative approach to political change and flexibility. Since similar characteristics are often attributed to the conservative and liberal positions generally we would suppose that law interpreting would be more closely linked to conservative decision making and law making to liberal decisions. (Vines, 1969:479)

Lawmakers and liberals are expected to be prochange while law interpreters and conservatives are expected to be antichange. If change in policy is the dependent variable, then this hypothesis makes at least some sense.

The dependent variable, decision behavior, is not, however, related to continuity or change. Instead the votes are classified in terms of whether the winning interest is an "underdog" in society. The hypothesis being tested is that lawmakers will vote liberally, not in the sense of social change, but rather in the sense of favoring underdogs (criminals, consumers, debtors, tenants, and so on) in society. This does not at all follow from the theory of lawmaking and law interpretation (and hence it is not surprising to find that the hypothesis is not supported by the data). *Indeed, there is no reason to expect a relationship between role orientations and liberal policymaking when role orientations are conceptualized as Vines has conceptualized them.*

What prediction does the lawmaker-law interpreter notion make? The reconceptualization of role orientations employed here might lead to the hypothesis that law interpreters will be more strongly influenced by statutes, precedents, and constitutions than will lawmakers. Conversely, lawmakers will rely more heavily on their own values (actually, on any of several extralegal factors) than will law interpreters. What is important, however, is that the role orientation does not tell us whether a judge's policymaking decisions will be liberal or conservative but instead tells us the criteria upon which the decision will be based.[6] In order for a decision to be liberal the theory predicts that the criterion upon which the judge bases his decision must itself predict a liberal decision. Two factors must therefore be known in order to predict decision: (1) what criteria the judge relies on, and (2) whether the criteria predict a liberal or conservative decision.

Figure 4-1, a diagram of this process, shows that both lawmakers and law interpreters are just as likely to be conservative as liberal. A lawmaker who makes conservative policy is predicted to have conservative policy preferences; if, however, he makes liberal policies he

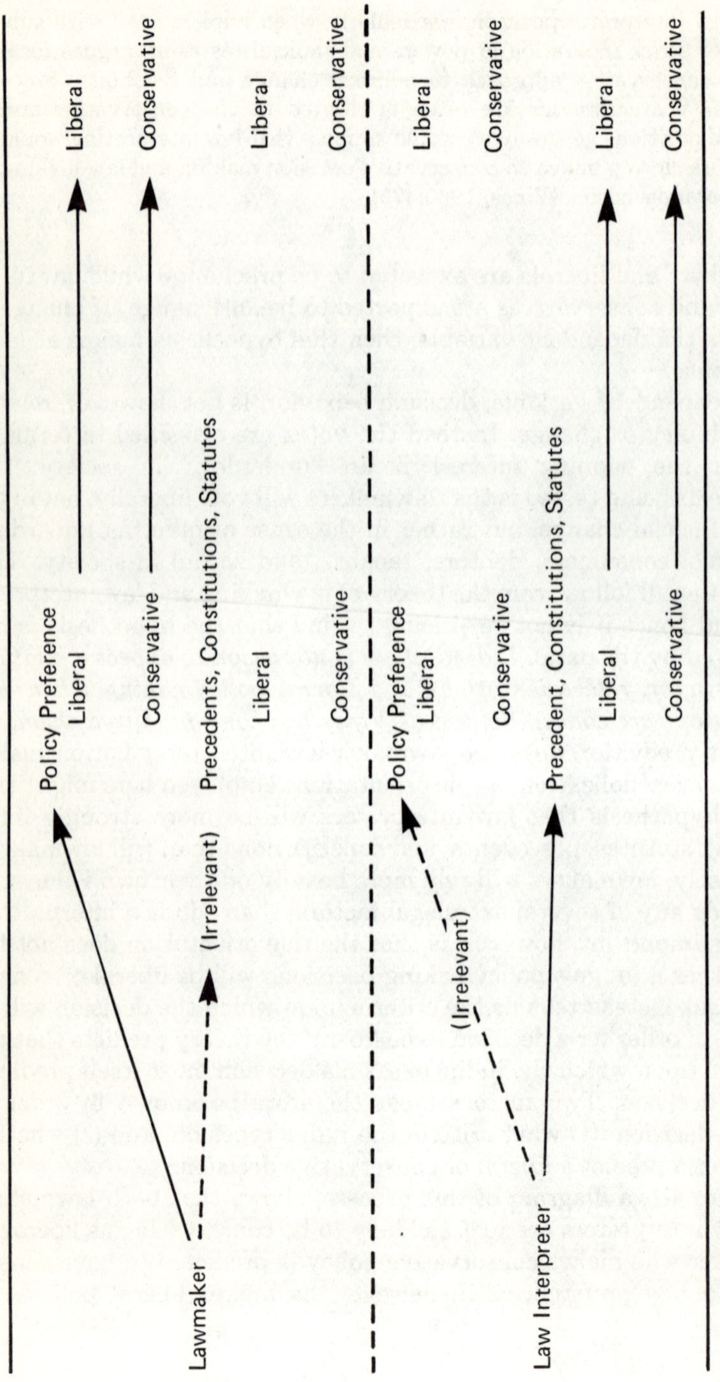

Figure 4-1. Hypothetical Relationships among Role Orientations, Decisional Criteria and Judicial Behavior

would be likely to have liberal preferences. Likewise, in the case of law interpreters, liberal policies result from liberal laws and conservative policies result from conservative laws. Role theory predicts which criteria the judge relies on, not whether his behavior will be liberal or conservative.

While this theoretical model *predicts* a correlation of zero between role orientations and behavior (a prediction consistent with previous empirical findings), role orientations are, in fact, a significant component of an equation that can be used to predict behavior. In this equation the independent variables are the *interactions* between role orientations and decisional criteria:

$$Y = b\,(Z_1X_1) + b\,(Z_2X_2) \ldots + b\,(Z_nX_n)$$

where:

Y = decisional behavior

X = criteria used to make decisions, and

Z = role orientation toward the type of criteria (that is, whether any criterion is considered a legitimate influence on decisions).

This equation is most easily understood by treating the role orientations as weights attached to different decisional criteria. If it is the belief of a judge that a particular criterion is improper, then the role orientation score is zero and that term drops out of the equation for the judge. Role orientations and decisional criteria interact: the influence of a criterion on behavior is contingent upon the score on the role measure. Neither the criterion nor orientation alone should predict behavior; only their interaction should have predictive power.

The use of multiple terms for role orientations and decisional criteria in the equation indicates that judges may be influenced by a variety of stimuli and that they may have different orientations toward different stimuli. This means that the model has a very high degree of generalizability. Previous models of decisional role orientations have not had this property: they have been quite narrowly focused upon precedents, statutes, and constitutions. Role theory can thus form the basis of a quite general theory of judicial decision-making.

ROLE THEORY AND CRIMINAL COURTS

Two issues must be resolved before we can turn to a consideration of how role theory may be applied to criminal courts. First, since much of the role research has been focused upon appellate court judges—as reflected in the conceptual centrality of "precedent"—it is legitimate to question whether role theory has any utility for the criminal court context where very few decisions are constrained by precedents. Second, role theory, especially as described here, emphasizes the attributes of the individual decision-maker as the major determinant of decisional outputs, whereas much contemporary research on criminal courts, especially that based on organization theory, tends to denigrate the significance of individual preferences. The compatibility of these approaches must therefore be addressed.

With regard to the first point, as noted earlier, role orientations need not be limited to precedent orientations. The conceptualization advocated here is highly generalized: judges' beliefs about the legitimacy of any criterion, including defendant attributes, organizational imperatives, community values, and so on, are quite easily incorporated into the model. Obviously, the particular "strictly legal" criteria relevant to trial and appellate court judges may differ somewhat, but conceptually the process is identical. Therefore, the irrelevance of precedents for criminal court decisions has no impact on the utility of role theory.

The second question is somewhat more complex. From the perspective of organization theory it is not fruitful to consider individual preferences, especially those of the judge,[7] because the decisions are a product of workgroup accommodation to various pressures. An appropriate answer to this question is obviously necessary in order to gauge the utility of role theory.

Generally, organization theory contends that

> . . . factors emanating from the collective efforts of judges, prosecutors, and defense counsel (the courtroom elite) to pursue common interests have important consequences for the processing of criminal cases. These collective efforts are manifested in the cooperative pattern of behavior reported in criminal courts. Further, to abstract a bit from what has been argued in these studies, these common interests can be defined as the shared desire to process cases expeditiously. It is this contention—that [it] is in the interests of the courtroom elite to process cases expeditiously—that makes this tradition organizational in nature and forms the basic premise in the mode of analysis. . . . (Nardulli, 1978:66)

Thus, from the organizational perspective, mutual self-interest is the dominant force in decision-making.

The interests of the participants structure the mode of decision-making and the goal of expeditious case processing results in negotiated decisions. Negotiation is facilitated because the principal actors all want the same thing. Decisions reflect the group consensus rather than individual, competing preferences. Presumably, no single actor can control decision-making; organizational norms overwhelm individual desires, severely constraining, if not eliminating, individual discretion. Further, unless judges participate in pretrial negotiations (and most do not) their function is considerably less significant than posited by the adversarial model. Mechanisms (sanctions, incentives) exist that compel each of the participants to acquiesce to group norms. Finally, because of the overwhelming domination of organizational imperatives, uniformity in the outputs of the system is assumed to exist. Thus organization theory posits that the criminal justice system is characterized by consensus, not dissensus, and as a consequence the values of individual participants do not influence decisions. Obviously, this contention is in very direct conflict with the model advocated here.

Yet the divergence in the two theories may be more apparent than real. Indeed, not only can organizational interests be incorporated straightforwardly into the equation predicting role behavior, but most of the major elements of organization theory can be interpreted in role theoretic terms.

Essentially, what organization theory argues is that a series of expectations prohibits major actors in the criminal justice system from making unilateral decisions. These expectations emanate from the other principal actors within the criminal justice system, sponsoring organizations, and a variety of external environmental actors. These expectations, especially those the principal actors hold for each other, become norms, or folkways, that may influence the decisions of each of the actors. Thus organizational imperatives structure the role expectations actors hold of one another and are therefore a significant constraint on the outputs of the criminal trial court.

The expectations actors hold of one another are essentially role expectations: they are the role alter's view of how the role occupant ought to behave. Prosecutors, for instance, expect judges to honor plea bargaining commitments—failure to do so may be seen, in the eyes of the prosecutor, to be improper behavior. Each of the actors incorporates, in one way or another, these expectations into an organizational role orientation: a belief about the proper degree of influence of organizational norms on decisions. The interaction term $R_o \cdot 0$, where R_o is the actor's orientation toward organizational norms and 0 is the norm itself, could easily be incorporated into the generalized equation. Thus role theory need not be insensitive to the organizational context of criminal courts.[8]

Both role theory and organization theory can incorporate contextual variables into their models of the decision process and thus are not fundamentally incompatible. The most significant difference between the approaches seems to be on the empirical question of whether role expectations are uniformly and faithfully translated into role orientations. The advantage of role theory is that it proposes a model for incorporating organizational factors; it is unclear that organizational theory even considers the impact of psychological properties of the individual participants on the organization or on its outputs.[9]

EMPIRICAL EVIDENCE ON THE UTILITY OF ROLE THEORY

As a means of further explicating role theory—but not confirming it—it seems fruitful to review some empirical evidence from studies applying this approach to decision-making in the criminal courts.

Case/Defendant Attributes and Role Orientations

The first piece of research to be considered was designed to investigate the utility of the activist-restraintist distinction within the criminal court context (Gibson, 1977). Appellate court research has demonstrated that there is considerable variation among Supreme Court justices (and within justices, across time) in the degree to which extralegal stimuli (for example, the race of the litigants) can predict decisions (Ulmer, 1974). Such variability is an indicator of the "behavioral activism" of the justices; that is, the degree to which decisions reflect stimuli other than precedents, constitutions, and statutes indicates how activistic each judge is in his decisions.

As suggested above, activism can be generalized by defining it in terms of any nonlegal criteria. Thus behavioral activism at the trial court level might well be indicated by predictive power on the part of such criteria as the defendant's race, sex, and plea; whether charge reduction occurred; the length of time between arrest and trial; whether the defendant was incarcerated prior to trial; and a measure of the pretrial sanctions imposed on the defendant.

In addition to describing behavioral activism it is of course important to account for variations in activist behavior. An obvious hypothesis is that behavioral activism is a function of role orientations: activist orientations should be related to activist behavior.

This hypothesis was tested using data from the Fulton County Superior Court in Atlanta, Georgia (Gibson, 1977). A measure of behavioral activism was constructed by using the seven case/defendant attributes in discriminant functions to predict sentence severity (after the sentences were adjusted to control for legally relevant criteria). These scores were then correlated with measures of the judges' role orientations, resulting in a Pearson correlation coefficient of .54, thus providing strong support for the hypothesis. The role orientations of the criminal court judges substantially affected the process through which they made decisions. Moreover, what is important to note about these results is that role orientations did not predict the substance of the decisions, but rather they predicted the process of decision-making.

Attitudes and Role Orientation

The Fulton County study suggests that role orientations influence decisional processes but it does not clearly test the relationship to substantive decisional outcomes. Such a test requires the use of the interactive model proposed above. Role orientations should not merely predict decisional processes but should, when considered in combination with decisional criteria (as in Figure 4-1), predict the decisions themselves.

Research has been conducted that directly tests the interactive model (Gibson, 1978a). Using measures of judges' attitudes and role orientations, as derived from personal interviews, and measures of sentence severity (corrected for the influence of legally relevant criteria) the model was tested on twenty-six criminal court judges from twenty-five counties in Iowa. By themselves, the attitudes of the judges had only a negligible impact on behavior: attitude explained only 14 percent of the sentencing variance. Similarly, role orientations alone accounted for a mere 8 percent of the variance. However, when attitudes and role orientations were placed in the interactive equation, 64 percent of the sentencing variance was explained. Judges with broad or activist role orientations apparently rely substantially upon their own values in making sentencing decisions, whereas more restraintist judges were able to insulate their behavior from their attitudes. That is, the influence of attitudes on sentencing behavior is contingent upon the degree to which the judge believes such influence to be legitimate.

Representational Role Orientations

A third research project also provides some support for the model (Gibson, 1976). Using the data from the twenty-five Iowa counties, research was undertaken to determine the degree to which judges modify their sentencing behavior in different counties (the system is a circuit court) in order to accommodate their perceptions of the seriousness of the crime problem in the county. Four variables were analyzed through path analysis: the judge's sentencing behavior in each county, the judge's attitudes toward the seriousness of the crime, the judge's perception of the seriousness of crime in each county, and the actual amount of crime in each county. The role model predicts that judges who perceive themselves as "delegates" (those believing it proper to include public opinion as a criterion in making decisions on sentencing) will be more strongly influenced by their perceptions of crime in each county, while "trustees" will be more strongly influenced by their own attitudes on crime. Thus representational role orientations are incorporated into the model as a conditional variable.

The data were quite supportive of the model: "delegate" judges were not only more accurate in their perceptions of the county (a path coefficient .59 versus .27) but these perceptions also had a much greater impact on sentencing (.55 versus .34). Further, the influence of the judge's own beliefs about crime was stronger (−.35 versus +.12) for "trustees" than for "delegates." Apparently, the judges' representational role orientations do perform the function of legitimizing the use of environmental characteristics for decision-making, precisely as predicted by the model.

Each of these pieces of research supports the model that posits role orientations as a quite important conditional variable. It must be stressed, however, that role orientations alone do not predict behavior, but specify the criteria that judges rely on to reach decisions. In combination with these criteria, then, role orientations are quite strong predictors of behaviors.

CONCLUSIONS

The purpose of this essay has been to demonstrate that, with proper reconceptualization, role theory provides a powerful predictor of decision-making in the criminal court context. A model of the relationship between role concepts and behavior has been explicated and some supportive empirical evidence has been produced. In addition to calling for further testing and refinement of the model, several important directions for future role research can be identified:

1. Origins of role orientations: a complete role model should incorporate an understanding of the process by which role orientations are formed. Judges, as lawyers, are subjected to a relatively homogeneous socialization process, yet great variability in role beliefs results. Why? This suggests that judges may be differentially receptive to external socialization forces. What accounts for variation in receptiveness? Although little research has been conducted on judicial role orientations, it has been suggested that personality characteristics may play a significant function in the process (Levinson, 1959), and some exploratory empirical work has begun (Gibson, 1978b). Role orientations

are not simple extensions of political beliefs, yet there is little understanding of their origin at this point.

2. Dimensional analysis of role orientations: as already suggested, the term "role orientations" stands for a complex set of beliefs about various decisional stimuli. The precise set of dimensions and the interrelationship, if any, among the dimensions have not been thoroughly investigated. Most research has focused on either precedent or representational role orientations, but these surely do not exhaust the list of possibilities.

3. Generalizability of the model: role theory has utility for understanding any institutional behavior. Research should be undertaken to determine how role concepts operate differently or similarly within different institutional contexts (for example, Gibson, 1978c). Only through cross-institutional analysis can a truly general theory be developed.

4. Finally, role theory has been limited primarily to on-the-bench decisional behavior. Judges, however, engage in many other types of role behaviors. Although a few studies have been sensitive to other role behaviors (Volcansek, 1977; Gibson, 1978c), much more research in these areas is needed.

Role theory burst upon the political science scene with much fanfare, touted as a means for developing a comprehensive understanding of institutional processes. Given such a grandiose claim, it is not surprising that intellectual disillusionment grew with each new set of empirical findings. I believe that role theory still holds great potential for understanding politics. If role analysts are sensitive to the complexity of roles in the real political world, theoretical payoffs may yet be realized.

NOTES

1. Among the earliest uses of role theory outside political science are Gross, Mason, and McEachern (1958), and Biddle and Thomas (1966).

2. On appellate court role research see Becker (1966), Flango, Wenner, and Wenner (1975), Howard (1977), and Wold (1974). Trial court role research is represented by Jaros and Mendelsohn (1967), Levin (1972), Ish (1975), and Gibson (1977, 1978c).

3. For a nice illustration of the manner in which role orientation can structure decisional behavior, see Grossman (1962).

4. Exceptions include Vines (1969), Becker (1966), and Howard (1977).

5. This section relies heavily on Gibson (1978a, 1977).

6. One of the few pieces of empirical research at the appellate level that is sensitive to this distinction is Ulmer (1974).

7. Eisenstein and Jacob are fairly specific about this point: "Some room is undoubtedly left for judges' personal values, but not much" (Eisenstein and Jacob, 1977:286).

8. In the same fashion, other approaches to criminal court decision-making can be incorporated into role theory. Representational role orientations (for example, delegate-trustee) can be combined with characteristics of the local political culture (see Levin, 1972); orientations toward particular "facts" or case stimuli mediate the impact of the stimulus on decisions (see Ebbesen and Konecni, 1975); and attitudinal influence is a function of the orientation of the decision-maker (see Hogarth, 1971). Virtually all of the factors thought by other scholars to be influential in the criminal court context can be integrated into the role model.

9. A partial exception to this can be found in Nardulli's (1978) notion of responsiveness.

REFERENCES

Becker, Theodore L. (1966). "A Survey Study of Hawaiian Judges: The Effect on Decisions of Judicial Role Variations." 60 *American Political Science Review* 677-86.

Biddle, Bruce J., and Thomas, Edwin J., eds. (1966). *Role Theory*. New York: Wiley.

Ebbesen, Ebbe B., and Konecni, Vladimir J. (1975). "Decision Making and Information Integration in the Courts: The Setting of Bail." 32 *Journal of Personality and Social Psychology* 805-21.

Eisenstein, James, and Jacob, Herbert (1977). *Felony Justice: An Organizational Analysis of Criminal Courts*. Boston: Little, Brown.

Flango, Victor E.; Wenner, Lettie McSpadden; and Wenner, Manfred W. (1975). "The Concept of Judicial Role: A Methodological Note." 19 *American Journal of Political Science* 277-90.

Gibson, James L. (1976). "Judges as Representatives: Constituency Influence on Trial Courts." Paper presented at the 1976 Annual Meeting of the American Political Science Association, Chicago, Illinois.

_______ (1977). "Discriminant Functions, Role Orientations and Judicial Behavior: Theoretical and Methodological Linkages." 39 *Journal of Politics* 984-1007.

_______(1978a). "Judges' Role Orientations, Attitudes and Decisions: An Interactive Model." 72 *American Political Science Review* 911-24.

_______ (1978b). "Personality and Elite Political Behavior: The Influence of Self Esteem on Judicial Decision Making." Paper presented at the 1978 Annual Meeting of the Western Political Science Association, Los Angeles, California.

_______ (1978c). "Decision Making across Institutions: Legislators and Lower Court Judges in California." Paper presented at the 1978 Annual Meeting of the Midwest Political Science Association, Chicago, Illinois.

Gross, Neal; Mason, Ward S.; and McEachern, Alexander (1958). *Explanations in Role Analysis: Studies of the School Superintendency Role*. New York: Wiley.

Hogarth, John (1971). *Sentencing as a Human Process*. Toronto: University of Toronto Press.

Howard, J. Woodford, Jr. (1977). "Role Perceptions and Behavior in Three U.S. Courts of Appeals." 6 *Journal of Politics* 916-38.

Ish, Joel S. (1975). "Trial Judges: Their Recruitment, Backgrounds, and Role Perceptions." Paper presented at the 1975 Annual Meeting of the American Political Science Association, San Francisco, California.

Jaros, Dean, and Mendelsohn, Robert I. (1967). "The Judicial Role and Sentencing Behavior." 11 *Midwest Journal of Political Science* 471-88.

Levin, Martin A. (1972). "Urban Politics and Judicial Behavior." 1 *Journal of Legal Studies* 193-221.

Levinson, Daniel J. (1959). "Role, Personality, and Social Structure in the Organizational Setting." 58 *Journal of Abnormal and Social Psychology* 170-80.

Nardulli, Peter (1978). *The Courtroom Elite: An Organizational Perspective on Criminal Justice*. Cambridge, Mass.: Ballinger Publishing Company.

Packer, Herbert L. (1968). *The Limits of the Criminal Sanction*. Stanford: Stanford University Press.

Ulmer, S. Sidney (1974). "Dimensionality and Change in Judicial Behavior." In James F. Herndon and Joseph L. Bernd, eds. *Mathematical Applications in Political Science-VIII*, pp. 40-67. Charlottesville: University Press of Virginia.

Vines, Kenneth N. (1969). "The Judicial Role in the American States: An Exploration." In Joel Grossman and Joseph Tanenhaus, eds. *Frontiers of Judicial Research*, pp. 461-85. New York: Wiley.

Volcansek, Mary L. (1977). "Extra-Judicial Roles: Perceptions of Texas District Judges." 6 *Public Affairs Forum* 1-8.

Wahlke, John C., and others (1962). *The Legislative System*. New York: John Wiley & Sons.

Wasby, Stephen L. (1978). "Accountability of the Courts." In Scott Greer, Ronald D. Hedlund, and James L. Gibson, eds. *Accountability in Urban Society: Public Agencies under Fire*. Beverly Hills, Calif.: Sage.

Wold, John (1974). "Political Orientations, Social Backgrounds, and Role Perceptions of State Supreme Court Judges." 27 *Western Political Quarterly* 239-48.

Chapter Five

Organizational Analyses of Criminal Courts: An Overview and Some Speculation

Peter F. Nardulli

During the past decade criminal courts have undergone a period of intensive examination, paralleled in quantity only by the research conducted during the 1920s, when a group of researchers closely connected to the municipal reform movement turned its attention to the criminal justice system. The recent literature, however, has been characterized by a more theoretical orientation. Political culture, the recruitment process, judicial attitudes, and role perceptions, among other concepts, have been used to explain patterns of behavior within and across criminal courts. The main theoretical thrust, however, has been in the application of organizational analysis to the study of criminal court phenomena.

An organizational approach to criminal courts, according to Herbert Jacob, "structures our thinking about courts in a different and useful way. It forces us to focus on the working relationships among the many actors in and around courtrooms. . . . It puts those relations into quite specific contexts that permit and even invite study. In addition, organizational theory leads us to focus on units of analysis in which real activity takes place rather than abstractions which exist only in the minds of the researcher" (Jacob, 1977, p. 1). What Jacob is suggesting, quite rightly, is that organizational approaches are theories of the conversion process in the criminal court system. They seek to elaborate upon the *context* of decision-making.

This focus on the context of decision-making differentiates organizational analyses from other approaches to the study of criminal courts. An organizational perspective recognizes that external factors affect internal operations, but it places less emphasis upon such factors than, say, a political culture approach. For a variety of reasons external factors almost never directly affect internal operations. Rather, they are normally implemented, interpreted, and diluted by personnel who have ongoing ties within the system; their ultimate impact is problematic at best. Organizational approaches also recognize the importance of individual-level considerations. Here again, however, less importance is accorded such factors than in approaches focusing upon role orientations or judicial attitudes. An organizational approach would place more emphasis upon the *constraints* upon individual deviations from group norms.

While one could legitimately contend that a common feature of organizational analyses is their emphasis upon the context of criminal court decision-making, these analyses appear to have little else in common. While they are perhaps organized around a common theme they evidence a myriad of emphases, concerns, and methodologies. As a result there has been little in the way of cumulative development of knowledge. This sense of unfocused development is enhanced by the lack of any attempts to examine systematically the course of thought in this field. This chapter tries to deal with some of these concerns.

The first section presents a brief overview of organizational analyses of criminal courts. Obviously no work of this length could provide a comprehensive review of the works in this area, and no such attempt is made. Rather this first section merely attempts to chart the development of thought in two areas. The first includes thought concerning the operations of the "court organization," that is, how the court processes its workload. These discussions attempt to summarize the contribution of various scholars to the development of an organizational theory of criminal courts. The second area relates to thought concerning the reasons for the prevalence of bureaucratic due process, that is, why do courts act like administrative bodies instead of adversary bodies? In these discussions the evolution of thinking in this area will be outlined. The second main section of this essay argues that there are certain commonalities in some of the later studies which have significant implications for future work in this field, especially with regard to the question of *how* courts function. These commonalities are identified and their implications for future analyses are discussed.

ORGANIZATIONAL ANALYSES OF CRIMINAL COURTS

A cursory examination of organizational analyses of criminal courts suggest three temporally organized groups of works—the seminal pieces of Blumberg and Skolnick, several transitional studies, and what may be termed second generation analyses. These three groups differ in terms of the extent to which they explicitly extend concepts derived from the organizational literature to criminal courts, the conceptual richness and cohesiveness of their analyses, and their attempts at hypothesis development and empirical examination. They also differ significantly in terms of their views concerning the reasons for the prevalence of bureaucratic due process.

Seminal Works

The appearance in the late 1960s of the works of two sociologists, Abraham Blumberg's *Criminal Justice* (1967) and Jerome Skolnick's "Social Control in the Adversary System" (1967), marked the beginning of a new era in the study of criminal courts. A generation earlier Raymond Moley (1930) had noted similarities between criminal court and administrative decision-making. Blumberg's and Skolnick's observations, however, were the first to have a lasting effect. Their work had such an impact because it came at a time when interest in the criminal justice system was on an upswing; Moley's observations had come at the end of an era. Blumberg's and Skolnick's work also stood in marked contrast to earlier studies. Unlike the spate of studies during the 1950s and 1960s which focused upon individual segments of the criminal process (bail, plea bargaining, sentencing), they viewed the process as an integrated whole tied together by mutual interests and a complex web of interrelationships.

Several things can be said about these works in terms of their contribution to an *organizational* theory of criminal courts. First, nothing even resembling a substantive organizational framework emerges from either work. Second, they borrow very little from the literature on organizations; they certainly do not explicitly apply, extend, or adapt organizational concepts or frameworks to the study of criminal courts. Finally, they do not develop empirical support for their observations. Indeed, they do not reach the hypothesis formulation stage.

These observations notwithstanding, these works merit the seminal role generally accorded them. They deserve this status because their insights led to the view of courts as organizations, even if they did not elaborate upon the implications of such a perspective. Their most significant observation is that courtroom behavior is characterized by cooperative, not adversary, relations. They view decision-making in the criminal court context as a group process in which individual actors tend to forego their formal prerogatives for the sake of consensus. The dominant concern of all, for a variety of reasons, is to "keep the calendar moving." The observation that courtroom behavior is cooperative and centered around common concerns is what leads to the view of courts as organizations; this is the primary theoretical contribution of Blumberg and Skolnick. That they leave this idea to later researchers to refine and extend is secondary.

Beyond merely noting that courtroom encounters are characterized by cooperative relations, Blumberg and Skolnick also address the reasons for the prevalence of bureaucratic due process. Simplistically their position in this regard could be summarized in one word: workload. In the final analysis both appear to attribute the demise of the adversary system to the overwhelming caseloads with which criminal court practitioners are saddled. In the introduction to "Social Control in the Adversary System" Skolnick (1967, p. 53) states that "the principal theme of the paper is that administrative requirements characterizing the American administration of criminal justice make for a reciprocal relationship between prosecutor and defense attorney that strains toward cooperation; that this relationship is based upon interests wider than those of the parties they represent, the State and the accused. . . ." It becomes clear in Skolnick's work that the "administrative requirements" he talks of are pressures emanating from heavy workloads.

Blumberg is even more direct concerning the role of case load pressure.

> Intolerably large case loads, which must be handled with limited resources and personnel, potentially subject the participants in the court community to harsh scrutiny from appellate courts and other public and private sources of condemnation. Thus there is an almost irreconcilable conflict; intense pressures to process large numbers of cases, on the one hand, and the stringent ideological and legal requirements of "due process of law," on the other. The dilemna is frequently resolved through bureaucratically ordained short cuts, deviations, and outright rule violations by members of the courts, from judges to stenographers, in order to meet production norms. (Blumberg, 1967, p. xi)

One thing should be mentioned about the role of the caseload thesis in these works: it was not as central as it was in earlier works decrying the demise of the adversary system. One gets the impression that both Blumberg and Skolnick believe that other, largely unarticulated considerations were as important as caseload pressure. This is perhaps most clear in Blumberg's work. While the importance of caseload pressure is a major theme in *Criminal Justice*, another seems to be that the displacement of adversary norms could not have taken place without corresponding changes in the environment of criminal courts.

More specifically, Blumberg is arguing that, like virtually all aspects of human existence, criminal courts have been affected by the emergence of mass, industrialized society, with its concomitant values of secularism and rationality.

> The kinds of values that produced due process and other Western notions of justice have been superseded. While the stated goals of the criminal court may still appear to be the same—at least as ritual affirmations—the instrumental structures used to achieve those goals are not. In fact, the evidence indicates that fundamental changes in values and accompanying changes in instruments in an industrial-urban society have so altered one another that virtually all that remains of the original criminal court goals are its ideological affirmations. . . . Concerns of secularism and rationality, based on modern values of efficiency, maximum production, and career enhancement, have deflected and perhaps displaced those goals. So there is also a new angle of vision more harmoniously in accord with the rationalization of justice. These perspectives are organizationally geared through bureaucratic discipline to mesh with the new goals. The impersonal relations inherent in this kind of social structure produce accusers and accused possessed of a self which is ideal for organizational purposes—one which is vulnerable to manipulation and capable of manipulating others. (Blumberg, 1967, pp. 75, 78)

For these reasons Blumberg looks skeptically at criminal courts reform proposals aimed merely at increasing available resources. In the closing paragraph of *Criminal Justice* he expresses the fear that additional resources will merely be absorbed by the prevailing structure.

Transitional Works

Several articles which first appeared in the early 1970s could be categorized as transitional works in the study of courts from an organizational perspective. They include pieces by George Cole (1970), Maureen Mileski (1971), and Malcolm Feeley (1973). With regard to their theoretical contribution it must be said that these transitional works again resulted in no general organizational frameworks being developed or empirically tested. They did, however, borrow more explicitly from the organizational literature and made more of an attempt to extend organizational concepts into the criminal court realm, even though the developments were not always cumulative. In addition they moved away further and more explicitly from the caseload thesis as a central factor in explaining the demise of the adversary system.

Cole. In "The Decision to Prosecute," George Cole (1970) explicitly applies one segment of organizational analysis to the courtroom setting.

Unlike Blumberg and Skolnick, however, Cole adopts an interorganizational perspective, focusing upon the participants as members of different groups with different aims. At one point he contends that "the legal system may be viewed as a set of interorganizational exchange relationships analogous to what Long has called a community game. The participants in the legal system (game) share a common territorial field and collaborate for different and particular ends. They interact on a continuing basis as their responsibilities demand contact with other participants in the process" (Cole, 1970, p. 314).

In contrast to the seminal works Cole's interorganizational approach tends to stress the differences among courtroom participants rather than their similarities. An implicit premise appears to be that in order to understand courtroom phenomena one must recognize that those who process criminal cases are representatives of different organizations with different goals. For example, at several points he compares the criminal court to a marketplace, giving rise to the impression of buyers and sellers competing in a zero sum or near zero sum situation. A more cynical view, perhaps attributable to someone like Blumberg, would be more apt to compare the criminal court to a group of OPEC oil ministers meeting to set prices and devise a strategy to enforce the agreed-upon rate. This difference in emphasis is important to note because it has important substantive implications. To stress the differences among the participants more than their commonalities suggests that, in the end, defense counsel are most concerned with the welfare of their clients, prosecutors are most concerned with community interests, and judges are dedicated to neutrality. Despite the centrality of these concerns they are never systematically addressed in the literature. Instead these conflicting emphases are permitted to coexist, drawing little discussion or research and reinforcing the impression that organization analyses of criminal courts are little more than a loosely organized, internally inconsistent group of works which do not lead to any common view of courtroom operations.

Mileski. Maureen Mileski's "Courtroom Encounters" (1971), unlike Cole's article, is not an attempt explicitly to extend some segment of organizational analysis to criminal courts. Rather it is a largely descriptive piece. Nonetheless what clearly emerges from it is a view of the court as an entity which routinizes, whenever possible, its procedures for handling cases. The aim of this routinization is to dispose of cases rapidly. She emphasizes the cooperative facets of courtroom behavior, but notes that those who deviate from established norms are sanctioned.

None of these observations was necessarily unique to Mileski. She does, however, provide more of an empirical grounding to them than earlier researchers. She outlines in detail some of the techniques and considerations used by courtroom personnel to perform various tasks and she discusses various methods of sanctioning recalcitrants. Mileski also introduces several conceptual innovations, such as the courtroom "team" which dominated the various "worksites." In addition she stresses the importance of such things as the seriousness of the cases, the orientation of the defendant, and the type of defense counsel as factors which affected the nature, as well as the outcome, of the proceedings. Finally, an important contribution of Mileski's work is that she engages in some quantitative analyses, however crude, of courtroom happenings. Unfortunately the quantitative analyses are only tangentially related to any organizational perspective which might be found in her work. It was, however, an important beginning.

Feeley. Malcom Feeley's "Two Models of the Criminal Justice System" is an attempt to "develop an explicit theoretical framework by which the practices in the administration [of criminal justice] can be depicted and explained" (Feeley, 1973, p. 402). Unlike earlier works, however, Feeley's article is not based upon empirical research. Rather it is a review of various studies of criminal courts in light of a modified version of Etzioni's discussion of two models of organizational analysis, a functional systems model and a rational goal model. While the article falls considerably short of its lofty objective it does serve useful functions. It sensitizes criminal justice researchers to at least one way of differentiating among approaches to studying organizations. Moreover, it outlines the thrust of each, analyzes their relative strengths, and assesses the potential each has to contribute to the study of criminal courts.

Feeley advocates the functional systems approach over the rational goal model. The latter tends to produce a "preoccupation with a set of formal goals and the observation of behavior primarily in terms of how it squares with these goals (or how the rules have altered previous patterns of behavior) is not conducive to theory building and the explanation of the observed patterns of behavior. It tends to produce an unidimensional picture of the process by placing undue emphasis on one set of goals and rules without adequately considering other factors which are, perhaps equally as important in shaping the behavior of the actors in the system" (Feeley, 1973, p. 412). The functional systems model, on the other hand, "lends itself to accurate description of actual behavior but also begins to identify and account for the causes and conditions leading to this behavior" (Feeley, 1973, p. 414).

Beyond a discussion of the relative merits of these two models,

Feeley makes a significant contribution to thought concerning the prevalence of bureaucratic due process. In this regard he edges a bit beyond the work of Skolnick and Blumberg. Whereas the latter two gave a qualified embrace to the caseload thesis developed in earlier works, Feeley comes close to questioning the viability, or at least the centrality, of it. After noting that Mileski observed "corner cutting" even when the court's workload was not great, he contends that "Blumberg has somewhat overstated the importance of heavy case loads" (Feeley, 1973, p. 418). While Feeley tends to view such things as long-term interactions and personal and administrative considerations as factors leading to cooperative patterns of behavior, he does not formally construct an alternative to the caseload thesis. Nor does he, at this time, present any empirical evidence relevant to the issue.

Second-Generation Analyses

Works by several researchers which emerged during the mid-1970s can be characterized as second-generation organizational analyses of criminal courts. Within this broad category, however, there are really two distinct subgroups. Works in the first focused upon only one facet of the dispositional process; works in the second attempted to present a more general framework. Studies by Carter (1975) and Fleming (1978) fall within the former category while works by Mohr (1976), Eisenstein and Jacob (1977), and Nardulli (1978) fall within the latter.

Second-generation analyses differ from earlier works in a number of important ways. With respect to *how* the courts operate, second-generation works are not so much descriptions of criminal courts or general overviews of organizational concepts; rather they are organizational *analyses* of criminal courts. Most are empirical studies that explicitly integrate concepts borrowed from the organizational literature into analyses of courtroom operations. Moreover, most of these works involve attempts to develop testable hypotheses and to examine them empirically, using either qualitative data, quantitative data, or some combination of both. With regard to the question of *why* bureaucratic due process is so prevalent, these works go beyond merely questioning the caseload thesis. Several challenge it outright by presenting compelling evidence to the contrary and constructing alternate explanations.

The Question of How: Carter. Leif Carter's *The Limits of Order* (1975) was the first book-length work which explicitly extended organizational concepts to a segment of the dispositional process. *The Limits of Order* is a study of the prosecutorial function in an anonymous California county—Varios County. Carter's theoretical orientation comes primarily from the work of James Thompson, especially the latter's concepts of organizational technology and environment. Carter focuses upon these two concepts because he contends that they have direct implications for resolving what he perceives as an internal contradiction in contemporary notions of justice.

> ... The concept of justice itself embodies two mutually incompatible standards: order and learning. The incompatibility arises because the objective of ordered application of law, unquestionably desirable in itself, presents a pragmatic tactical question: What administrative apparatus can achieve it? The conventional administrative apparatus for making behavior uniform—bureaucracy—imposes costs of its own. Specifically, bureaucratic controls can interfere with the alternative conception of justice as learning. This alternative conception requires that those who do justice maintain the capacity to learn new information about the cases they handle, about social preferences concerning crime, and about the consequences of punishment. (Carter, p. 2)

An organization's technology is its prevailing combination of desirable outcomes and beliefs about cause/effect relationships. Thompson identifies several important theoretical dimensions to the concept of technology. One important dimension concerns the extent to which the organization's standards of desirability are crystallized (or ambiguous). Another important dimension concerns the extent to which knowledge concerning cause and effect relationships is complete. These are important dimensions because they have important implications for organizational operations.

The prosecutor's technology is ambiguous because there is little indisputable guidance concerning what is to be maximized or minimized, such as social cost, crime, traditional due process values, or rehabilitation. This makes the concrete specification of desirable outcomes impossible. The prosecutor's technology is uncertain because, even if there were agreement over desirable ends, there is little causal knowledge about the relationship between work strategies and outcomes. Both factors mitigate against the centralized, hierarchical control needed to insure the attainment of "order" because the lack of clear goals and/or knowledge of how to attain them eliminates tools essential to such a structure. In the prosecutor's office control devices such as office rules become either too broad to be effective or too rigid to be useful, leading to widespread circumvention. The fact that the prosecutor's technology is intensive (that is, it requires professionals to choose from a wide variety of treatments; information relevant to application of treatment comes from the client) also mitigates against hierarchical control.

An organization's environment is important to consider when analyzing organizational behavior because no organization is completely closed. Initially it recruits individuals from its environment; it also relies upon its environment for information as well as supplies and other types of supports. Moreover,

> just as the nature of its technology affects the way an organization does its work, Thompson suggests that different environments produce different organizational patterns. Thompson argues that organizations dealing with *homogeneous* environments (environments that contain people and institutions with similar interests and needs) and with *stable* environments (environments that make predictable demands on the organization) will develop structures and procedures that differ considerably from organizations dealing with *heterogeneous* and/or *shifting* environments.
>
> Confronted with a heterogeneous environment (one that makes competing and inconsistent demands on the organization) and a shifting environment (where these demands and pressures change), organizations, Thompson argues, will adopt flexible and decentralized operations that do not rely heavily on rules. (Carter, 1975, p. 18)

In the case of the prosecutor's office many environmental factors lead to the ineffectiveness of centralized control. First, the office has to recruit lawyers who are socialized to professional autonomy norms and who have no long-term commitments to the prosecutor's office. A second factor working against the feasibility of centralized control is the way prosecutors have to learn the facts essential to handling their cases.

> To get their work done, prosecutors must rely on the calculations and perceptions of others—police, defense attorneys, judges, and sometimes probation officers—whose values and interests and understanding of facts vary among themselves and from case to case. Because prosecutors learn from fragmented and competing sources, their sense of what is true remains tentative, and this continuous factual tentativeness and uncertainty (they are rarely sure that they know the entire story) further reduces the possible payoffs to the organization of any attempts to control prosecutorial behavior by rules. (Carter, 1975, p. 19)

Among other things this factual tentativeness and uncertainty lead to the development of informal relationships across organizational boundaries. To the extent that hierarchical controls would interfere with these relationships they would be counterproductive and circumvented by line personnel. The shifting and inconsistent nature of the office's political environment also enhanced as well as dictated a flexible and decentralized organizational structure.

The empirical section of Carter's work is an elaboration of his general thesis. He argues quite convincingly, using largely qualitative observational data, that the Varios County prosecutor's office had a great deal of difficulty implementing centralized policies. These policies ranged from a petty "no more than two prosecutors in an office" rule to one which outlawed sentencing commitments in guilty plea cases to a seven-day rule which discouraged the acceptance of guilty pleas within a week of the trial date. He also analyzes the deficiencies of three broad control strategies as they were used in Varios County.

Flemming. In a recent paper, "Pretrial Sanctioning Processes: Felony Bail Practices in Baltimore and Detroit," Roy Flemming (1978) presents perhaps the most insightful analysis of bail to date. In it he lays a "conceptual foundation for the empirical study of the pretrial sanctioning process that is theoretically rooted in the literature on organizational choice and empirically nurtured by extensive field work conducted in the two cities and by samples of felony cases processed in their courts during 1972" (Flemming, 1978, p 1). Flemming's focus is on two facets of the bail process—the bail tariff and the mode of choice (routine, situational, or bargaining).

In discussing the structure of the bail tariff, by which Flemming appears to mean a fairly routinized decision function used to determine bail outcomes, he identifies three important factors. One is ecological, the political environment; two are contextual, risk and resources. In Flemming's analysis the notion of political environment refers mainly to variations in local political cultures. He notes that Baltimore courts worked with a much more conservative environment than Detroit courts. This is important because the environment can have indirect effects upon such things as average bail amounts, release-on-recognizance (ROR) rates, jail facilities, and so on. While this in itself is not a major conceptual innovation, the strength of the work is that Flemming is able to integrate this notion with the contextual factors noted above to construct a convincing argument explaining variations in Baltimore and Detroit bail tariffs (Baltimore's system has higher average bail amounts, lower overall release rates, and is less apt to use ROR than Detroit's).

For example, Flemming identifies three components to the notion of risk—uncertainty, threat, and vulnerability. Uncertainty is a consideration because there is incomplete causal knowledge of the consequences of different bail options. This was less of a problem in Detroit than in Baltimore, however, because Detroit judges had more reliable and complete information on defendants than did Baltimore magistrates. Detroit judges also had a better understanding of the consequences of their decisions. They handled a case from indictment to sentencing while Baltimore magistrates were only responsible for setting bail. The threat structure was also different in these two systems. Because of the conservative political environment Baltimore magistrates were severely sanctioned for making the wrong decision (releasing a dangerous defendant) but seldom applauded for making the right decision. This led to a cautious bail strategy, mitigating against the use of ROR. In Detroit the political environment was more diverse, with active reform groups advocating defendant rights. This led to a more liberal ROR policy. The vulnerability of bail personnel also differed in the two systems. Baltimore's magistrates were appointed and ranked very low in terms of power, prestige, and salary. Detroit judges, on the other hand, were elected officials with a political following and relatively high salaries and prestige.

The second contextual factor which Flemming discusses, resources, also played an important part in the determination of bail policies. While both had ROR programs with staffs available to analyze candidates for release, Baltimore's program was much more conservative than Detroit's. The real differences in resources, however, concerned jail capacities. Detroit labored under a court-imposed quota on the number of defendants it could assign to the local jail; Baltimore did not. Hence Detroit's jail capacity, relative to its caseload, was much lower than Baltimore's, necessitating a more liberal bail policy.

Although Flemming devotes more attention to the question of bail tariff, his analysis of the determinants of the mode of choice has a similar structure. He argues that "the amount of time officials have to review and evaluate cases, their availability to other actors such as defense attorneys, prosecutors, or police, the severity of the cases they handle, and the quantity and quality of pertinent information before them when they make their bail selections all influence the manner in which bail decisions are made" (Flemming, 1978, p. 19). Greater workloads, more serious cases, less variation in the type of case, more complete and reliable information, and less contact with interested parties led to a largely routinized bail process in Detroit. Baltimore's process was characterized by a situational mode of choice.

Mohr. Lawrence Mohr (1976) was the first, and at this point the only, organization theorist to examine the operations of criminal courts. In "Organizations, Decisions, and Courts" he begins his analysis by noting that, because courts have been observed to lack such things as hierarchies and effective compliance systems, important branches of organization theory are not relevant to the study of courts and that the potential contributions of the organizational literature are correspondingly limited. This notwithstanding, he contends that some recent theoretical developments concerning the determinants of organizational goals and structure are relevant. But, rather than straining the analogy between courts and more conventional objects of organizational analysis, he advocates conceptualizing courts as decision-making systems. Relevant strands of organization theory can then be applied in a straightforward manner. In suggesting this, however, he cautions that there is no reason to expect that one model of decision-making will explain courtroom operations in all court systems under all conditions. Indeed he suggests as one of the primary objects of inquiry the determinants of mode of choice.

With mode of choice (style of decision-making) as the primary concern, Mohr discusses the essential characteristics of four different submodels of choice behavior—termed submodels to emphasize that each could occur in different systems or within the same system under different conditions. He views three of these as having some relevance to courts. The first, the firm submodel, emphasizes satisficing, and the dominant instrumental activity is bargaining. The rational submodel emphasizes maximization of goals, and the dominant activities include analysis and persuasion. The third submodel Mohr outlines is the political, meant to connote contention, struggle, and the attempt to overpower with superior force. The choice mechanism here is domination: the dominant actor decides. Mohr contends that much plea bargaining activity fits within the firm submodel, trial activity before submission to the jury might fall best within the political, and many jury deliberations may fall within the rational.

Mohr also outlines various contextual factors, culled from the works of organization theorists such as Cyert, March, Olsen, and Dalton, which are expected to have an effect upon the dominant mode of decision-making in a given system. These factors include goal compatibility of the participants in the decision-making process; the consistency of the participants (a two-dimensional concept, which operates multiplicatively, concerning the extent to which the participants meet in face-to-face interactions and on a recurring basis); resource constraints; and norms against redistribution (the existence or strength of norms against making one of the participants in an interaction relatively worse off than before the interaction).

Table 5-1 summarizes the hypothesized relations between the contextual factors and the three different modes of decision-making.

Mohr concludes with a brief review of some contemporary works on criminal courts in light of his model. He notes that the dominant mode of choice in criminal courts should be the firm model because com-

Table 5-1. Decision Submodels

Choice Mechanisms:	*Firm Satisficing*	*Rational Maximizing*	*Political Domination*
Typical Instrumental Behavior:	*Bargaining*	*Analysisis, Persuasion*	*Contention, Struggle, Force*
Contextual Variables			
1. Goal compatibility	Mod	High	Low
2. Consistency of participants	High	Low-Mod	Low
3. Resource constraints	High/Mod	Low	Low
4. Norms against redistribution	High	High	Low

Source: Mohr (1976), p. 634.

patibility is moderate and the other three factors are high. He notes, however, that different conditions, such as a strange defense counsel in a highly publicized, serious case, can bring about a different mode of choice.

Eisenstein and Jacob. James Eisenstein and Herbert Jacob's *Felony Justice* (1977)—a comparative study of felony courts in Baltimore, Chicago, and Detroit—is the most comprehensive and influential work to date on criminal courts from an organizational perspective. They begin their analysis by briefly reviewing—and rejecting—the more traditional explanations of courtroom phenomena.

> Neither defendant characteristics, nor characteristics of judges, nor features of the felony disposition process such as plea bargaining, the kind of defense counsel, or pretrial release provides us with a sufficient explanation of the felony disposition process. Nor can these variables be combined in a simple fashion. But the evidence is strong that each has some effect on the disposition of cases; moreover, they exist close to each other and visibly interact with one another. If we cannot simply sum them together, we must find more complex models which combine their effect on the final disposition of cases. (Eisenstein and Jacob, 1977, p. 9)

A basic thesis in this work is that a profitable way to uncover how these rather traditional factors, and others, affect courtroom operations is to understand the organizational context within which they interact. Indeed, *Felony Justice* can best be understood as an attempt to outline and elaborate upon the important facets of this context. To do this Eisenstein and Jacob borrow explicitly from a diverse body of literature on organizations. Most of their theoretical development is at the workgroup level and concerns two important sets of factors: workgroup characteristics and ecological influences upon workgroups.

In discussing the structure of workgroups, Eisenstein and Jacob note several features which are important for understanding courtroom operations. One such feature is that criminal court workgroups are sets of professionals who provide a service; they dispose of criminal cases. Performing this service implies a given set of tasks, even though the actual tasks may vary slightly across jurisdictions. Each participant has a highly specialized role within the workgroup. To perform their respective role tasks workgroup participants can utilize any of three "work techniques": unilaterial decisions, adversary proceedings, or negotiations. Criminal court workgroups also have an established authority structure. While the judge is the formal leader, this structure is modified by informal patterns of influence. The result is that no workgroup leaders in other organizations have (for example, budgetary, personnel control). Moreover, the formal authority structure is modified by informal patterns of inflence. The result is that no one member usually dominates, although the actual distribution of power varies across workgroups.

Another important feature of these workgroups is the nature of their goal structure. While the formal roles of the main participants (judge, prosecutor, defense counsel) imply markedly different orientations, Eisenstein and Jacob argue that these participants actually share basic values and goals. They identify four goals

> [which] . . . are produced by the interaction of two dimensions: the function performed (expressive or instrumental) and the origins of the goals (external or internal to the group). Expressive goals serve symbolic functions and infuse meaning into activity. Instrumental goals serve material functions and help get things done. Externally oriented goals are imposed by the workgroup's environment. Internal goals are produced by the need of the members to share perspectives that sustain the organization itself, (Eisenstein and Jacob, p. 25).

Table 5-2 outlines this goal structure. The desirability of the various goals is quite obvious. What is important to note, however, is that while the instrumental goals are mutually supportive the expressive are not. "Doing justice" may conflict with the maintenance of group cohesion. Moreover, across workgroups the relative importance of these goals is expected to vary, although not to any great extent.

Familiarity is a final important workgroup characteristic. It is a reflection of two factors, the stability of assignments and the size of

Table 5-2. Goals of Courtroom Workgroups

Function of Goal	*Origins of Goal*	
	External	*Internal*
Expressive	Doing justice	Maintaining group cohesion
Instrumental	Disposing of caseload	Reducing uncertainty

Source: Eisenstein and Jacob (1977), p. 25.

the personnel pool. Familiarity has important implications for how workgroups perform their basic tasks. Where it is high they can utilize the most informal of the various work techniques, negotiation, to dispose of cases, thus enhancing cohesion. Unfamiliarity, however, breeds adversary proceedings, introducing stress and uncertainty.

Because courts are not autonomous bodies, the ecology of workgroups is also important to consider in attempting to understand how courts operate. In discussing ecological factors Eisenstein and Jacob outline three types. The first includes the workgroup's physical surroundings. This layout—like that of supermarkets—is structured to have an impact. Courtrooms are designed to awe. The high ceilings, the elevated bench, the jury box, the enclosed chambers, and so on are all intended to create a specific aura. There are, however, also unintended consequences. The courtrooms, for example, are isolated from one another and separated from the formal offices of most of the participants. This means that periods of formal inactivity are consumed by socializing and negotiating rather than by more conventional types of legal activity.

A second important facet of the workgroup's environment consists of the participants' sponsoring organization. One fairly unique feature of these workgroups is that the participants are formally agents of several distinct organizations (a prosecutor's office, for example). While much of these individuals' work is done outside of their office and is highly discretionary, the sponsoring organizations are important for several reasons. They often recruit and assign personnel as well as determine the resources available to the workgroups. Sponsoring organizations also attempt to influence directly workgroup procedures by adopting formal or informal policies in designated areas.

The third ecological factor discussed in *Felony Justice* concerns entities in the workgroup's task environment, which include suppliers, regulators, and customers. Sponsoring organizations and police departments are the primary suppliers, but they also regulate. Moreover, they share this regulatory function with groups such as legislatures, appellate courts, the news media, political organizations, and prison authorities. These latter groups have both direct and indirect effects (through sponsoring organizations).

After elaborating upon the above-mentioned factors in some detail, Eisenstein and Jacob expend a good deal of effort analyzing each of the three cities studied in light of their theoretical framework. These discussions are one of the strengths of the work inasmuch as they flesh out the rather abstract theoretical concepts and provide significant insights into the operations of criminal courts. For example, they note that, for a variety of reasons (rapid personnel turnover, shifting personnel assignments, case assignment procedures), workgroup familiarity in Baltimore is quite low. Other factors (geographical dispersion, low pay and prestige) made the control of sponsoring organizations quite weak. In addition, Baltimore's conservative political culture, baited by an active media, reflected great concern for law and order. These factors led to such things as judge dominated proceedings, the extensive use of trials, and relatively severe bail and sentencing levels.

Chicago, unlike Baltimore, had high workgroup familiarity and relatively powerful sponsoring organizations. The prevalence of the Daley machine insulated Chicago workgroups and their sponsoring organizations from external groups such as the media. Moreover, most criminal court personnel were socialized into a political culture which emphasized negotiations. These factors led to a fairly even distribution of power within the workgroups since sets of common understandings were permitted to emerge; the goals of cohesion and uncertainty reduction took on more importance than in Baltimore. Guilty pleas were the dominant mode of conviction. Detroit courts, like Chicago's, were characterized by very strong sponsoring organizations and workgroups which were almost as familiar as Chicago's. Unlike Chicago, however, the task environment of Detroit courts was characterized by the presence of several active, defendant oriented watchdog groups. The policies of sponsoring agencies and the familiarity of workgroups led to high guilty plea rates, but sentences and bail policies were quite liberal.

In addition to these qualitative analyses articulating the differences in the processes across these three cities, Eisenstein and Jacob also engage in a good deal of quantitative analysis. The analyses are largely aimed at outlining factors affecting different facets of the dispositional process. Many of their multivariate analyses are interesting and powerful. They do not, however, contribute as much to the development of their theoretical model as their qualitative analyses. The principal reason for this is that, while the theoretical discussions are mainly at the workgroup level, the quantitative analyses use the individual defendant as the unit of analysis. The two levels of analysis are not sufficiently meshed. In addition Eisenstein and Jacob lacked the data to measure many of the concepts which they developed so elaborately in their theoretical analysis.

Nardulli. The last relatively general organizational framework to be discussed is that set forth by Nardulli (1978) in *The Courtroom Elite*. In this study he attempts to set forth, elaborate upon, and empirically examine a mode of analysis appropriate for studying criminal courts based upon several fundamental concepts derived from the literature on organizational behavior. He argues that, because of certain institutional characteristics of criminal courts, there are important parallels between the operations of these courts and the operations of goal oriented collectivities. These institutional characteristics include its closely knit interest structure and its monopolistic power structure. A basic premise of the study is that it is in the mutual interest of the judge, prosecutor, and defense counsel (that is, the courtroom elite) to process cases expeditiously. He also contends that these individuals control most of the important facets of courtroom operations.

This monopolistic power structure permits members of the courtroom elite to effectuate common concerns. For this reason the literature on organizations is believed to be relevant to the study of criminal courts—much of the organizational literature revolves around the notion of collective efforts to achieve common ends. But the relevance of organization theory does not stop there.

> The organizational literature is also useful because it leads one to consider the effect of external constraints upon the coalition's pursuit of its common ends and sensitizes one to the fact that the implications of these collective efforts may be different in different settings. All three factors—the interests of the courtroom elite, external (environmental) considerations, and the court's setting—are essential in viewing courts from an organizational perspective. Indeed, perhaps the most significant contribution that an organizational mode of analysis could make to the study of criminal courts would be an understanding of how the courtroom elite's efforts to pursue common interests are manifested in different settings and how this coalition responds to changes in environmental constraints. (Nardulli, 1978, p. 67)

After discussing and analyzing the significances of these three factors (Nardulli, 1978, pp. 66-77), Nardulli discusses how they can be used to understand courtroom operations. He contends that they have implications for the structure of the court's dispositional strategy as well as for the criteria used in making important decisions. Differences in the setting of criminal trial courts may, for example, have implications for the dominant dispositional modes used in a system. External considerations may demand that most dispositions be convictions; internal considerations may dictate that they be expeditious. The court's immediate setting may, however, influence whether a slow plea or guilty plea system prevails. Where case assignment procedures are unstable and where indigent defense is provided for by reimbursing private attorneys at reasonable rates, the slow plea may emerge as the dominant mode of conviction procurement. Stable case assignment procedures and public defender systems may result in a guilty plea system.

The implications of Nardulli's suggested mode of analysis for decision-making can be illustrated with reference to the sentencing decision. Internal considerations make expeditious conviction modes such as the slow plea and guilty plea satisficing modes of disposition, but external considerations dictate that nonsatisficing modes, such as adversary trials, always be available. This has implications for the structure of the sentencing decision. In a guilty plea system, for example, the basic implication is that there are really two sets of sentencing decision rules—one for satisficing situations (guilty pleas) and one for nonsatisficing situations (adversary trials). In both situations case seriousness is expected to be the primary determinant of sentencing, for external reasons. But the similarity is expected to end there. Guilty plea cases of comparable seriousness are expected to receive significantly lower sentences than trial cases, for internal reasons. If a cost were not levied for deviating from accepted, beneficial norms, it would be difficult for members of the courtroom elite to realize their common interests. In addition to different sentencing levels in the two situations, other criteria relevant to the determination of sentence are also expected to vary. In guilty plea cases factors relevant to the relative bargaining positions of the parties are expected to affect sentence. In trial cases nothing remains to be bargained. What is relevant is the extent to which informal norms were violated. Grievous offenders are expected to receive longer sentences than others, if all other factors are held constant.

Nardulli's empirical examination of his proposed organizational perspective consists primarily of a set of multivariate analyses of several important processes (the screening process, conviction procurement, the decision to pursue a case to trial, sentencing) in Chicago's felony court system. While he uses Eisenstein and Jacob's data base (plus some supplementary data), he structures his analyses somewhat differently. He introduces and operationalizes a set of concepts relevant to the suggested mode of analysis and appropriate for micro-level analyses. These include such things as the seriousness of a case, the evidentiary strength of the state's case, the responsiveness of the various participants to internal needs and norms, the susceptibility of the defendant to organizational pressures, and a set of measures indicative of resistance to informal norms. He attempts to analyze the relevance of the various concepts to each of the decisions analyzed in light of the overall framework, explicitly outlining expected relationships. The results are mixed. Some analyses lend strong support to his arguments (the sentencing analysis) and others produce less supportive results (the decision to pursue a case to trial).

The Question of Why. Second-generation studies devote a good deal of attention to the reasons for the prevalence of bureaucratic due process; the analyses go well beyond the traditional arguments which are grounded in the notion of heavy caseloads. Moreover, several works explicitly challenge the caseload thesis, presenting empirical evidence to support their arguments. For example, Milton Heumann (1978), in *Plea Bargaining*, conclusively demonstrates that trials have played a minor role in both high- and low-volume Connecticut criminal courts since the 1880s. Malcolm Feeley (1975), in "The Effects of Heavy Caseloads," like Heumann, empirically examines the caseload thesis in a macro-level analysis of Connecticut lower level trial courts. He compares aggregated statistics on courtroom outputs in a high-volume court with those in a low-volume court and finds no significant differences in trial rates, average number of motions filed, release statistics, bail structure, and sentencing structure. There appears to be, however, some differences in guilty plea and overall conviction rates which were consistent with traditional expectations. These notwithstanding, Feeley concludes that traditional expectations concerning the impact of heavy caseloads were not supported.

In another recent challenge to the caseload thesis, "The Caseload Controversy and the Study of Criminal Courts," Nardulli (1979) examines the impact of variations in caseloads at a micro level. He uses two measures of caseload (a judge measure and a system measure) over an eighteen-month period in conjunction with a sample of felony cases selected from the trial courts of Chicago. He examines the impact of substantial variations in caseloads upon dismissals, guilty pleas, and sentences in guilty plea cases. No statistically significant findings emerge, even when interactive effects (between the two caseload measures) and anticipatory and lag effects are examined.

Second-generation organizational analyses of the prevalence of bureaucratic due process go beyond earlier works in another important way. They develop alternate explanations of courtroom phenomena which do not rely upon the notion of caseload pressure. Heumann's explanation for the prevalence of plea bargaining, for example, is grounded in the court system's adaptation process. Adaptation is the process by which "a newcomer learns and is taught about his role obligations, and the related processes in which he translates these obligations into a perspective on plea bargaining. . . . The learning component refers to the newcomer's discovery that the reality of local criminal courts differs from what he expected. The teaching component refers to the use of rewards and sanctions by others in the court system to direct newcomer behavior down a particular path" (Heumann, 1978, pp. 2-3).

In developing his adaptation theory of plea bargaining Heumann begins with the well founded premise that most recruits know very little about their new roles or the reality of criminal courts. They normally have a very idealistic conception of criminal adjudication and are serious about complying with the formal dictates of their respective roles. Initially they question the legitimacy of techniques like plea bargaining. Imperceptibly, however, their views change. As they become immersed in the courtroom setting, they experience a period of "frenzied drifting" as they grope for ways to deal with various problems. At the same time the newcomer "is learning and is being taught about plea bargaining. He learns that the reality of the local criminal court differs from what he expected, and that compelling reasons to negotiate cases are often a product of this 'reality'; he also is taught by rewards and sanctions that benefits are attached to plea bargaining and that costs may be levied for a trial" (Heumann, 1978, p. 154).

The general lack of disputable legal or factual issues in criminal cases is the most important of the realities to which Heumann refers. In addition to this, the defense attorney learns that most defendants readily admit their guilt, are desirous of a good bargain, and that the prosecutor's offers are usually too good to turn down. The prosecutor, on the other hand, learns that he can minimize uncertainty and maximize "professional concerns" through plea bargaining. The judge finds that plea bargains permit him to do his job more easily, reduce the risk that his decisions will be reversed, and enable him to move the business of the court more efficiently. The net result of these factors is that after a successful adaptation period each participant moves from a presumption of trial to a presumption of plea bargaining.

Given the ascribed importance of these realities for the behavior of the participants Heumann argues that, while teaching is an essential part of adaptation, learning is the heart of the process.

> Independent of rewards and sanctions newcomers will plea bargain most of their cases. . . . Newcomer adaptation is not simply a process in which

> well-motivated idealistic newcomers are coerced to cooperate in a bureaucracy obsessed with moving the business. Without sanctions for trial, without rewards for plea bargaining, the newcomer would still learn that plea bargaining serves his interests in many cases. (Heumann, 1978, p. 154)

Feeley (1975) also gives some thought to an alternate explanation for the prevalence of bureaucratic due process. He attributes this phenomenon to two factors. The first concerns the organization of the court's work. It is structured in such a way that as soon as the docket is completed everyone can leave the courtroom. This is important because everyone who "counts" has somewhere else to be and something else to do. Because of this a good deal of grumbling and sanctioning takes place when the smooth flow of cases is impeded. The gist of this first point is that there will always be too many cases on the daily docket.

A second factor, which reinforces the impact of the first, is the prevalence of the belief that "disputes settled through negotiation and/or pleas of guilty provide mutually advantageous benefits for *all* the involved parties." (Feeley, 1975, p. 37) Normative support for this position derives from the commonly held belief that all defendants are guilty of something and that the real issues presented concern the question of what to do with the case. The determination of an "appropriate disposition" does not require a formal trial. Rather, a substantive justice can be obtained through informal proceedings which are mutually advantageous to all concerned, including the defendant.

A third explanation for the prevalence of bureaucratic due process is offered by Nardulli (1979). He argues that expeditious dispositional procedures exist and persist because they further the interests of those who control the process. He makes several arguments—unrelated to caseload pressure—to lend support to the view that it is in the common interests of the courtroom elite to process cases expeditiously. (Nardulli, 1978, pp. 67-71) Financial considerations play a crucial role for the private defense counsel; the structure of the court's workload is important for other courtroom regulars (judge, public defender, prosecutor). Like Feeley, Nardulli views as crucial the fact that once the day's docket is cleared the formal courtroom responsibilities of the public officials are completed. The impact of this factor is increased by the perception these individuals have of their workload and the social setting of criminal courts. These officials tend to view cases as rather mundane, presenting few disputable issues worthy of adversary adjudication. The fact that these officials are professionals and get no overtime pay is also important; it means there are neither professional nor financial incentives to engage in adversary proceedings. Finally, everyone has somewhere else to be, as well as the ability to communicate their desires to other workgroup members. Thus there are limits on the ability of individuals to ignore consistently the desire of others.

Nardulli places a great deal of significance upon the shared interests of the courtroom elite as a factor in explaining the prevalence of bureaucratic due process because of the nature of the power structure in criminal courts. Not only do members of the courtroom elite enjoy a virtual monopoly of power within the courtroom, but it is distributed among them in such a manner that, in the long run, none can dominate. This is not an uncommon situation in organizations. Moreover, according to organization theorists such as James Thompson, such a situation is conducive to the development of an intraorganizational coalition which can then exercise a good deal of control within the organization. Nardulli argues that this is, indeed, what has occurred in criminal courts. Its significance lies in the fact that what holds the coalition together is the mutual interest in the expeditious handling of cases. This, in turn, accounts for the predominance of bureaucratic due process.

TOWARD THIRD-GENERATION ANALYSES

This brief review leaves one with two conflicting impressions of developments in this field of study. The first is: We've come a long way; the second is: We haven't gotten very far. Both are correct. On the one hand, when compared with earlier studies, second-generation organizational analyses are much more refined. In different ways the various works have begun to explore the conceptual, empirical, and practical implications of the insights developed in the seminal works. Moreover, researchers have moved from an initial acceptance of the traditional caseload thesis to much more sophisticated explanations for the prevalence of bureaucratic due process.

On the other hand, one is struck by the lack of continuity or cumulative development of ideas or empirical evidence. There is no readily apparent common thrust, even in recent works. Some researchers see criminal courts as a marketplace in which competitors meet to do business; others see them as collusive enterprises; still others merely observe the existence of shared goals or interests. While some theorizing exists at the environmental, contextual, and individual level, there appears to be little consistency within levels. For example, most works attribute a good deal of influence to environmental factors, although the level of ascribed importance varies considerably. Furthermore, some view the environment as important because it affects the content of decisions. Others, notably Carter, emphasize the environment's impact upon the structure of the process by which decisions are made. A good deal of diversity also exists at the contextual level. Flemming, for example, emphasizes the importance of resource constraints and the structure of risk; Eisenstein and Jacob stress various workgroup characteristics; and Nardulli dwells upon the significance of the power and interest structure as well as the setting. Finally, even in the work on factors contributing to the prevalence of bureaucratic due process, where there are supportive empirical results, there are substantial disagreements over the reasons for those results.

While the latter set of observations may not be encouraging, the outlook for a cohesive, broadly based organizational theory of criminal court operations is not as dim as it may seem. First, it may be that it is too early to expect the emergence of a common, tightly knit, organizational framework. It has, after all, been only ten years since this approach was first suggested. Second, as disparate as even the later works appear, certain common concerns do emerge which offer promise for the direction of future research, especially with regard to the question of *how* courts operate. A discussion of these commonalities, as broad as they are, can lend insights into how the various approaches just reviewed might be integrated into a more sophisticated way of studying criminal courts. Later studies, utilizing these insights, may eventually take us closer to a cohesive theory of courtroom operations.

Commonalities in Second-Generation Analyses

Succinctly stated, what emerges from second-generation analyses is a concern with the substantive considerations reflected in various criminal court decisions as well as the factors affecting how these substantive considerations are reflected in criminal court decisions. An analysis of each of these concerns together with a discussion of how they interface will shed some light on directions which future criminal court research could take.

The concern with substantive factors reflected in various criminal court decisions is especially prominent in the research of Eisenstein and Jacob (1977) and Nardulli (1978). In addition, however, it should be noted that this concern is shared in nonorganizational approaches to criminal courts such as role theory (Gibson 1976, 1978a, 1978b) and political culture (Kritzer, 1979). The result has been a plethora of factors whose effect on various criminal court decisions has been hypothesized about and sometimes demonstrated. Eisenstein and Jacob talk about such factors as the offense, the evidence, the defendant's characteristics, the identity of the courtroom, and so on. Nardulli suggests such things as the responsiveness of the participants, the susceptibility of the defendant, the defense's resistance to informal norms, case seriousness, the weight of the evidence, and dispositional value. Those concerned with political culture and criminal courts have suggested such things as the community's political conservatism, progressivism, and orientation toward violence. In addition the relevance of various judicial attitudes has been suggested.

Several things are important to note about this array of variables. First, despite their numbers (included above is only a sample of variables actually considered) and seeming diversity, there is some overlap among them and there are ways to categorize them to make them more manageable. One could, for example, group them in terms of environmental, contextual, and individual level factors, although within each of these categories there is still a good deal of diversity. Another important point about these variables is that none has consistently been shown to have a strong effect upon various facets of courtroom operations. Several things may account for this. There may be a need for more refined definitions or measures, as well as more thoughtful specifications of interrelationships. Also, the various theoretical approaches may have to be reexamined in an effort to identify relevant concepts previously overlooked. Finally it might be necessary to consider more systematically the factors which affect how substantive considerations are woven into various decisions. This would permit a more sophisticated application of relevant variables to various decisions across different settings.

This last point is of particular interest because, as noted above, a second commonality observed in second-generation analyses is a concern with factors affecting how substantive considerations are reflected in various decisions. This concern is not as manifest as the concern with substantive factors, but a careful review of second-generation analyses reveals its significance. The discussions of mode of choice or work techniques in the work of Eisenstein and Jacob (1977), Flemming (1978), and especially Mohr (1976) illustrate the centrality of this concern. The brief discussion of the effects of political insulation by Nardulli (1978, p. 119) would also fall into this category, as might discussions of concepts such as workgroup stability, risk structure, resource constraints, and role orientations. Beyond these discussions, an analysis of second-generation studies suggests that a consideration of certain dimensions of criminal court decisions themselves would shed some light on how different substantive factors are reflected in them.

Prospective Insights

To demonstrate how these observed commonalities might be used to guide future research some examples will be given. Different substantive factors will be discussed in light of the mode of choice as well as different decisional characteristics. Before presenting the examples, however, a few words need to be said about modes of choice and decisional characteristics.

In his discussion of relevant modes or techniques of decision-making, Mohr identifies the firm, rational, and political models; Flemming identifies the routine, situational, and bargaining modes; and Eisenstein and Jacob identify unilateral decisions, negotiations, and adversary proceedings as the three dominant work techniques. While each typology is somewhat different, "adversary" and "situational" seem enough like "political," and "unilateral" and "routine" seem enough like "rational," to argue that there appear to be at least three important modes of choice utilized in criminal courts. While later studies may want to refine this observation somewhat, it is sufficient for present purposes.

Criminal court decisions undoubtedly have a variety of unique characteristics. The characteristics that are of concern here, however, are only those which have implications for the relevance of different decision cues. To date these characteristics have not been discussed to any great extent. This is unfortunate because an examination of several studies suggests that a consideration of decisional characteristics may shed some light on why different researchers rely on different types of factors in explaining criminal court decision-making. Sensitivity to such concerns may, for example, explain why Flemming (1978) places so much emphasis upon external factors in his examination of bail while Eisenstein and Jacob (1977) and Nardulli (1978) place more emphasis upon contextual- and individual-level factors in their analyses. Differences in the decisions which they examined may have had an impact upon the factors to which they attribute most importance.

This having been said, however, it is no small task to identify the relevant dimensions of criminal court decisions. Several plausibly relevant dimensions do, however, come to mind. These include the formal characteristics of the decision, its visibility, and its relationship to the goals or interests shared by courtroom participants. A fuller discussion of these characteristics and how they affect the substantive factors reflected in a decision—alone and in conjunction with the mode of choice—will hopefully provide some guidance for third-generation analyses.

Formal Characteristics. These characteristics include such things as the legal variables that are supposed to affect a decision and the identity of the individual who is formally empowered to make the decision. These factors are important not because there is a one-to-one correspondence between formalities and realities in criminal court decision-making, but rather because, while they have only a limited impact, this impact varies from decision to decision as well as across modes of decision-making.

Legal variables include such things as the weight of the evidence, the seriousness of the case, the defendant's criminal record, and his ties to the community. They are so called because they have some foundation in legal theory. But their relevance varies from decision to decision. The latter three, for example, are more relevant to sentencing and bail decision than to the determination of guilt or innocence (conviction procurement), where evidentiary matters are formally the most important.

Like legal variables, the formal power to make decisions varies considerably across decisions. The judge is normally responsible for the sentencing and bail decisions, the prosecutor controls the charging decision, and the defendant is the only one who can waive certain rights such as the right to a trial. This variable is important because it suggests that the applicability of various substantive factors varies with the locus of formal responsibility. The ties between environmental-level factors such as political conservatism would, for example, be more indirect to decisions vested in the defendant than in the judge or prosecutor. Likewise, the impact of individual-level attributes (attitudes, for example) would be expected to be greater in decisions controlled by the individual whose attributes are considered than those controlled by others. The prosecutor's attitudes may, for example, be more relevant to the charging decision than to the decision to plead guilty.

A consideration of the mode of decision-making complicates these matters even further. For example, the impact of evidentiary factors upon the attainment of a conviction may be stronger when the decision is made by political or adversary means (a trial) than by negotiation. The impact of certain defendant characteristics upon the sentencing decision may be greater when the sentence is negotiated (by a guilty plea) than when it is made unilaterally (after a trial). Various attitudes on the part of the judge, on the other hand, may have a greater impact upon sentencing when he makes the decision unilaterally than when it is negotiated.

Visibility of Decision. This dimension concerns the extent to which a decision is visible to entities in the criminal court's environment. Certain facets of courtroom operations are less visible than others. Screening—the decision to dismiss a case or refuse to issue a warrant—is not, for example, as visible as the bail decision. The bail decision is made at a point in time close to the event and has a great deal of symbolic importance to different external entities (the police, victims, newspapers, civil liberties groups). The decision to dismiss, on the other hand, is often made several months after the incident, when tempers have cooled. Some sort of informal resolution may even have been effectuated.

The visibility of a decision is important because it has implications for the impact of different types of factors. More specifically, the greater the visibility the greater the impact of environmental-level considerations, all other factors considered equal. Thus, as Flemming (1978) suggests, environmental factors may be very important in determining bail policies. These same factors may not, however, have the same impact upon screening policies. Here again, however, the types of factors reflected in a decision may vary depending upon the mode of decision. Thus, while environmental factors may be highly influential when bail is set in a routine mode, they may be less influential in a situational or adversary mode. In the latter situation more immediate concerns become significant and may dilute the impact of more distant environmental considerations.

Relationship to Shared Interests. One of the most characteristic features of organizational analyses of criminal courts is the contention that those who control criminal court operations share certain common interests or goals. (Eisenstein and Jacob, 1977, p. 24; Mohr, 1976, p. 635; Nardulli, 1978, p. 66) These common goals or interests have generally been identified as the desire to process cases expeditiously. This desire, in turn, has important implications for the structure of decision-making, but its implications and relevance varies by decision. For example, since sentencing is the most potent tool to induce expeditious convictions, certain contextual factors related to these shared interests are expected to play a significant role in the sentencing decision (Nardulli, 1978, chapter 8). These factors may not, however, be very important in setting bail. Bail is temporally far removed from conviction procurement, and the relationship of the former to the latter may not be all that clear due to the uncertainty of bail consequences (Flemming, 1978).

A final point is that, as before, the impact of various contextual factors may vary with the mode of decision. Sentences arrived at through bargaining may reflect contextual factors such as relative bargaining positions and the relationship among the participants. Unilateral sentencing decisions (those made after a trial) may reflect such things as the extent of the defendant's resistance to informal norms. There is even some empirical evidence to support these last points (Nardulli, 1978, chapter 8).

CONCLUSION

It should be emphasized that the final section of this chapter merely outlines some rough suggestions for the direction of third-generation organizational analyses. Others may advocate more compelling research agendas. Moreover, before the suggestions offered here can be made operational a good deal more thought needs to be given to the types of substantive considerations reflected in various criminal court decisions, as well as the factors which affect how these considerations are meshed in the decision-making process. While pursuing this line of inquiry will entail considerable investments of time and resources, its benefits could also be considerable. It could result in a more integrated approach to the study of criminal courts in which "nonorganizational" factors could be meshed with "organizational" factors within a framework in which knowledge could be cumulative. Thoughtful consideration of the issues raised here could also lead to a body of third-generation analyses which builds upon the insights of seminal works and which coheres more closely than second-generation analyses.

REFERENCES

Blumberg, Abraham (1967). *Criminal Justice*. Chicago: Quadrangle Books.

Carter, Lief (1974). *The Limits of Order*. Lexington, Mass.: Lexington Books.

Cole, George (1970). "The Decision to Prosecute." 4 *Law & Society Review* 313-43.

Eisenstein, James, and Jacob, Herbert (1977). *Felony Justice: An Organizational Analysis of Criminal Courts*. Boston: Little, Brown.

Feeley, Malcolm (1973). "Two Models of the Criminal Justice System: An Organizational Perspective." 7 *Law & Society Review* 407-26.

_____ (1975). "The Effects of Heavy Caseloads." Paper presented at the 1975 Annual Meeting of the American Political Science Association.

Flemming, Roy (1978). "Pretrial Sanctioning Processes: Felony Bail Practices in Baltimore and Detroit." Paper presented at the 1978 Annual Meeting of the Law and Society Association, Minneapolis, Minnesota.

Gibson, James L. (1976). "Judges as Representatives: Constituency Influence on Trial Courts." Paper presented at the 1976 Annual Meeting of the American Political Science Association, Chicago, Illinois.

_____ (1978a). "Judges' Role Orientation, Attitudes and Decisions: An Interactive Model." 72 *American Political Science Review* 911-24.

_____ (1978b). "Personality and Elite Political Behavior: The Influence of Self Esteem on Judicial Decision Making." Paper presented at the 1978 Annual Meeting of the Western Political Science Association, Los Angeles, California.

Heumann, Milton (1978). *Plea Bargaining: The Experiences of Prosecutors, Judges, and Defense Attorneys*. Chicago: University of Chicago Press.

Jacob, Herbert (1977). "A Second Look at Organizational Analysis of Trial Courts." Paper presented at the 1977 Annual Meeting of the Midwest Political Science Association, Chicago, Illinois.

Kritzer, Herbert (1979). "Political Cultures, Trial Courts, and Criminal Cases." In Peter F. Nardulli, ed. *The Study of Criminal Courts: Political Perspectives*. Cambridge, Mass.: Ballinger Publishing Company.

Mileski, Maureen (1971). "Courtroom Encounters: An Observation Study of a Lower Court." 5 *Law & Society Review* 473-538.

Mohr, Lawrence (1976). "Organizations, Decisions, and Courts." 10 *Law & Society Review* 621-42.

Moley, Raymond (1930). *Our Criminal Courts*. New York: Minton, Balch.

Nardulli, Peter F. (1978). *The Courtroom Elite: An Organizational Perspective on Criminal Justice*. Cambridge, Mass.: Ballinger Publishing Company.

_____ (with the assistance of Kathleen Proch) (1979). "The Case Load Controversy and the Study of Criminal Courts." 70 *Journal of Criminal Law and Criminology*.

Skolnick, Jerome (1967). "Social Control in the Adversary System." 11 *Journal of Conflict Resolution* 52-70.

Chapter Six

Political Cultures, Trial Courts, and Criminal Cases

Herbert M. Kritzer

In recent years several studies have appeared which focus on state political cultures in the United States (Johnson, 1976; Elazar, 1966, 1970; Patterson, 1968; Sharkansky, 1969, 1970; and Luttbeg, 1971), and much recent work in the area of state politics and policy has focused on differences that may be attributable to variations in those political cultures (for example, Sharkansky and Hofferbert, 1969; Hutcheson and Taylor, 1973). The notion of geographically based political subcultures is immensely useful in studying and explaining the variations that mark local politics around the United States. Grossman and Sarat (1971) have argued that political culture can be usefully applied to the study of the judiciary. The goal of this chapter is to apply the concept of political cultures to the study of criminal courts, both federal and state, in order (1) to determine the degree to which the concept can be used to increase our understandings of those courts and (2) to suggest potentially fruitful paths for future research.

The potential value of the concept of local political cultures in the study of courts and court systems has been demonstrated in several studies which have focused on state supreme courts. The best, an explicitly comparative study, is Glick's (1971) analysis of judicial role in four state supreme courts; Glick found notable differences among the

[a]An earlier version of this chapter was presented at the 1978 Annual Meeting of the American Political Science Association, New York Hilton Hotel, New York, August 31-September 3, 1978. I would like to thank Peter Nardulli, Ira Sharkansky, Stephen Wasby, and Herbert Jacob for their valuable comments. Some of the data used in this analysis were provided by the Inter-University Consortium for Political and Social Research; the consortium bears no responsibility for the analyses and interpretations presented here.

role conceptions of the justices in the states he studied, and the pattern of the variations clearly suggested state political cultures as an explanatory variable.

A second area of research that suggests an examination of political culture explanations is a group of studies concerned with the relationship between party identification and decision-making by state supreme court justices. Schubert (1959), Ulmer (1962), and Feeley (1971) found clear evidence that party identification was related to decision-making (in at least some types of cases) by the Michigan Supreme Court; Bieser and Silberman (1971) found mixed evidence regarding the New York Court of Appeals (depending upon the specific time period examined); and Adamany (1969) found no evidence of such a relationship for the Wisconsin Supreme Court. While the formal political systems of Michigan and Wisconsin are quite similar, the political cultures of the two states are quite different, particularly as regards the court systems; Adamany summarizes the differences as follows:

> The differential situational circumstances of judges in the two states is a reasonable explanatory variable. In Michigan, party continues to be an important factor in judicial behavior because of the partisanship of the judicial constituencies and the absence of a resident court with procedural methods which encourage accommodation. In Wisconsin, the influence of party diminishes because judicial constituencies are bipartisan and the Court's procedures create a considerable personal interaction between the justices which maximizes the opportunities for accommodation and compromise. (1969, p. 73)

In the same way that the political cultures concept can be used to explain variations at the appellate court level, it can be used to increase our understanding of trial courts.

We can dichotomize the potential relationships between trial courts and the local political culture along two dimensions. The first dimension is the internal-external dimension. External aspects involve decisions made outside the judicial subsystem by the larger political system (that is, the legislature, executive, electorate, and so on) about things such as the structure of the judicial subsystem and the selection of judicial personnel. Internal aspects involve decision-making within the judicial system itself, including patterns of disposition, delay, and so on. The second organizing dimension is the federal-state dimension. Research on the judiciary has generally focused either on the state courts or on the federal courts; seldom have researchers considered both systems together.

It is perhaps most difficult to see how local political cultures can affect external aspects of the federal district courts. The structure of the federal district courts is established by the national government (Title 28 of the *U.S. Code*) and federal district judges are appointed by the president (subject to confirmation by the U.S. Senate). However, as has been well documented (see Chase, 1972), U.S. senators have a large voice (and frequently the dominant voice) in the actual selection of who will be nominated for federal trial judgeships, though the president makes the formal nomination; how the individual senators go about designating their choices and who the senators actually choose may reflect the local political cultures from which the senators come. As for structure of the district courts, the boundaries of the federal judicial districts (and division within districts) are subject to manipulation, and that manipulation is probably attributable (at least in part) to pressures arising from local politics within the state involved.

It is easier to see how local political cultures can affect decision-making by federal district judges. Richardson and Vines (1970, pp. 36-54) argue that federal district judges reflect the orientations and attitudes of the local areas from which they come; that is, federal judges, by and large, are "local" in their orientation (ibid., pp. 70-73). Most federal district judges were born and raised in the states in which they serve, most attended college and law school in the states in which they serve (the exceptions most likely attended Yale or Harvard), and most were active in local political affairs prior to becoming judges. While federal judges are appointed for life and are insulated from formal political pressures, they are not protected from the informal pressure that arises from their neighbors, social acquaintances, and professional colleagues. Studies of variations in the behavior of federal district judges in such areas as civil rights (Vines, 1964) and sentencing of draft resisters (Kritzer, 1978a; and Graebner, 1973) found evidence that those variations can be attributed, at least in part, to differences in the local political cultures in which the judicial actions occurred.

When we turn to state and local courts, there are clear a priori reasons to expect to find relationships between local political cultures and both external and internal aspects of the judicial system. Each state establishes its own judicial system, and there is every reason to expect that variations in the structures of the systems reflect local political cultures (see Glick and Vines, 1973, pp. 14-35), particularly if we view those structures and cultures within a historical context (see Vines and Jacob, 1971, pp. 279-81, 288-91). The role of various political actors in the selection process for judges should also reflect the nature of the local political context. While studies of the differences that arise as a result of variations in formal selection processes show only minor differences in the characteristics of the judges selected (Jacob, 1964; Canon, 1972), the studies of the Michigan and Wisconsin supreme courts cited above suggest that variations in the informal norms governing selection may lead to important differences.

The final area to be discussed below will be the impact of local political culture on the internal workings of state trial courts, including both the process of decision-making and the outcomes of that process. There are a variety of mechanisms by which local political cultures can affect the internal workings of trial courts; please note that we are not arguing that we can isolate these mechanisms in practice but rather that the mechanisms provide a useful framework for exploring the role of local political cultures in the workings of trial courts. The four specific mechanisms that will be considered below are

1. Formal legal situation: variations in local courts may reflect differences in formal norms (statutes), procedural rules, and so on.
2. Socialization: judges are creatures of the local political culture in which they were socialized, and their socialization into that culture leads to a certain set of political attitudes and values (see, for example, Gaylin, 1974).
3. The influence of constituency pressure.
   - Mass constituencies: judges in election-based systems must stand for reelection and consequently must be in some sense responsive to their constituencies; furthermore, judges may believe that part of their job is to "represent" the values of the community in which they serve (see Walker, 1973), and consequently they may seek to exercise their discretion (for example, when imposing criminal sanctions) in a way they view as consistent with the attitudes of their "constituents" (see Gibson, 1976).
   - Elite constituencies: in some areas, local trial judges are in a real sense creatures of the local party organizations and consequently are responsive to the demands of those organizational constituencies; this can be true for both state trial courts (see Jackson, 1974, pp. 186-97) and federal district courts (see Goulden, 1974, pp. 114-57).
4. Social pressures: even if a judge is formally insulated from constituency pressures by such means as life tenure, a judge is subject to the social pressures of the community in which he resides; such pressures can take the form of either "subtle" signs from social and political peers that a judge should do a certain thing in a given case or set of cases (the threat here being social ostracism) or direct physical intimidation by means of threats, rock throwing, and so on (see, for example, Kluger's description of the pressures directed at a

South Carolina judge who favored school integration in the early 1950s, 1975, pp. 295-305).

THE CONCEPT OF POLITICAL CULTURE

Before we can examine the relationship between political culture and various aspects of the judicial system it is necessary to define and operationalize what we mean by political culture. Political culture is a somewhat murky concept that has been most often used as a residual explanatory variable; that is, geographic variations that could not be explained by other variables are attributed to "political culture." This approach can be found throughout the comparative study of political phenomena, including the study of the courts. One example, pointed out by Grossman and Sarat (1971, p. 185), is to be found in Jacob's *Debtors in Court* (1969, p. 92). In seeking to explain the differences in the rate of court use for private purposes in four Wisconsin cities, Jacob suggests that "political culture may be a significant explanatory device for accounting for differences in litigation rates." Despite this argument, Jacob does not provide any real test to the culture argument; no doubt this is because it would be difficult to carry out any statistically valid test with only four "cases."

If we are to look systematically at the explanatory power of political culture, we must have some way to measure it, and in order to measure it we must first define the concept in such a way that measurement is possible. The basic definition that is commonly used is derived from the work of Gabriel Almond: "Political culture is the pattern of individual attitudes and orientations toward politics among members of a political realm which underlies and gives meaning to political actions" (Almond and Powell, 1966, p. 50; see also Almond, 1956). This broad definition permits many systems of classification of relevant orientations; Almond and Powell suggest a functional classification scheme involving cognitive, affective, and evaluative orientations. This particular classification primarily reflects the popularity of "functional" analysis among students of comparative politics during the 1960s; other schemes can be equally useful. Elazar has suggested three dimensions of political culture which he believes to be particularly suited for the study of the political cultures of the American states: "(1) the set of perceptions of what politics is and what can be expected from government, held by both the general public and the politicians; (2) the kinds of people who become active in government and politics, as holders of elective offices, members of the bureaucracy, and active political workers; and (3) the actual way in which the art of government is practiced by citizens, politicians, and public officials in light of their perceptions." (1966, pp. 84-85) Elazar argues that in fact

American politics can be seen as rooted in two contrasting conceptions of what the American political order should be; one views the political order as a "commonwealth" in which there is something which could be labeled the "public interest" or the "common interest," while the other sees politics as a marketplace serving the self-interests of the participants. He goes on to combine his various arguments to identify three "ideal type" political cultures: the *moralistic* political culture, which sees politics as a "positive sum game" seeking to achieve the good society; the *individualistic* political culture, which sees politics as a "zero sum game" in which it is legitimate for individuals and groups to use politics as a means of social mobility and personal enrichment; and the *traditionalistic* political culture, which views politics primarily as something to be done by the elite who, in a paternalistic fashion, will seek to serve the needs of the public while maintaining the status quo.

Does this conceptual approach outlined by Elazar have any empirical validity? The work of several political scientists (Sharkansky, 1969; Clynch, 1972; and Ritt, 1974) suggests that it does in fact have *construct* validity. All of these studies used Sharkansky's unidimensional score for political culture, which goes from the moralistic through the individualistic to the traditionalistic (1969, p. 70), and all of them found that the variables Elazar suggests should correlate with political cultures do, in fact, tend to correlate. The basic problem with his approach is whether, in fact, there is only a single dimension or whether there are several dimensions underlying the concept of political culture used by Elazar. Drawing on Elazar's suggestion that the various political cultures are traceable to the migration patterns of various religious and ethnic groups in the United States, Johnson (1976) used census data on religious affiliation to construct indexes for each of the three types of cultures. Using his three indexes, Johnson was able successfully to match Elazar's classification for thirty-five of forty-eight states (by chance alone, he would have been able successfully to predict only seventeen states); in addition, he found that his indexes correlated, in the expected way, with six of eight political characteristics (even after introducing some controls). But does this mean that political culture, as it should be applied to the American states, is a one-dimensional characteristic, a three-dimensional characteristic, or an *n*-dimensional characteristic?

In fact, there is no definitive way to resolve this question. However, for our purposes, there is a way to determine an empirically usable measure, or set of measures, of political culture. It should be emphasized that the approach below is intended only as a way to resolve the dilemma of operationalizing political culture; there are many other ways that it could be done. The first step is to seek to determine the dimensionality of political culture as it should be applied for purposes of analysis. Elazar suggests several "areas" of importance (see above) which, on close reading, appear to be interrelated; for example, the perceptions of what politics is about would most likely be related to who is involved in politics. Unfortunately, we do not have any direct measures of the areas suggested by Elazar; however, we do have four measures of political culture, one developed by Sharkansky and three developed by Johnson, that seek to combine those areas to measure type of political culture. As a first step, we factor analyzed the correlation matrix of those measures.

The intercorrelations among these measures and the results of the factor analysis are shown in Table 6-1. While the table shows only one principal components analysis, we in fact carried out several additional analyses, all of which were consistent with the results shown in the table. Table 6-1b clearly suggests that there are two dimensions underlying the various measures of political culture that are based on Elazar's typology, one following the individualistic dimension and one following the moralistic dimension; the two dimensions account for almost 95 percent of the variance in the four measures. When we analyzed only the three measures developed by Johnson, we found

Table 6-1. Analysis of Measures of Political Culture

	(1) Correlations			
		Johnson's Measures of		
	Moralism	*Individualism*	*Traditionalism*	*Sharkansky's Measure of Political Culture*
Moralism	1.00			
Individualism	.03	1.0		
Traditionalism	–.59	–.82	1.00	
Political culture	–.67	–.54	.81	1.00

	(b) Factor Analysis of Four Measures[a]	
	Factor 1	*Factor 2*
Moralism	–.018	–.983
Individualism	–.997	.001
Traditionalism	.813	.556
Political culture	.567	.738
Proportion of total variance explained		
Before rotation	.697	.252
After rotation	.494	.455

[a]Loadings shown are after a varimax rotation.

that two dimensions accounted for 99.9 percent of the variance in the three measures. Clearly, if we are to obtain empirically useful and substantively understandable information, we need some additional insights into the underlying dimensions of political culture.

In order to accomplish this we added ten more variables to our factor analysis; these variables were seen as "indicators" of political culture. The first three were the proportions of statewide presidential vote that went conservative in the presidential elections of 1964, 1968, and 1972 (proportions Republican in 1964 and 1972, and proportion Republican plus proportion Wallace in 1968). Two were party competition measures: party dominance (Sorauf, 1972, p. 34), ranging from 0 for total Republican dominance to 1 for total Democratic dominance; and party competition, which was computed by subtracting .5 from party dominance and taking the absolute value, producing an index that ranged from 0 for highly competitive states to .5 for uncompetitive states. Other measures included in the analysis were Walker's (1969, p. 881) innovation index, Vines and Jacob's (1971, p. 292) legal professionalism index, the overall Uniform Crime Index (UCI) for each state for 1974 (LEAA, 1977, pp. 450-60), the level of education as indicated by the proportion of registrants failing the mental portion of selective service preinduction examinations in 1970 (National Center for Educational Statistics, 1972, p. 13), and a dummy variable for region (scored 1 for South and 0 for non-South). The results of this factor analysis are shown in Table 6-2; the analysis included a

Table 6-2. Factor Analysis of Political Culture Indicators[a]

Variable	*Factor 1 Role of Government*	*Factor 2 Role of Politics*	*Factor 3 Role of Legal System*
Legal professionalism	–.19	–.56	.67
UCI	–.07	–.06	.88
Vote 1964	.25	.83	–.09
Vote 1968	.28	.88	–.11
Vote 1972	.32	.81	–.23
Party dominance	.87	.30	–.03
Lack of party competition	.76	.41	–.31
Innovation	–.13	–.64	.46
Lack of educational achievement	.78	.41	–.00
Region	.78	.50	–.13
Moralism	–.89	.17	.14
Individualism	–.31	–.80	.09
Traditionalism	.77	.54	–.15
Political culture	.80	.41	–.12

[a]Results shown have been subjected to a varimax rotation.

total of fourteen variables. Three factors emerged from the analysis, accounting for 80.7 percent of the total variance. An examination of the loadings shown in Table 6-2 clearly indicated that the third factor is based primarily on the two law-related variables, UCI and Legal Professionalism; in fact, if these two variables are deleted from the analysis, two factors emerge, accounting for 79.4 percent of the variance, with loadings virtually identical to the first two factors of the larger analysis.

These results suggest an interesting interpretation for the dimensions of political culture. The first factor is aligned with Elazar's moralistic political culture which is defined as primarily focused upon government activity aimed at achieving the common good. A number of other indicators also load on this factor, including region, lack of educational achievement, party dominance, and lack of party competition. Taken together, these loadings suggest that the first underlying factor of political culture involves beliefs about the "role of government." Specifically, low (negative) values on the factor indicate an orientation toward an interventionalist government with a welfare state goal while high values indicate a laissez-faire role for the government. The second factor has extreme loadings on the political conservatism measures and on the individualism measures; at first this may seem confusing, since the "rugged individualist" is usually associated with a conservative ideology; in fact, Elazar means something different in his use of the term individualist. Elazar sees the individualistic culture as one in which the orientation toward politics is "everyman for himself"; politics is seen as just another way for each individual to achieve his or her personal goals. This orientation appears to define the low (negative) end of the second dimension; the high (or positive) end is defined in terms of voting for conservative political candidates. Notice that state party dominance does not load on this factor, only presidential voting in the three years when the presidential elections had a strong ideological component.

We interpret the two poles of this factor as representing "politics as self-interest" (low values) versus "politics as conservative ideology" (high values); thus we have labeled the second general factor as the "role of politics." There are only three variables that load on the third factor: legal professionalism, Uniform Crime Index, and innovation (which also loads on factor 2); all of these variables are closely related to the role of the legal subsystem in the larger political system (many of the innovations included in Walker's index are "legal" innovations such as child labor laws). We suspect that this factor may be tapping the legal subculture versus democratic subculture dimension identified by Richardson and Vines (1970, p. 89); however, for the time being we have labeled the third factor "the role of the legal system," with high positive values indicating a strong reliance on the legal system as a distinct part of the larger political system and low values indicating a lack of such a reliance on the legal system.

In the analysis below we will seek to relate these dimensions of political culture to a variety of characteristics of the courts and the way courts handle criminal cases. For state-level analyses we computed factor scores for each of the three factors. For the federal district level analysis we do not have sufficient information to compute factor scores: for that analysis we have relied upon a rough indicator of the second dimension obtained by summing the three voting measures (see McKennell, 1977, p. 206, for the rationale for this simple way of combining individual items) plus the region variable as gross measures of different political cultures.

EXTERNAL INFLUENCES

There are three external aspects of the criminal court system that are subject to influence by local political cultures: court structure, personnel selection, and formal legal context. Only the first two are applicable to the federal system, while all three are important in understanding the role of political cultures in state judicial systems.

Federal Trial Courts

The structure of the federal trial courts is established by the Congress (Title 28 of the *U.S. Code*), and the basic structure is only loosely tied to the local influences. However, one aspect of the federal trial court structure may be influenced by local cultures: the drawing of district and division boundaries. The federal judicial district is the basic administrative geographic unit of the federal trial courts. Judges are appointed to specific districts (although some judges serve "at-large" within a few multidistrict states); other court-related personnel (for example, marshalls and U.S. attorneys) also serve in specific districts. Divisions are units within districts, primarily organized around places at which court sessions are actually held. Over the last two decades there have been four major realignments of districts within states, one minor change to district boundaries, and numerous smaller adjustments to division boundaries.[1] Richardson and Vines (1970, pp. 48-51) have called this process "the politics of constituency development."[2]

There are four types of structures within a state: the state comprises a single district with no divisions, the state comprises a single district with divisions, the state is divided into two or more (at present the maximum is four) districts and the districts do not have divisions, and the state is divided into two or more districts and at least one district is further divided into divisions. Table 6-3 shows the current structure for each state. If the major consideration in structuring federal judicial districts was administrative, one would expect districts to be most prevalent in states with large populations (and hence much court business) and divisions in geographically large states (to minimize travel problems of litigants). While to some degree the former expectation is borne out by the information in Table 6-3, there are interesting inconsistencies; as for the latter expectation, there appears to be little relationship between physical size and a division structure. The lack of relationship between physical size and the presence of a division structure probably reflects the fact that most districts hold court at more than one location whether or not there is a formal divisions structure; only three districts are authorized to hold court sessions at a single location (Delaware, Hawaii, and Rhode Island). All but two of the states that currently have divisions are located either in the South or in the Midwest. A possible explanation for this trend is that in these two areas the political culture dictates a maximum of "local control," and the division structure provides a modicum of such control (or at least the illusion of control); however,

Table 6-3. Organization of the Federal District Courts by State

Single District, No Divisions	*Single District with Divisions*	*Multi-District, No Divisions*	*Multi-District with Divisions*
Alaska	Maine	California	Alabama
Arizona	Minnesota	Florida	Arkansas
Connecticut	North Dakota	Kentucky	Georgia
Colorado	South Carolina	New York	Illinois
Delaware	South Dakota	North Carolina	Indiana
Hawaii	Utah	Oklahoma	Iowa
Idaho		Pennsylvania	Louisiana
Kansas		Virginia	Michigan
Maryland		Washington	Mississippi
Massachusetts		West Virginia	Missouri
Montana		Wisconsin	Ohio
Nebraska			Tennessee
Nevada			Texas
New Hampshire			
New Jersey			
New Mexico			
Oregon			
Rhode Island			
Vermont			
Wyoming			

none of our three political culture dimensions correlates with the presence of a division structure. It may be that the division structures found in the South and Midwest reflect historical accident more than explicit cultural influences.

There have been no published studies of the politics underlying changes in district and division boundaries. One unpublished study (Laymon, 1978) examined the creation of the Middle District of Louisiana which came into existence in 1971, and the consolidation of the Eastern and Western Districts of South Carolina into a single district in 1965. The rationale expressed for both of these changes was administrative efficiency; however, Laymon questions the reality of such justifications, calling them "the myth of efficiency." This myth is most obvious in the Louisiana case. The argument was made that the then existing Eastern District had a serious backlog problem and the creation of a new district would alleviate this problem. However, the new Middle District had only one judge and the new Eastern District lost one judgeship, going from ten to nine; the caseload (new cases commenced) per judge for the first half of FY1973 for the Eastern District was 221.56, compared to only 177 for the Middle District (Administrative Office, 1974, pp. A-6, A-31). In fact, the creation of the Middle District increased the caseload for judges in the Eastern District. The alternate explanation suggested by Laymon (pp. 19-23) is a possible desire on the part of various parties to create a judicial constituency for the Baton Rouge area that was independent of New Orleans (perhaps New Orleans was perceived as being too "cosmopolitan" for the folks in Baton Rouge).

There is little need to go into detail on the role of local political influences on the selection of federal district judges since this has been well documented elsewhere (Chase, 1972; Richardson and Vines, 1970, pp. 70-73). Local influences operate through the practice of senatorial courtesy which gives senators of the president's party (and other senators who occupy key positions) a major, if not dominant, role in the selection process. The result is that most federal district judges are localists with strong ties to the local political culture. This view of federal district judges should not be pushed too far; despite the loud voice of senators in the selection process, the president still sets the bound of ideological acceptability. A recent study of decisions published by federal district judges (Rowland and Carp, 1978) found sharp differences between Nixon appointees and appointees of other presidents; furthermore, the Carter administration is trying to "depoliticize" the selection process by using an informal merit selection process involving nominating commissions. Thus, while local political cultures play a role in the selection process, other factors must be considered in understanding the staffing process for the federal trial courts.

While the literature on federal judicial selection leaves little doubt that local politics play a role in the selection process, those studies have focused on the nature of the selection process rather than on how local political cultures influence the process. We know that federal trial judges *usually* reflect the basic outlook of their home environments; beyond this we have only anecdotal evidence regarding the degree to which local cultures shape expectations regarding the type of individuals who should be selected as judges (see Goulden, 1974, pp. 114-57). We might expect states in which the local judiciary is "nonpartisan" to have norms that constrain the range of the possible alternatives open to those states' senators; this might also be true of "partisan" states where federal judgeships might simply be part of a party's larger patronage operation. The studies of federal judicial selection have by and large neglected the possibility of local variations in the selection process; such variations would probably reflect differences in local political cultures.

State Trial Courts

Studies of sentencing in criminal cases have consistently found that the most important predictors of the sanctions imposed upon persons convicted of criminal acts are legal factors such as the statutory minimum and maximum sentence, prior record, number of courts, and so on. These are factors that are written into law by state legislatures. The law, as written by state legislatures, reflects the local political cultures in which individual legislators are acting. The statement that law reflects political cultures is almost a cliché; in its broadest sense, law reflects the views of those in power (see Quinney, 1970), who in turn reflect their political cultures.[3]

Historically it is easy to link variations in law across the United States to differences in local political cultures. This is true both in terms of what is defined as illegal behavior and in terms of the penalties set for illegal behavior. The most obvious example is the South, where penalties for such acts as rape were more severe than in the North, and where the whole set of Jim Crow laws (see Woodward, 1966) uniquely defined a wide class of behavior as illegal. However, variations in law have by no means disappeared. One contemporary example is the de facto legalization of the possession of marijuana in some communities (particularly university communities). Can such variations be directly linked to differences in political cultures? The answer to this question is yes; such links can be demonstrated in both a case study fashion and in a systematic, quantitative fashion.

Lundsgaarde (1977) has done a fascinating study of homicide in Houston, Texas. He quotes (p. 159) Article 1, Section 3 and Article 1, Section 23 of the Texas constitution:

> Every citizen shall have the right to keep and bear arms in the lawful defense of himself or the state.
>
> The Legislature shall have power, by the law to regulate the *wearing of arms,* with a view to prevent crime [emphasis added], (Lundsgaard, p. 159).

Despite the "limitation" provided for in section 23, Lundsgaarde finds that "the right to bear and use dangerous weapons by far outweighs any corresponding and opposite duty on the part of the citizenry to refrain from exercising this right in all but the most life-threatening situations." The political culture of Texas is to be found not only in the state constitution, but also in the statutes concerning what constitutes justifiable homicide. Lundsgaarde quotes William M. Ravkind (p. 161):

> The provisions of the [Texas] Penal Code concerning justifiable homicide and their judicial interpretation do not reflect the tempo of our modern day society, but rather are representative of the code of the "old west." Much of the Penal Code has remained unchanged since the date of its enactment in 1856. Specifically, in the area of justifiable homicide, no significant attempt on the part of the legislature has been made to modernize the law, (Lunsgaard, p. 163).

Lundsgaarde points to several aspects of the Texas statutes on justifiable homicide as indicative of the Texas culture (or, to use the phrase of one legal scholar writing in the *Texas Law Review* in 1942, "the Texas point of view," quoted by Lundsgaarde, p. 163). Until 1974 a husband had, under Texas law, the right to kill his wife if he caught her in the act of adultery; he could also kill (perhaps was expected to kill?) his wife's paramour. This right existed only if the adulterous couple was caught while actually engaged in intercourse, or while still together. It is noteworthy that a wife did not enjoy the same right to kill an adulterous husband and his mistress (Lundsgaarde, p. 162). Lundsgaarde points out a second article in the Texas statutes dealing with justifiable homicide:

> If homicide takes place in preventing a robbery, it is justifiable if done while the robber is in the presence of the one robbed or is flying [*sic*] with the property taken by him.

Thus, if one returned home late at night and saw a person fleeing down the street with one's color television, one would have the right in Texas to kill the fleeing burglar even though there is no threat of personal injury to the victim.[4] No doubt there are other states that share some of these provisions with Texas, but those states probably also share aspects of political culture with Texas.

To our knowledge, there have been no attempts systematically to link provisions of criminal law to local political cultures in the United States. Using information in *Sourcebook of Criminal Justice Statistics-1976* (LEAA, 1977), it is possible to do so for one aspect of criminal law: gun-control laws. An examination of gun-control laws can be seen as going beyond the simple question of firearms. A state's position on gun control in fact reflects the attitude of the state toward crime prevention and the source(s) of crime. Using information on gun-control laws in the *Sourcebook* (p. 294), we constructed a scale that ranged from 0 to 14. This score was then correlated with our measures of political culture; the correlations were computed for all forty-eight continental states, and separately for nonsouthern states.[5] These correlations are shown in Table 6-4; several are statistically significant. The presence of gun-control laws is associated with the role of politics index, with such laws most prevalent in areas that do not view politics as fundamentally ideological (particularly conservative). When we exclude the South, we also find a strong correlation with the role of government factor. These results clearly suggest that the "legal environment" is in fact a product of the local political culture.

The structure of state courts has been linked to historical time periods (Glick and Vines, 1973, pp. 18-28), and this is one facet of local cultures. Can we link aspects of judicial structure to contemporary measures of political culture? Here we are defining structure very broadly to include the formal structure of the court system, legal professionalism, and resources available to the judicial system. Vines and Jacob (1971, pp. 290-93) have reported some analyses of the correlates of an index that they call legal professionalism. This index is in fact an indicator of the nature of the organization of the judicial system. It includes judicial selection, court organization, judicial administration,

Table 6-4. Correlations between Gun-Control Index and Measures of State Political Culture

	48 States	*35 Nonsouth States*
Role of government	.24	.46[a]
Role of politics	−.37[a]	−.48[a]
Role of legal system	.11	.16

[a]Significant at .01 level.

tenure systems, and salary level. Here we will examine correlations between legal professionalism plus two of its individual components (court organization and judicial salary levels) and indexes of local political culture. The measure of court organization is taken from Vines and Jacob (1971, p. 290), with low values indicating "modern" forms of court organization and high values indicating "traditional" forms; the salary measure is the salary level of judges of major trial courts (LEAA, 1977, p. 148).[6] The correlations are shown in Table 6-5; as before, we have computed correlations with and without the southern states. We would expect correlations with the third factor because one of the major components of the factor is legal professionalism; what about the other two dimensions of political culture? Once again we find a number of significant correlations, suggesting that, at the state level, the structure of a state's judicial system is related to that state's political culture.

What about allocation of resources to the criminal courts? Does it, too, reflect local political values? To test this we correlated our political culture indicators with measures of allocation priorities. The first set of allocation measures used was a group of per capita expenditure measures derived from data in the *Sourcebook* (LEAA, 1977, pp. 60-69); the measures included total direct expenditure per capita on the criminal justice system, per capita expenditure on judicial activities, and per capita expenditure on prosecution activities. We computed partial correlations controlling for total per capita expenditures; this control variable was intended to take care of variations in general level of expenditures in the states. The partial correlations are shown in Table 6-6a. All but one of the significant correlations are with the role

Table 6-5. Correlations between Judicial Structure and Political Culture

	48 States		
	Legal Professionalism	*Court Organization*	*Judicial Salaries*
Role of government	−.14	−.04	.15
Role of politics	−.56	.02	−.30[a]
Role of legal system	.67[c]	−.54[c]	.43[b]
	35 Nonsouth States		
	Legal Professionalism	*Court Organization*	*Judicial Salaries*
Role of government	.38[a]	−.19	.51[b]
Role of politics	−.40[a]	−.07	−.40[a]
Role of legal system	.73[a]	−.60[b]	.39[a]

[a]Significant at .05 level.

[b]Significant at .01 level.

[c]Significant at .001 level.

of legal system factor. The one exception is the modest nonsouth correlation between per capita expenditures on prosecution activities and the role of politics factor; ideological states appear to spend more on prosecution activities. From the results in Table 6-6a, one would probably conclude that resource allocation to the criminal justice system (once we control for overall expenditure level) does not reflect variations in the general political culture but rather reflects the "needs" of the system.

We must modify these conclusions if we focus on expenditures per crime rather than per capita. The analysis above was repeated using expenditure per crime; the crime figures were taken from the Uniform Crime Index. The results are shown in Table 6-6b; here we find substantial correlations both in all states and in nonsouth states with all three culture dimensions. These correlations indicate that high (per crime) expenditures are most prevalent in "individualistic" states and, excluding the South, in states oriented toward the "common good." Thus there is evidence to support the argument that the allocation of resources to the criminal courts is related to political culture.

The final external aspect of state trial courts that might be related to political cultures is the selection process. There are a variety of types of formal selection systems used in the states; these have been discussed and described extensively elsewhere (see, for example, Glick and Vines, 1973, pp. 39-42). There is some evidence that formal judicial selection mechanisms are a reflection of political cultures, since different types of systems seem to be concentrated in different areas; systems that formally recognize party politics tend to be concentrated in the Northeast and South, and those that seek to exclude party politics are concentrated in the Midwest and West.

There is a variety of evidence that suggests that method of selection does make a difference, both in terms of who is selected and in terms of who has a say in who is selected. Jacob found that the Missouri plan favored persons who had attended in-state law schools (1964, p. 108); this is not surprising, since the Missouri plan maximizes the input of members of the legal profession, and persons who attended in-state law schools are likely to have more professional contacts than persons who went to law school out of state.[7] In electoral systems Green and Walker (1975, pp. 18-19) report that, as one might expect, candidates perceive the party as having more influence on outcomes in partisan systems than in nonpartisan systems;[8] the reverse is true regarding the influence of professional organizations. The effect of this is to create differing perceptions of what constitutes the judicial "constituency"; Levin (1977) found that judges in Minneapolis, who were selected by means of a nonpartisan electoral system, came out of legal careers and looked almost entirely to professional groups and professional norms as reference points in their judicial actions. In Pitts-

Table 6-6. Correlations between Allocation of Resources to the Criminal Justice System and Political Cultures

	48 States			*35 Nonsouth States*		
	Criminal Justice Entire	*Judicial Activities*	*Prosecution Activities*	*Criminal Justice Entire*	*Judicial Activities*	*Prosecution Activities*
(a) Per Capita						
Role of government	.02	–.00	–.35[b]	.19	.16	–.17
Role of politics	.04	.04	.15	.18	.08	.39[a]
Role of legal system	.80[c]	.62[c]	.54[b]	.83[c]	.62[c]	.58[a]
(b) Per Crime						
Role of government	–.12	–.12	–.41[b]	.42[b]	.37[a]	–.02
Role of politics	–.34[b]	–.34[b]	–.15	–.30[a]	–.31[a]	.11
Role of legal system	.83[c]	.74[c]	.64[c]	.84[c]	.70[c]	.61[c]

[a]Significant at .05 level.
[b]Significant at .01 level.
[c]Significant at .001 level.

burgh, on the other hand, where judges were products of a highly partisan political system and had "political" rather than professional backgrounds, the judges were more able to identify with persons of working class backgrounds; while Levin does not attribute this to "constituencies," it may well reflect a recognition of the importance of electoral constituencies (that is, the person being sentenced today as a result of a fight at the neighborhood tavern will be a voter tomorrow).

There seems little doubt that local political cultures affect the selection of state trial judges; the formal mechanism of selection reflect the values of the culture in terms of who should have the major "say" in the selection process. In addition, local culture determines the informal norms that transform the formal rules of selection into a working reality. Thus while there is nothing to stop the governor of Minnesota from making partisan choices when he is called upon to fill judicial vacancies, in fact party considerations appear to have had little importance in such appointments (Levin, 1977, p. 51). It is probably true, though there is no general evidence on this point, that informal norms regarding judicial selection reflect local political cultures even more than does the formal selection process.

INTERNAL WORKINGS

How does local political culture affect the internal workings of the criminal courts? This is the question that we will turn to now. Political culture can affect the internal workings of the court in three ways. It can have direct effects, effects in which the courts are responding directly to some aspect of the political culture (for example, a community belief that criminals should be dealt with harshly). The political culture can have indirect effects on the courts; that is, the culture can set the norms of selection so that the individuals selected believe that criminals should be dealt with harshly. Finally, there can be what might be termed complex or interaction effects; that is, the political culture might serve to modify the nature of the relationship between two or more other variables thus, an important consideration in one type of culture might be the race of the defendant, while in another culture race would be an unimportant variable. In the discussion below we will seek to touch on each of these types of effects; we will first look at the federal trial courts, and then at the state trial courts.

Federal Trial Courts

There have generally been two types of studies of the impact of local political cultures on the internal workings (i.e., decision-making) of federal trial courts.[9] The first of these concern primarily civil cases in areas such as civil rights (Vines, 1964; Heike, 1977, 1978) and civil liberties and labor (Richardson and Vines, 1970, pp. 100-105); these studies generally support the argument that local culture is an important variable in understanding decision-making patterns of district court judges. The types of effects found are generally of the indirect (Vines, 1964) and complex (Richardson and Vines, 1970, p. 104) types. The second body of literature deals with sanctioning decisions of federal district judges focusing on a single type of case: Selective Service violation (Markham, 1972; Note, 1969; Cook, 1973a, 1973b, 1977; Graebner, 1973; and Kritzer, 1978a, 1979).[10]

In this latter set of studies one can find discussions of each of the three types of effects (direct, indirect, and complex). Two types of direct influences are examined: public opinion and elite attitudes. The evidence on public opinion is mixed; some studies report or suggest that judges were responsive to opinion toward the war (Graebner, 1973; Cook, 1973a), though the weight of the evidence suggests that judges did not adjust their sentences in accordance with local opinion (Kritzer, 1978a, p. 48; 1979). On the other hand, there is some good evidence linking together elite attitudes and sentencing of draft offenders (Kritzer, 1978a, p. 49), but the nature of linkage (direct, indirect, or spurious) is unclear.

We can employ the same state-level data used to look for possible relationships between opinion and sentencing of draft offenders to examine the relationship between our political culture measures and sentencing of draft offenders. We will use three measures of sentencing: proportion of convicted offenders *not* jailed, average jail term received by offenders sentenced to prison, and average jail sentence received by all convicted offenders (those receiving no jail term were counted as zero); a state-year combination was included only if the sentencing measure could be based on at least ten cases. Table 6-7 shows these correlations by fiscal years for the period of the Vietnam War. The clearest correlations are between the role of government dimension and the length of jail term measures; twenty-four of twenty-eight are positive and sixteen of the positive correlations are statistically significant. There are no clear trends either between the other cultural dimensions and sentencing trends or between the probability of a jail term and the cultural dimensions. These results suggest that draft offenders in areas with a "common good" orientation tended to receive shorter prison terms for their noncooperation with the draft; judges' sentencing decisions in these cases appear to have reflected their local political cultures (for more evidence on this point, see Kritzer, 1978a, p. 48).

Finally, Cook (1973a) has found a variety of complex effects of political culture by looking at correlations between the sentencing of

Table 6-7. Correlations between Sentencing of Selective-Service Violators and Political Culture

Year	Dimension	Proportion Not Jailed		Average Jail Term: Jailed Offenders		Average Jail Term: All Convicted Offenders	
		All States	Nonsouth States	All States	Nonsouth States	All States	Nonsouth States
1966	Role of government	.41	.23	–.18	.67[a]	–.17	.56[a]
	Role of politics	.28	–.28	–.33	.16	–.26	.25
	Role of legal system	–.12	.06	.10	–.07	.07	–.11
1967	Role of government	.11	.02	.36[a]	.60[b]	.23	.70[b]
	Role of politics	.18	.08	–.17	–.35	–.26	–.43
	Role of legal system	.34	.41	–.11	.08	–.20	–.04
1968	Role of government	–.45[a]	–.13	.46[a]	.42	.56[b]	.36
	Role of politics	–.19	.36	.23	.09	.24	–.15
	Role of legal system	.15	.09	–.12	.24	–.15	.07
1969	Role of government	–.40[a]	.12	.44[a]	.64[b]	.43[a]	.21
	Role of politics	–.30	.15	.22	–.14	.29	–.08
	Role of legal system	.21	.16	–.25	–.09	–.25	–.16
1970	Role of government	–.46[a]	–.14	.49	.46	.44[a]	.48[a]
	Role of politics	–.31	.20	.24	.08	.32	–.01
	Role of legal system	.17	.09	–.14	.27	–.20	–.06
1971	Role of government	–.14	.43[a]	.57[a]	.58	.34	–.53[a]
	Role of politics	–.22	–.10	.04	–.55	.37[a]	.29
	Role of legal system	.12	.09	–.54	–.21	–.28	–.27
1972	Role of government	–.06	.18	.85[c]	.64[a]	.54[b]	.22
	Role of politics	–.06	.02	.52[a]	–.07	.33[a]	–.11
	Role of legal system	–.03	.05	–.16	.01	–.15	–.23
1973	Role of government	.10	.50[a]	.61	.65	.34	–.43[a]
	Role of politics	–.24	–.17	.14	–.43	.43[a]	.46[a]
	Role of legal system	.15	.26	–.07	–.02	–.49[b]	–.30

[a]Significant at the .05 level.
[b]Significant at the .01 level.
[c]Significant at the .001 level.

draft offenders and a variety of other variables within individual judicial circuits. For example, Cook found a significant, negative correlation between sentence severity and the judge's propensity to join cultural organizations in the seventh circuit, but no such relationship in three other circuits (1973a, p. 16a).

There have been virtually no studies of the impact of local political cultures in the disposition of the other types of criminal cases (other than Selective Service) handled by the federal trial courts, though some unpublished work by Rathjen (pp. 13-61; see also Rathjen and Ungs, n.d.) points toward possible cultural explanations for variations in dispositional patterns of federal criminal cases. The only clear evidence is on the impact of public opinion in criminal case decision-making by federal trial judges: there is no relationship with opinion. This is true both for sentencing decisions and for decisions on matters such as *habeas corpus* and criminal procedure (Kritzer, 1979).[11] The results of a recent study of federal sentencing patterns (Sutton, 1978) suggest that political culture may be producing a variety of complex effects in sentencing patterns. For example, the study reports that in the Southern District of New York and in the Southern District of Texas whites tend to receive harsher sentences than blacks while in the Central District of California blacks tend to receive harsher sentences than whites (ibid., p. 25). The author of the study does not speculate on the basis of these complex effects, but it is likely that they, at least in part, reflect differences in political culture.

Can broader aspects of local political cultures be used to explain the outputs of the federal trial courts in criminal cases? To look at this we correlated measures of judicial decision-making within the eighty-nine federal judicial districts[12] with our general measures of political culture; we also checked for complex relationships by looking separately at the southern and nonsouthern districts. We used two different types of decision-making variables. The first was taken from data published by the Administrative Office of the U.S. Courts (1971, pp. 152-55) forFY 1969.[13] These measures are indicators of the severity of sentencing decisions in the federal district courts. Using a sentence weight scale (A.O., 1971, p. 52) the Administrative Office reports the actual average sentence received by all defendants in each district during the year and the expected average sentence if each defendant had received the national average sentence for his or her offense. Thus, if the actual average sentence is less than the expected average sentence, the sentencing decisions of judges in the district are less severe overall than the national average; and if the actual is greater than the expected, judges are more severe. Using this information we computed two indexes of relative sentence severity:[14]

$$\text{Index 1} = \text{Actual} - \text{Expected}$$

$$\text{Index 2} = \frac{(\text{Actual} - \text{Expected})}{\text{Expected}}$$

These two indicators take into account the "mix" of offenders in each judicial district and provide measures of relative sentence severity controlling for the nature of the cases that are heard in each district. The second set of measures is based upon data made available by Robert Carp (see Rowland and Carp, 1978) and looks at decisions of federal district judges on questions such as habeas corpus, motions related to criminal trials, and contempt of court. Carp compiled information on all cases dealing with criminal procedure that were reported in the *Federal Supplement* for the period 1964 through 1972;[15] decisions in 4,688 cases were coded as either liberal or conservative (cases that could not be so coded were omitted). From these data, three indexes were created: proportion of liberal decisions for all judges, proportion of liberal decisions by Democratic judges, and proportion of liberal decisions by Republican judges.[16] We have used the two measures of political culture that we have for the judicial district (role of politics and region) as the independent variables.

The correlations are shown in Table 6-8. Since the sentencing measures are coded so that high values indicate severity and low values indicate leniency, we would expect to find positive correlations with our political culture measure (high values indicate "conservatism," since the measure was simply created by adding together electoral results); we would expect to find negative correlations between voting and the measures derived from published judicial opinions, since the latter measures are based on the proportion of the decisions that are "liberal." The results with opinion-based measures of judicial decision-making are pretty clearcut: there is no relationship between the decisions made by federal judges on criminal procedure related questions and the political conservatism of their judicial districts. When we look at our region dummy variable we find evidence of a relationship between region and the liberalness of federal district judges' decisions in crime-related cases. There is one exception, and this one is quite interesting: when we isolate published opinions of Democratic judges, we find that southern Democrats are no more conservative than northern Democrats when it comes to making decisions in the area of criminal procedure. At least in this one area Democratic presidents have been successful in "nationalizing" the federal trial judiciary; it would be interesting to repeat this analysis with opinions since 1972 to see if this same type of "nationalizing" influence can be

Table 6-8. Political Culture and Decision-making in Federal District Courts

	Sentencing Behavior		*Published Opinions*		
	Index	*Index 2*	*All Judges*	*Republican Judges*	*Democratic Judges*
"Role of politics"[a] (all districts)	.22[b]	.23[b]	.07	.06	−.16
"Role of politics" (southern districts)	.02	.01	−.28	−.33	−.38
"Role of politics" (nonsouthern districts)	.10	.13	−.07	−.05	−.19
Region (South [1] v. North [0])	−.25[c]	−.26[c]	−.28[c]	−.27[b]	−.06

[a]Computed by summing the three measures of voting, so that the resulting index is effectively a measure of political conservatism.

[b]Significant at .05 level.

[c]Significant at .01 level.

found in the more recent decisions of Nixon and Ford appointees, particularly in light of the more conservative tone of the Supreme Court in the last few years. When we turn to the sentencing measures, we at first find what appears to be an expected relationship with our political conservatism measure ("Role of Politics"); however, when we control for region this relationship disappears. The correlation *with* region does clearly suggest a relationship, probably reflecting regional differences in political culture. Thus this analysis does provide modest evidence to support the argument that decision-making in federal trial courts is influenced by variations in local political culture.

State Trial Courts

When we turn to state courts, there are many ways in which the local political culture can and does influence internal decision-making. The most obvious type of effects comes from variations in the formal legal norms. Lundsgaarde's study of Houston provides many examples of such influences at work:

> The killer and victim, both Mexican-Americans, had little, if any, awareness of each other's existence before the shotgun slaying that took place in June, 1969. The killer, a male, age 35, was a neighbor of the victim's nephew. . . . The trouble began when the victim, a 50-year-old male, arrived together with his wife to visit his nephew and family. As they pulled up in front of the nephew's house they parked in such a way that the neighbor's driveway was blocked. The neighbor came to the house shortly thereafter and requested that they move the car. The car was

> moved to permit the neighbor to drive his truck out of the driveway. The victim's car, however, was again parked in front of the neighbor's driveway. This led to an argument between the two men. The killer went into his house, loaded his shotgun, and returned to the driveway where he openly stated that he would kill the 50-year-old man unless he moved his car away once and for all. The man unwisely chose to heed the advice of the Nemesis and thus held his ground. He refused to acknowledge and respond to the verbal threat. One shot was fired and the victim fell over dead. The victim was not armed nor, according to several eyewitnesses, did he verbally or physically threaten the killer except, as noted, by holding his ground. An ambulance and the police arrived and the killer was arrested and charged with murder. Trial was set for October, and the killer entered a plea of guilty. He was judged and admonished by the court. He was then given a five-year probation sentence! (Lundsgaarde, 1977, pp. 109-10)

This case would seem to have all of the elements one normally associates with what is commonly called first-degree murder: lack of an apparent physical threat to the killer, premeditation, and malice. However, in Texas law, the *machismo* mentality has been institutionalized into law, and it is applicable to property as well as to the person; in the words of Article 1225 of the Texas penal code,

> The party whose person or property is so unlawfully attacked is *not bound to retreat* in order to avoid the necessity of killing his assailant [emphasis added; quoted in Lundsgaarde, 1977, p. 164].

Since it would be "unmanly" to retreat, such an action is not required in Texas law. However, in the case cited above, Texas law did not excuse the actions of the killer; the defendant, after all, was convicted. Texas law does truncate the right to kill an assailant with the following statement in Article 1226:

> The attack upon the person of an individual in order to justify homocide must be such as produces a reasonable expectation of fear of death or some serious bodily injury. (quoted in Lundsgaarde, 1977, p. 164)

Nonetheless, in this case, the tone of Texas law served to mitigate and effectively excuse the actions of the killer.

This case study from Texas is more suggestive than definitive. Could we demonstrate a consistent empirical link between the legal norms which define criminal behavior and set the penalties for such behavior and the actual "outputs" of the criminal courts? While the thrust of research on sentencing suggests that we should find such links, there have in fact been no empirical studies which have demonstrated linkages of this sort; the studies which have argued that legal norms are the most important determinants of sentencing decisions have reached these conclusions by examining decisions within the same legal jurisdiction for several types of crimes. Would these conclusions hold up if we looked at variations in sentencing behavior for the same offense across jurisdictions? This is an important question which we must at this time leave to future research.

There have been a number of studies of decision-making in state and local criminal courts which have used either an implicit or explicit "political cultures" approach. The earlier studies of this type were the crime surveys of the 1920s (see Nardulli, 1978, pp. 3-39). Over a period of about ten years, the crime surveys collected extensive data on criminal court dispositions in at least seventy-five jurisdictions; the data were such that they offered the opportunity for comparative analysis (see Table 1-2 in Nardulli, 1978, pp. 24-27): some of the individual surveys were explicitly comparative, collecting and analyzing data from different "types" of areas (that is, urban versus rural areas). The results of the analyses were mixed; some differences were found but not fully understood (often these differences were unexpected); other expected differences did not appear in the data.

Of the more contemporary studies of criminal courts there have been several that have used a political cultures approach. One of these studies focused on what we have termed direct effects. Gibson (1976) sought explicitly to apply the test to a "constituency influence model" of the type used by students of legislative institutions (for example, Miller and Stokes, 1963). Using the district courts of Iowa, Gibson assembled data on sentencing decision, "local" public opinion regarding crime, judges' attitudes toward crime, and judges' perceptions of local public opinion about crime. The results of the analysis provided little support for the argument that judges were responsive to public opinion; while judges' sentencing decisions were positively correlated with their perception of local concern about crime, their perceptions were inversely correlated with actual opinion. There seemed to be no link between the judges' own concerns about crime and sentencing decisions. Gibson revised his model, replacing the measure of actual public opinion with a surrogate, per capita crime rate; the argument cited for this change was that judges may rely on the amount of crime in the county as a cue for citizen concern, thus assuming that citizen concern is related to the actual amount of crime (1976, p. 13). The results of this analysis were more encouraging; the expected links in the constituency influence model were found to be present. The introduction of a variety of intervening variables seemed to provide additional support for the contention that judges do respond to their local political environments (for more on Gibson's approach, see the chapter by him in this volume).

Balbus (1973), in a study of the response of the judicial system to the ghetto revolts of the 1960s, sought explicitly to link the nature of those responses to the nature of political environments in which the courts functioned. Specifically, Balbus was interested in determining to what degree the judicial response to the crises created by the ghetto revolts was influenced by the nature of the authority structures in the three cities he studied (Detroit, Chicago, and Los Angeles). To put this into the framework being used in our analysis, to what degree did the criminal courts respond to the demands of elite constituencies that the court systems assist in restoring and maintaining order? The three cities selected by Balbus had elite structures that varied considerably in cohesion; one might have expected that cities with the strongest "pro-law and order" elite structures would produce the severest judicial response.

The case studies used by Balbus seem to support this contention for minor ghetto revolts (1973, pp. 242-48). Chicago, which had a highly cohesive authority structure and a largely disorganized counterstructure, responded to minor outbreaks with sanctions that were far more severe than those for criminal offenses that were not related to disorders. The opposite was true in Detroit, where the authority structure lacked cohesion but was confronted with a well-organized defense response; the result there was that sanctions were less severe than those for "normal" offenses. Los Angeles saw a response that closely approximated "normal" times, reflecting the fact that neither the authorities nor the defense were well coordinated. This suggests that the criminal courts do respond to elite constituencies in times of minor crisis, provided that that constituency can present its demands to the courts in an unambiguous fashion; this conclusion must be very tentative because we do not have a case in which a cohesive authority structure was confronted by an equally cohesive defense community.

While the courts may be responsive to outside constituencies during minor crises, Balbus found that this was not true of major outbreaks. He found that the judicial response to major outbreaks, in terms of case flow and sanctions, was similar in all three cities, and in all three the resulting case outcomes were less severe than for "normal" times. While the initial response was to keep most persons who had been arrested in detention in order to end the revolt as quickly as possible, as case processing progressed, the demands of "organizational maintenance" forced the courts to seek to dispose of the large caseload by permitting a large number of defendants to escape any significant sanctions. The one exception to this was Chicago, where about 25 percent of the arrestees received jail sentences; however, Balbus attributed this not to demands of elite constituencies but rather to the fact that Chicago's revolt did not come until 1968, giving the court system time to learn from the experiences of other cities (1973, p. 242). Thus Balbus concluded that the judicial system is responsive to the demands of elite constituencies when those constituencies are cohesive in nature; however, the importance of elite demands varies inversely with the degree of crisis with which the political system is confronted (1973, p. 249).

Levin's exploratory study of Minneapolis and Pittsburgh (1972a, 1972b, 1977) explicitly sought to determine (1) whether there was a link between the political cultures of the two cities and the actions of the criminal court judges, and (2) what was the basis of any such linkages that might be found. Levin found that judges in Minneapolis had substantially different orientations and reference groups than did judges in Pittsburgh; he attributed this primarily to differences in the nature of the pre-judicial career experiences of judges in the two cities (1977, p. 147). These differences in turn resulted from the norms of the selection systems; the Minneapolis system selected individuals who had pursued legal careers while the Pittsburgh system sought out lawyers who were also "politicos." Thus Levin concluded that the influence of the political system in the two cities is indirect, with no evidence of direct influence on individual criminal cases (1977, pp. 152-53).

What Levin basically found was that the nature of the self-perceptions of the role played by the judges is different in the two cities, and the type of self-perceptions is a result of the norms of the political culture in which the judges must function. This is potentially an extremely important finding. There have been a number of pieces of research that suggest that the nature of a judge's role conception has both direct effects on judicial behavior (Walker, 1973; Galanter, Palen, and Thomas, 1977; Sarat, 1977) and complex effects that serve as inhibitors or catalysts for effects of other variables (Gibson, 1978). Levin's findings potentially add much to our understanding of the sources of these role orientations and the rich and complex influences of political cultures on judicial decision-making.

Eisenstein and Jacob look at three cities in their study of *Felony Justice* (1977). While their primary analytic framework, drawn from organization theory, focuses on the nature of courtroom workgroups (judge, prosecutor, and defense counsel) they include in their analysis a consideration of the political environments in which the courts are situated (ibid., pp. 58-59) and they devote substantial attention to the description of the larger environments in the three cities. Eisenstein and

Jacob rely on environmental factors to help explain some of the features they find in the three cities (for example, they argue that the lack of plea bargaining in Baltimore reflects, in part, the "law and order" political environment (ibid., p. 96). The authors never actually try to isolate political culture per se as an explanatory variable though their work suggests that culture would be of importance, and they specifically mention culture in their conclusions:

> We found sharp differences among the three cities on several important dimensions. . . . It is unlikely that [the] different outcomes [found in the analysis] are spurious, or that they resulted from differences in the characteristics of defendants, the evidence gathered against them, or the kinds of crimes they commit. Rather, differences in procedures and case outcomes result from the combined effects of structures and rules mandated by state law, local political and cultural values, the structure and policies of sponsoring organizations, and the characteristics of courtroom workgroups. (ibid., p. 300)

The potential importance of political culture as an aid to understanding is most clear in looking at the differences in relationships among variables. For example, the strength of evidence accounts for a sizable proportion of the variance in the decision to convict or acquit in Detroit but accounts for none of the variance in Baltimore, while in Baltimore the characteristics of the defendant account for much of the variance (ibid., pp. 241-42). This suggests that the culture of Detroit probably tends toward the legalistic while in Baltimore it tends toward the individualistic. It is likely that Eisenstein and Jacob's failure systematically to consider political culture as an explanation for these differences in the nature of relationships is largely a result of a lack of any kind of framework for using the concept of political culture in this way; we will suggest some possible solutions to this problem in our conclusions.

In recent years there has been a growing interest in the field of judicial administration (see, for example, Berkson, Hays, and Carbon, 1977; Wheeler and Whitcomb, 1977). Students in this field have sought to examine the sources of many of the administrative problems facing the courts and to suggest remedies for those problems (for example, Church and others, 1978a; Flanders, 1977). A recent study of court delay in twenty-one metropolitan courts (Church and others, 1978b) found little support for many of the traditional explanations for delay; as an alternative explanation, the authors of the study suggest that delay may in fact reflect the norms of the local legal culture (ibid., pp. 41-42). They argue that if the cultural explanation is correct, one should find that separate courts in the same cultural environment have similar patterns of delay even though the courts handle different types of cases, have different caseloads, and have different rules of procedure; the similar delay patterns would arise from shared cultural values held by attorneys practicing in the two courts. In support for this argument, Church and associates show that delay patterns are similar in the federal and state courts in the metropolitan areas they studied (ibid., p. 45); statistics computed from the data they present show a .60 correlation between state and federal "civil disposition time" and a .49 correlation between state and federal "time for trial" (both correlations are significant at the .05 level). What this analysis does not make clear is the relationship between what Church and associates call "legal culture" and what we have identified as "political culture"; we would argue that legal culture is one aspect of the broader political culture, though it may not be tapped by the specific dimensions which we have used to measure political culture.

Church and associates is the last of the comparative studies of criminal courts. However, there are many studies of criminal courts in individual jurisdictions, or in groups of similar jurisdictions. These studies can be combined to provide insights into the role of political cultures in the criminal courts. In a recent article Hagan (1974) sought to assess the influence of "extralegal attributes" on criminal sentencing by examining previous individual sentencing studies; while he does not explicitly consider political cultures as an explanatory variable for differences in results reported in the literature, he briefly touches on culture in his consideration of race as a predictor of sentence severity. Hagan reports that while several studies report statistically significant differences in the sentences received by white and black defendants, most of these differences are very small and many disappear after controlling for type of offense and/or prior record (1974, pp. 362-69). The major exception to this is when one looks at the race of both defendant and victim in cases carrying a potential death penalty; in three of the five studies examined by Hagan the interaction of victim and defendant race was significant, and for at least one study the relationship was quite large. What is important for our purposes, however, is the fact that all three of the studies that found victim-defendant race to be significant used data from southern states; the one study that looked at nonsouthern cases reported no relationship between sentence outcome and victim-defendant race (Hagan, 1974, pp. 371-72). This example suggests that groups of prior studies could be used to answer carefully constructed questions about the effect of political cultures on the criminal courts.

There is one final approach to studying the relationship between political cultures and decision-making in the criminal courts; this approach involves the analysis of aggregate, state-level statistics on the performance of the criminal courts. Specifically, are there correlations between such statistics and indicators of political cultures like those used in our analysis of external decisions regarding the court system? Since aggregate data on court outputs are not readily available, we used data reported by Gibbs (1968, pp. 520-21) on the certainty and severity of sanctions for homicide during 1960 for an exploratory analysis. Table 6-9 shows the correlations between Gibbs's data and our measures of political culture; note that our measures involve data for time periods that come after the period covered by Gibbs's data. Because this is an exploratory analysis, we have not predicted the direction of relationships, and the significance tests shown in the table are two-tailed. The table shows several significant, though modest, correlations. Severity is inversely correlated with the role of the legal system (severity appears to decline as the degree of legalism increase) and inversely correlated with an ideological approach to politics. Certainty is correlated with a "public good" cultural orientation, and in the nonsouthern states it is correlated with an ideological approach to politics. These very tentative results suggest that additional research in this area might be fruitful.

CONCLUSIONS

The purpose of this chapter was to examine the applicability of the concept of political culture as a tool for understanding variations in the nature of and operation of the various judicial systems in the United States. Previous studies of the judiciary that have referred to political culture have used it primarily as a residual category, to be used to explain variations that could not be attributed to other explanatory variables; in this discussion we have sought to make "political culture" a primary explanatory factor for variations in a number of aspects of the judicial systems.

Specifically we sought to examine the impact of political culture on

Table 6-9. Correlations between Sanctions for Homicide and Political Culture

	48 States		*35 Nonsouth States*	
	Severity	*Certainty*	*Severity*	*Certainty*
Role of government	–.21	–.32[a]	–.13	–.36[a]
Role of politics	–.26[a]	.11	–.22	.32[a]
Role of legal system	–.38[a]	–.05	–.42[b]	–.10

[a]Significant at .05 level.

[b]Significant at .01 level.

both internal and external aspects of the state and federal courts. We operationalized political culture along three dimensions: role of government, role of politics, and role of the legal system. We found a large number of correlations between external features and characteristics of the court systems and both the role of politics dimension and the role of legal system dimension; we found somewhat fewer relationships between the external aspects and the role of government dimension. We found a number of relationships between internal aspects of the courts and each of our dimensions of political culture. We believe that the evidence presented above persuasively shows that political culture should be considered at the beginning stages of research on the judiciary and should not be saved as something to be used at the end of the research process to explain the unexplainable.

We do not mean to suggest that political culture should be viewed as the primary explanatory variable in judicial studies. As a "direct" explanatory variable political culture is really only a part of a larger complex of variables—the environmental context in which the judicial subsystem exists. This environment includes a number of components in addition to culture: resources, structure, habit, historical background, and so on. Some of these other components are consequences of political culture, some are causes of culture, and some are both causes and consequences: to untangle thoroughly this complex of variables which we have labeled as environment is probably an impossible task. At the same time, we must consider the relationship of courts to their environments, or what might properly be referred to as the study of the "ecology of the courts" (note that this usage flows directly from the definition of *ecology*, which is the study of the relations between something and its environment); students of the trial courts have only recently begun explicitly to consider environmental factors and, despite the use of the term *ecology* in several recent publications (Eisenstein and Jacob, 1977, pp. 40-64; and Kritzer, 1979), those studies have not really been concerned with the interrelationship (that is, two-way relationship) between courts and their environments which would be required if the studies were truly interested in the ecology of the courts. One clear direction for future research on the courts would involve the potential two-way relationships between the courts and their environments; the focus on systems theory as a framework for the analysis of the courts (see Goldman and Jahnige, 1971; and Sheldon, 1974, pp. 164-99) has involved the notion of "feedback," but seldom have studies considered how such back" might actually modify the larger environment in which the courts are situated.

While as a direct explanatory variable political culture needs to be included as part of this larger notion of environment, political culture has some unique aspects which make it more important than the other components of environment in our efforts to understand the courts. In both our review of other studies and in some of the original analysis presented above we have argued that political culture can also explain variations in the nature of relationships among other variables (for example, differences in the effect of defendant race on criminal case disposition in various regions of the country); that is, political culture serves to structure the nature of the causal relationships which we look for in trying to understand the judicial system. We need to understand why relationships found at one time and place are not found at another time and place; the likely explanation for those differences has to do with political culture. A political culture with one set of expectations will lead to one set of relationships, while a different political culture with a different set of expectations will lead to another set of relationships. In general, our tendency to focus on "linear" models for explanation has led us away from the consideration of more complex, interactive models (see Blalock, 1969, pp. 155-65; Wright, 1976; and Southwood, 1978). Because of the nature of the data available to us in preparing this analysis, we have not been able to devote a substantial amount of attention here to possible interactive models involving political culture; however, recent explicitly comparative studies (for example, Eisenstein and Jacob, 1977; Levin, 1977) suggest that such may be coming in the future. In addition, recent work by Gibson (1978) involving interactive models in the study of judicial decision-making (though not involving political culture) suggests that nonlinear (or modified linear) models of this type may be very fruitful in developing our understanding of the courts. What is needed in future research is an explicit consideration of the ways in which political culture might modify the relationships among the primary variables in the study, and efforts to include in such research tests for nonlinearities involving political culture.

NOTES

1. The basic unit that is juggled in creating districts and divisions is county. Unlike congressional districts, which often split counties into many little pieces, all judicial district boundaries are contiguous with county boundaries.

2. Richardson and Vines have argued that little juggling of district boundaries takes place, and that district lines are usually set at the time states enter the Union. While historically this is true, all four of the major changes that have occurred in recent years have taken place in the Sun Belt, and this may be indicative of future changes that are to come as the population shift to the Sun Belt continues (assuming it does in fact continue).

3. For a comparative analysis of criminal law, see Mueller (1970).

4. Compare the situation in Texas to a recent case in Wisconsin in which an accused robber was suing a sales attendant who had shot him in the course of a robbery attempt; the robber claimed that the attendant had used excessive force.

5. Hawaii and Alaska were omitted because some items of data were unavailable for them. The southern states were Alabama, Arkansas, Florida, Georgia, Kentucky, Louisiana, Mississippi, North Carolina, Oklahoma, South Carolina, Tennessee, Texas, and Virginia.

6. Some states allow local areas to supplement judicial salaries; this analysis does not include those supplements in the judicial salary data.

7. See Ashman and Alfini (1974) and Watson and Downing (1969) for studies of the actual workings of the Missouri Plan.

8. This perceptual data is consistent with recent studies of aggregate election statistics (Dubois, 1977).

9. See Goulden (1974) for a journalistic discussion of the federal trial courts; Goulden suggests a number of political culture links (see particularly chapter 3).

10. There have been several general studies of criminal case dispositions in the federal district courts that have not focused on local cultures as an explanatory variable (for example, Tiffany, Avichai, and Peters, 1975; Finkelstein, 1975), though presenting in at least one case (Rau, 1972) some data on regional variations in sentencing.

11. It should be noted that the study cited above is based on an analysis of thirty-four federal judicial districts for which public opinion data were available. It is possible that a relationship with opinion could be found if other districts were examined. It is also possible that these results are time bound (the data are from the late 1960s) and that a relationship could exist at another time.

12. The Federal Judicial District for the District of Columbia has been omitted in this analysis, along with the "territorial" district courts.

13. The year 1969 was selected because these same data were used in the opinion analysis (Kritzer, 1979) discussed above, and because 1969 comes in the middle of the period covered by the voting data we have.

14. Both indexes have a value of zero when the expected and actual average sentences are the same; the indexes are positive for harsher sentencing patterns and negative for more lenient patterns.

15. In fact, Carp's work covers a much longer time period and a variety of other decisional areas.

16. If there were fewer than five cases upon which to base the index, the index was coded as missing.

REFERENCES

Adamany, David (1969). "The Party Variable in Judges' Voting: Conceptual Notes and a Case Study." 63 *American Political Science Review* 57-73.

______, and Dubois, Philip (1976). "Electing State Judges." 1976 *Wisconsin Law Review* 731-779.

Administrative Office of the U.S. Courts (1974). *1973 Semi-Annual Report of the Director*. Washington, D.C.: Government Printing Office.

_____ (1971). *Federal Offenders in the U.S. District Courts 1969*. Washington, D.C.: Government Printing Office.

Ashman, Allan, and Alfini, James J. (1974). *The Key to Judicial Merit Selection: The Nominating Process*. Chicago: American Judicature Society.

Balbus, Isaac D. (1973). *The Dialectics of Legal Repression: Black Rebels Before the American Criminal Courts*. New York: Russell Sage Foundation.

Beiser, Edward N., and Silberman, Jonathan J. (1971). "The Political Party Variable: Workmen's Compensation Cases in the New York Court of Appeals." 3 *Polity* 521-31.

Berkson, Larry C., Hays, Steven W., and Carbon, Susan J. (1977). *Managing the State Courts*. Minneapolis: West Publishing Co.

Blalock, Hubert M. (1969). *Theory Construction: From Verbal to Mathematical Formulations*. Englewood Cliffs, N.J.: Prentice-Hall.

Cannon, Bradley (1972). "The Impact of Formal Selection Processes on the Characteristics of Judges—Reconsidered." 6 *Law & Society Review* 579-93.

Chase, Harold (1972). *Federal Judges: The Appointing Process*. Minneapolis: University of Minnesota Press.

Church, Thomas, and others (1978a). *Pretrial Delay: A Review and Bibliography*. Williamsburg, Virginia: National Center for State Courts.

_____ (1978b). "Justice Delayed: The Pace of Litigation in Urban Trial Courts." 2, 4 *State Court Journal* 3-8, 41-47.

Clynch, Edward (1972). "A Critique of Ira Sharkansky's 'Utility of Elazar's Political Culture.'" 5 *Polity* 139-41.

Cook, Beverly Blair (1973a). "Decision-Making by Federal Trial Judges: Reference Groups and Local Culture." Paper presented at Meetings of the American Political Science Association, Jung Hotel, New Orleans, Louisiana, September 4-8.

_____ (1973b). "Sentencing Behavior of Federal Judges: Draft Cases." 42 *University of Cincinnati Law Review* 597-633.

_____ (1977). "Public Opinion and Federal Judicial Policy." 21 *American Journal of Political Science* 567-600.

Dolbeare, Kenneth M. (1967). *Trial Courts in Urban Politics: State Court Policy Impact and Functions in a Local Political System*. New York: John Wiley & Sons.

Dubois, Philip L. (1977). "Judicial Elections and Judicial Policy: The Case for Partisan Election of Judges." Paper presented at Meetings of the American Political Science Association, Washington Hilton Hotel, Washington, D.C., September 1-4.

Eisenstein, James, and Jacob, Herbert (1977). *Felony Justice: An Organizational Analysis of Criminal Courts*. Boston: Little, Brown.

Elazar, Daniel (1970). *Cities of the Prairie*. New York: Basic Books.

_____ (1966). *American Federalism: A View from the States*. New York: Thomas Y. Crowell Co.

Feeley, Malcolm M. (1971). "Another Look at the 'Party Variable' in Judicial Decision-Making: An Analysis of the Michigan Supreme Court." 4 *Polity* 91-104.

Finkelstein, Michael O. (1975). "A Statistical Analysis of Guilty Plea Practices in the Federal Courts." 89 *Harvard Law Review* 293-315.

Flango, Victor Eugene (1975). "Court Administration and Judicial Modernization." 35 *Public Administration Review* 619-24.

Galanter, Marc; Palen, Frank; and Thomas, John M. (1977). "The Crusading Judge: Judicial Activism in Urban Trial Courts." Paper presented at Meetings of the Midwest Political Science Association, Pick-Congress Hotel, Chicago, Illinois, April 21-23.

Gaylin, Willard (1974). *Partial Justice: A Study of Bias in Sentencing.* New York: Alfred A. Knopf.

Gibbs, Jack (1968). "Crime, Punishment, and Deterrence." 48 *Southwest Social Science Quarterly* 515-30.

Gibson, James L. (1976). "Judges as Representatives: Constituency Influence on Trial Courts." Paper presented at Meetings of the American Political Science Association, The Palmer House, Chicago, Illinois, September 2-5.

_____ (1978). "Judges' Role Orientations, Attitudes and Decisions: An Interactive Model." 72 *American Political Science Review* 911-24.

Glick, Henry (1971). *Supreme Courts in State Politics: An Investigation of the Judicial Role.* New York: Basic Books.

_____, and Vines, Kenneth N. (1973). *State Court Systems.* Englewood Cliffs, N.J.: Prentice-Hall.

Goldman, Sheldon, and Jahnige, Thomas P. (1971). *The Federal Courts as a Political System.* New York: Harper & Row.

Goulden, Joseph C. (1974). *The Benchwarmers: The Private World of the Powerful Federal Judges.* New York: Weybright and Talley.

Graebner, Diane B. (1973). "Judicial Activity and Public Attitude: A Quantitative Study of Selective Service Sentencing in the Vietnam War Period." 23 *Buffalo Law Review* 465-97.

Green, Justin J., and Walker, Thomas G. (1975). "Partisan and Professional Influences in the Recruitment of Judicial Candidates." Paper presented at Meetings of the Midwest Political Science Association, Pick Congress Hotel, Chicago, Illinois.

Grossman, Joel B., and Sarat, Austin (1971). "Political Culture and Judicial Research." *Washington University Law Quarterly* 177-207.

Hagan, John (1974). "Extra-Legal Attributers and Criminal Sentencing: An Assessment of a Sociological Viewpoint." 8 *Law & Society Review* 357-83.

Heike, Susan J. (1977). "Federal District Judges and Public School Desegregation: A Study of Judicial Decision-Making." Unpublished Ph.D. Dissertation, Emory University.

_____ (1978). "Federal District Judges and School Desegregation: Social Background Factors Reconsidered." Paper presented at Meetings of the Southern Political Science Association, Atlanta, Georgia, November 9-11.

Hutcheson, John D., Jr., and Taylor, George A. (1973). "Religious Variables, Political System Characteristics, and Policy Outputs in the American States." 17 *American Journal of Political Science* 414-21.

Jackson, Donald Dale (1974). *Judges*. New York: Atheneum.

Jacob, Herbert (1964). "The Effect of Institutional Differences in the Recruitment Process: The Case of State Judges." 13 *Journal of Public Law* 104-19.

Johnson, Charles A. (1976). "Political Culture in American States: Elazar's Formulation Examined." 20 *American Journal of Political Science* 491-509.

Kluger, Richard (1975). *Simple Justice*. New York: Vintage Books.

Kritzer, Herbert M. (1978a). "Political Correlates of the Behavior of Federal District Judges: A 'Best Case' Analysis." 40 *Journal of Politics* 25-58.

______ (1978b). "Enforcing the Selective Service Act: Deterrence of Potential Violators." 30 *Stanford Law Review* 1149-76.

______ (1979). "Federal Judges and Their Political Environments: The Influence of Public Opinion." 23 *American Journal of Political Science* 194-205.

Law Enforcement Assistance Administration (1977). *Sourcebook of Criminal Justice Statistics—1976*. Washington, D.C.: Government Printing Office.

Laymon, Mary (1978). "Efficiency and Justice Competing Symbols in Judicial Structure and Processes." Unpublished paper, University of Wisconsin, Department of Political Science.

Levin, Martin A. (1972). "Urban Politics and Judicial Behavior." 1 *Journal of Legal Studies* 193-221.

______ (1972b). "Urban Politics and Policy Outcomes: The Criminal Courts." In George F. Cole, ed. *Criminal Justice: Law and Politics*, pp. 330-63. Belmont, Calif.: Duxbury Press.

______ (1977). *Urban Politics and the Criminal Courts*. Chicago: University of Chicago Press.

Lungdsgaarde, Henry P. (1977). *Murder in Space City: A Cultural Analysis of Houston Homicide Patterns*. New York: Oxford University Press.

Luttberg, Norman R. (1971). "Classifying the American States: An Empirical Attempt to Identify Internal Variations." 15 *Midwest Journal of Political Science* 703-21.

Markham, Walter Gray (1971). "Draft Offenders in the Federal Courts: A Search for the Social Correlates of Justice." Unpublished Ph.D. Dissertation, University of Pennsylvania.

McKennell, A.C. (1977). "Attitude Scale Construction." In C.A. O'Muircheartaigh and C. Payne, eds. *The Analysis of Survey Data: Exploring Data Structures*, pp. 183-220. New York: John Wiley & Sons.

Miller, Warren E., and Stokes, Donald E. (1963). "Constituency Influence in Congress." 57 *American Political Science Review* 45-56.

Mueller, Gerhard O. (1970). *Comparative Criminal Law in the United States*. New York: Criminal Law Education and Research Center, New York University.

Nardulli, Peter (1978). *The Courtroom Elite: An Organizational Perspective on Criminal Justice*. Cambridge, Mass.: Ballinger Publishing Company.

National Center Educational Statistics (1972). *Digest of Educational Statistics 1971*. Washington, D.C.: Government Printing Office.

Note (1969). "Sentencing Selective Service Violators: A Judicial Wheel of Fortune." 5 *Columbia Journal of Law and Social Problems* 164-96.

Patterson, Samuel (1968). "The Political Culture of the American State." 30 *Journal of Politics* 187-209.

Quinney, Richard (1970). *The Social Reality of Crime*. Boston: Little, Brown.

Rathjen, Gregory (n.d.). "Law and Reorder: A Comparative Assessment of the Johnson and Nixon Administrations of Justice." Unpublished manuscript.

_____, and Ungs, Thomas (n.d.). "U.S. Attorneys and the Administration of Criminal Justice: An Exploration of the Nixon and Johnson Years." Unpublished manuscript.

Rau, Richard M. (1972). *Sentencing in the Federal Courts*. Washington, D.C.: National Institute of Law Enforcement and Criminal Justice.

Richardson, Richard J., and Vines, Kenneth N. (1970). *The Politics of Federal Courts*. Boston: Little, Brown.

Ritt, Leonard (1974). "Political Cultures and Political Reform: A Research Note." 5 *Publius* 127-32.

Roland, Claude, and Carp, Robert (1978). "The Influence of Background Characteristics on the Voting Behavior of Federal District Judges." Paper presented at Meeting of the American Political Science Association, New York Hilton, August 31-September 3.

Sarat, Austin (1977). "Judging in Trial Courts: An Exploratory Study." 39 *Journal of Politics* 368-98.

Schubert, Glendon (1959). *Quantitative Analysis of Judicial Behavior*. New York: The Free Press.

Sharkansky, Ira (1969). "The Utility of Elazar's Political Culture: A Research Note." 2 *Polity* 66-83.

_____ (1970). *Regionalism in American Politics*. Indianapolis: Bobbs-Merrill.

_____, and Hofferbert, Richard (1967). "Dimensions of State Politics, Economics, and Public Policy." 63 *American Political Review* 867-79.

Skogan, Wesley G. "The Validity of Official Crime Statistics." 55 *Social Science Quarterly* 25-38.

Sorauf, Frank J. (1972). *Party Politics in America*. Boston: Little, Brown.

Southwood, Kenneth E. (1978). "Substantive Theory and Statistical Interaction: Five Models." 83 *American Journal of Sociology* 1154-1203.

Sutton, L. Paul (1978). *Federal Sentencing Patterns: A Study of Geographical Variations*. Washington, D.C.: Government Printing Office.

Tiffany, Lawrence P.; Avichai, Yukov; and Peters, Geoffrey W. (1975). "A Statistical Analysis of Sentencing in Federal Courts: Defendants Convicted after Trial, 1967-1968." 4 *Journal of Legal Studies* 369-90.

Ulmer, S. Sidney (1962). "The Political Party Variable in the Michigan Supreme Court." 11 *Journal of Public Law* 352-62.

Vines, Kenneth N. (1964). "Federal District Judges and Race Relations Cases in the South." 26 *Journal of Politics* 337-57.

_____, and Jacob, Herbert (1971). "State Courts." In Herbert Jacob and Kenneth N. Vines, eds. *Politics in the American States: A Comparative Analysis*. Boston: Little, Brown.

Walker, Jack (1969). "The Diffusion of Innovations among the American States." 63 *American Political Science Review* 880-99.

Walker, James L. (1973). "Role Perception as a Linkage between Urban Courts and the Local Political System: Are Trial Judges Reactionary?" Paper presented at Meetings of the American Political Science Association, Jung Hotel, New Orleans, Louisiana, September 4-8.

Watson, R., and Downing, R. (1969). *The Politics of Bench and Bar: Judicial Selection under the Missouri Non-Partisan Court Plan*. New York: John Wiley & Sons.

Wheeler, Russell, and Whitcomb, Howard (1977). *Judicial Administration*. Englewood Cliffs, N.J.: Prentice-Hall.

Woodward, C. Vann (1966). *The Strange Career of Jim Crow*. New York: Oxford University Press.

Wright, Gerald C. (1976). "Linear Models for Evaluating Conditional Relationships." 20 *American Journal of Political Science* 349-73.

Part III

Policy Issues in Criminal Courts

Chapter Seven

Punishment before Trial: A Political Choice Model of Policy Changes in Pretrial Sanctioning

Roy B. Flemming

For nearly fifty years American bail practices have been criticized as overly harsh, generally unjust, often capricious, frequently corrupt, and rarely guided by either the letter of the Constitution or the spirit of the "presumption of innocence" (Beeley, 1966; Foote, 1955, 1958, 1965; Goldfarb, 1965). Yet during the last fifteen years, while concern over crime in the streets and law and order was rife throughout the country, bail policies apparently changed greatly to the advantage of defendants (Thomas, 1976). No one, however, knows exactly why or how these changes occurred.

At first glance bail reform seems a logical and obvious answer. Pretrial release agencies have proliferated to permit the release of defendants on their own recognizance. Local and state rules have been changed to allow security or 10 percent deposit bail instead of surety bonds. In many instances these reforms eliminated the long disparaged role of the bondsman and added a measure of equity into financial release since most of the deposit was refunded to defendants. Conditional release programs designed for defendants too poor to post cash bails but too risky for recognizance have also become popular (Thomas, 1976).

To single out reform, however, is to confuse cause with effect. Reform often reflects the adroit use by reformers of the opportunities for change created by bail bondsman scandals, as in Illinois. The initial diffusion of recognizance reform in the 1960s relied as much on the flush of national excitement engendered by the emerging concern over poverty during the Kennedy administration and the ensuing flow of federal funds for the projects, as on the well-publicized success of the

Manhattan Bail Project (Friedman, 1976). Later recognizance programs instituted during the Nixon years were often financially backed by the Law Enforcement Assistance Administration to help local courts cope with mounting jail problems brought about by prisoner riots, lawsuits over jail conditions, and an increased willingness by higher courts to take a hand in the administration of the facilities (Thomas, 1977; Goldfarb, 1975).[1]

In other words, various, perhaps disparate, local and national events created the context for change. Little is known, however, about the process through which criminal courts reformed their bail practices, how the factors involved in this process affected the extent or stability of the change, or what role bail reform measures played in this process. This study seeks to supply answers to these questions. It lays out a theoretical perspective of pretrial sanctioning and the process of change, then shows how one large urban criminal court eventually decided to reform its pretrial policies.

A PERSPECTIVE OF PRETRIAL SANCTIONING

Current theories about organizational behavior were used to develop a perspective of pretrial sanctioning. It shares the emphasis these theories place on an organization's efforts to control its environment or at least insulate itself to some extent from its effects (Thompson, 1967; Warwick, 1975). It also incorporates the concepts of uncertainty, risk, slack resources, and the general notion that courts behave like satisficing organizations (March and Simon, 1958; Cyert and March, 1963). A central assumption behind this perspective is that the choice behaviors of courts have equilibrating tendencies and that policy changes occur primarily when equilibrium is disturbed. Figure 7-1 portrays the relationships among the basic elements making up this perspective. Briefly stated, the pretrail sanctioning behavior of court officials and the scope and severity of these sanctions are seen as reflecting the effects of risk and resources as they are shaped by the court's political environment which in turn may change as it reacts to the court's policies and their outcomes.

Risk, which combines the elements of both uncertainty and threat, permeates pretrial release choices. Bail decisions—the decision to release defendants from custody and the price, if any, they are forced to pay for their freedom—are often calculated gambles by court officials made for the most part on the basis of intuition, hunches, past experiences, and personal favors to courtroom participants (Flemming, 1977). No valid, reliable causal theory guides these decisions, and so they are gambles in two respects. First, court officials cannot be

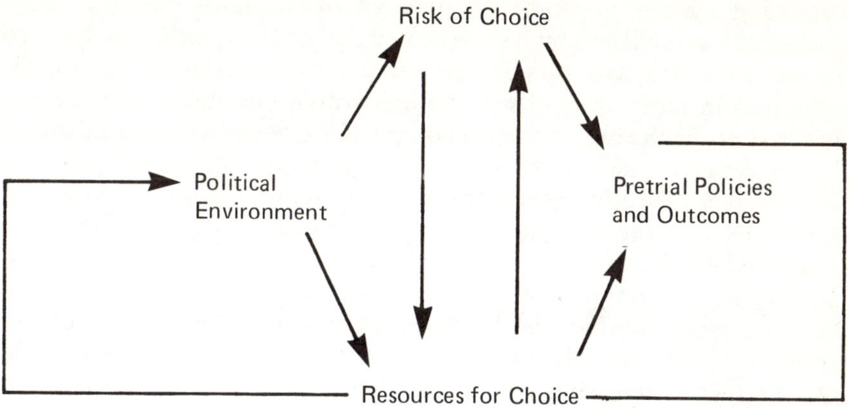

Figure 7-1. A Perspective of Pretrial Sanctioning Determinants

sure how defendants will behave if they are released or detained, whether their decisions were "fair" or will deter undesirable behavior, or how the court's envionment will react to their choices and their results. Second, because different segments of the political setting have varying substantive and symbolic stakes in pretrial policies, they may try to preserve or change these policies by mustering whatever political resources they have at their disposal to sanction court officials with whom they are displeased. In New York City, for example, the police successfully pressured the court to reassign a judge, whom they had nicknamed "Turn 'Em Loose Bruce" because of his liberal bail practices, to the civil bench, an action which the judge labeled as his "banishment" (*New York Times*, February 11, 1975).

Resources include laws, rules, and pretrial release agencies. But the critical factor is the jail, since it is the fulcrum of pretrial sanctioning. Cash bails work only because defendants know they will be incarcerated if they do not post them. Remands or denials of bail and high cash bails intended to detain defendants depend on the existence of some means of incarceration. Even recognizance and conditional release carry the threat of jail for defendants who violate the stipulations of their release. Jails, therefore, provide the key resource needed to achieve the various operative goals of bail such as preventive detention or assuring the trial appearances of defendants. Accordingly it is not farfetched to hypothesize that the punitiveness of pretrial policies varies directly with the detention resources made available to criminal courts.

Jails, it should be noted, can be surprisingly elastic facilities. Overcrowding clearly expands a jail's detention limits beyond those putatively established by its "design capacity" and, until the upsurge in jail riots and lawsuits in the early 1970s, was often politically tolerated in most large cities. A more subtle but equally efficacious method of increasing or maintaining a jail's detention capabilities is by accelerating the turnover rate of its prisoner population.

Turnover refers to the ratio between the daily outflow and inflow of prisoners. A number of factors affect this ratio. The volume of arrainged defendants, the severity of their charges, court bail practices, bondsman behavior, and the economic status of defendants combine in complex ways to affect both the numerator and denominator of the ratio. A major variable affecting the outflow of jail prisoners is the court's own disposition policies and the length of time it takes to dispose of its trial docket.

A court can stabilize the jail population or reduce it—without changing bail policies and thus the current rate of detention—by quickening the pace of dispositions to the point where the outflow of prisoners equals or exceeds the influx of newly detained defendants. Delay is obviously a slack resource in its own right which is distributed within courts to meet the interests of courtroom participants (Levin, 1977, pp. 226-45). However, it will be argued shortly that, when existing policies no longer satisfactorily balance the competing forces impinging on a court, revision of disposition procedures taking up this slack will be more politically attractive than changes in the court's bail policies.

The scope and severity of pretrial sanctioning, then, are shaped by a court's efforts to cope with the uncertainties and penalties of bail choice and facilitated by the detention capabilities of the jail as determined by its size, the willingness of the community to ignore overcrowding, and the court's pretrial policies affecting the turnover of the jail's population. In the instance of both major concepts in this simplified perspective, a court's environment assumes a major role. Its interorganizational ties with the police, prosecutor, jail, bondsmen, and others make its policies vulnerable to actions or changes in policies taken by these actors, and its political links and dependencies make it susceptible to the threat or imposition of sanctions.

A PROCESS MODEL OF POLICY CHANGE

The basic elements of a pretrial sanctioning model have been introduced. An outline of the process through which courts alter their pretrial policies as the elements affecting these policies change, still remains to be discussed, however. Figure 7-2 illustrates a basic process

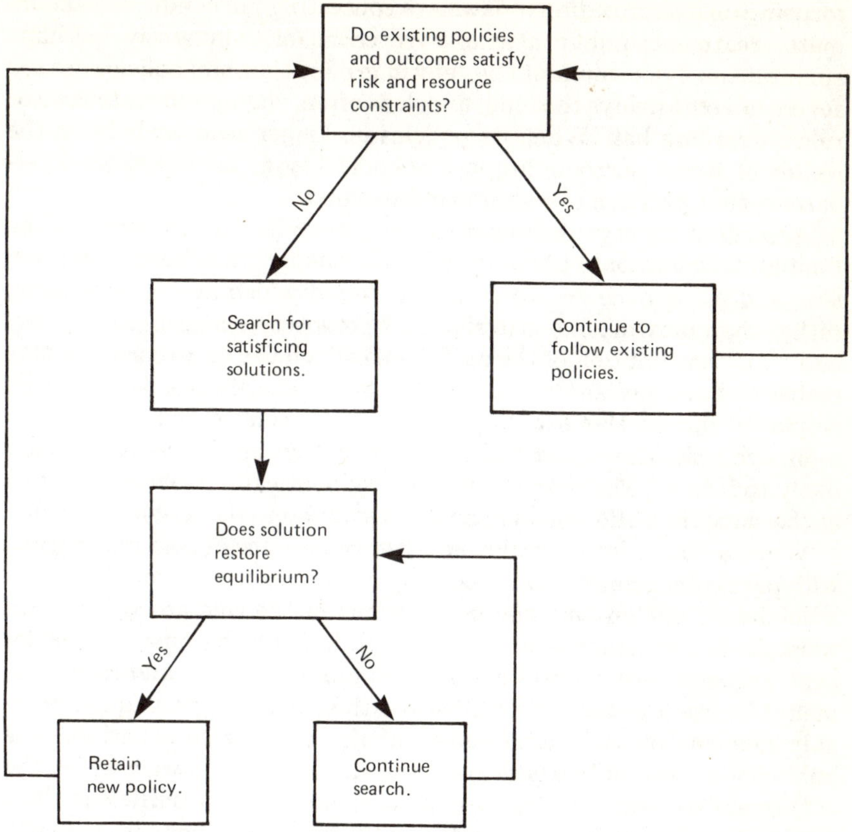

Figure 7-2. A Process Model of Policy Change in Criminal Courts

model based on the seminal work of March and Simon (1958) and Cyert and March (1963).

Bail and disposition policies are conceived as the means courts use to effect an approximate equilibrium between their environmental concerns and their detention resources. As long as these constraints are satisfied, the scope and severity of pretrial sanctions remain largely the same from one time to another. Environmental factors are assumed to be the primary causes of policy change and central considerations in the selection of alternatives.

This initial state of equilibrium can be upset by a number of things. Some common ones include shifts in the volume or composition of arrests or crime patterns; inmate riots or a sudden rash of inmate suicides, homosexual rapes, or beatings in the jail; media attention focusing on overcrowding or lawsuits contesting jail conditions and inmate treatment; public alarms over crime or, conversely (perhaps simultaneously), complaints by reform groups that bail policies are too severe or court delays too long; and, less often, changes in state laws or rules regarding bail. When its policies no longer seem to balance the welter of forces surrounding it, the court begins to search for alternatives that promise to restore equilibrium.

According to organization theorists, search activity tends to be limited, focusing only on alternatives in the neighborhood of a problem, and stops once an alternative is found which meets satisficing, rather than maximizing, criteria. This perspective highlights the second major assumption of the model, one which lies at its core. For this model to have any analytical bite, it should specify the decision rule employed during this search process. It is assumed courts prefer to minimize risk. They choose policy options that are perceived as least likely to increase the changes of negative political repercussions while at the same time offering an immediate solution to the problem at hand.

When a public furor breaks out after the release of persons charged with particular crimes or an especially dramatic crime is committed by a defendant out on bail, the implications of the rule are straightforward. In most instances succeeding bail decisions become more stringent; recognizance releases are granted more sparingly and cash bails mount in size (Corman 1974). Whether this change is permanent probably depends on the vulnerability of the officials to sanctions, the publicity generated by these episodes, the seriousness with which the events are treated by influential actors, and whether sufficient slack exists in the jail to hold the additional volume of defendants who will have difficulty making bail.

The rule's implications are less clearcut and the process more complex when overcrowding is no longer politically tolerable or its detention capabilities become strained, or if the court faces significant challenges demanding liberalization of its bail practices. To avoid risk, courts are expected to search for options that will satisfy these shifts in constraints but shun drastic changes in bail practices as counter productive, since extensive reform would entail alterations in the existing distribution of substantive and symbolic benefits produced by the court's present bail policies. When jail problems arise, a valuable source of policy slack, and hence opportunities for adjustment, can normally be found in its disposition procedures.

Policy options in this area are preferred by courts to bail reform for three reasons. First, and most important, changes in bail policies introduce greater uncertainty and higher risks into the choice process than speedy trial programs because less consensus exists as to what constitutes effective and fair bail policies than regarding the importance of prosecuting and trying defendants as quickly as possible. Second, if the past is prologue when bails are set, many officials may harbor considerable doubt about the sagacity of releasing on their own recognizance persons accused of crimes or with prior criminal records who formerly would have been detained or at least forced to post a substantial bond. Given these concerns a more attractive choice will be the increasing of the tempo of dispositions, since detained defendants spend less time in jail while the perceived risks attending their release are not increased. Finally, courts often lack the institutional means to enforce new bail rules on recalcitrant members of the bench. Unless there is a clear and pressing reason to change bail habits, courts will try other alternatives before struggling to gain the cooperation of these officials in overhauling bail policies.

If various changes in disposition policies fail to stabilize the relation between risk and jail resources or if the court's current bail practices are criticized as too punitive, some changes in bail procedures may be required. Adoption of bail reform measures, nevertheless, need not result in dramatically less punitive policies. Many changes in court procedures can be made that fall short of sweeping reform but which will meet the court's need to satisfy the demands facing it. For example, it may establish a pretrial release agency to assist in evaluating defendants for recognizance release, but use the option so sparingly that the reform becomes merely symbolic (Dill, 1972). Another option is to have pretrial investigators review bails for detailed defendants on the basis that deserving defendants occasionally are passed over inadvertently for recognizance release during the rush of arraignments or their circumstances may change in some way while in jail and thus a lower bail or recognizance is warranted. Defendants whose bails are reduced and who subsequently gain their release benefit from this change, of course. But substantial change may be unlikely, since the pretrial release agency must second-guess many original bail decisions and persuade officials to change their minds if they set the bails or revise the bails set by their colleagues, and in either case they may be reluctant to do so very often.

If more than marginal changes are required, courts can still minimize the changes of political sanctions by tinkering with the size of their bails or by utilizing security bails more frequently if state or court rules permit it. The appearance of reform, and obviously to a degree its substance, can be achieved if customary bails are reduced as defendants receive a break in purchasing their release from custody. Security bonds remove the bondsman as a middleman in the pretrial release process and defendants may gain their freedom more readily than if they had to post surety bonds. But since defendants still deposit a sum of money before being released, the court does not appear quite as lenient as when recognizance releases are granted, and the risks of change are minimized accordingly. Political opposition may be reduced even further, since the elimination of bondsmen, long the bête noire of local justice in America, generally attracts considerable support within the legal community.

As each policy alternative is found and adopted, the choice process comes to a rest if equilibirum is reestablished. If not, the process resumes with the cycle of search and adoption repeating itself, using the same general rule of risk avoidance to select alternatives, until a new balance is struck. Whether policy revisions increase or decrease the incidence and punitiveness of pretrial sanctions, and to what degree, quite clearly depends on the nature of the environmental shock disturbing the status quo and the court's perception of its strength and possible consequences if it ignores it. An equally important factor influencing the court's response is the kind and amount of slack existing in the pretrial sanctioning process as a whole. Slow-moving or quick disposition procedures and the relationship between detention resources and the factors affecting the inflow and outflow of prisoners structure a court's array of policy options and thus the nature of the policy changes it makes in reacting to environmental disturbances.

The following case study of Detroit illustrates the process of change in a large urban court. It provides not only an interesting example of this process, but also lays a basis for a more elaborated model resting on the concepts and assumptions discussed in these first two sections.[2]

A CASE STUDY OF POLICY CHANGE IN DETROIT'S FELONY COURT

The Political Setting: 1960-1973

Recorder's Court has jurisdiction over felony cases arising within the city of Detroit. Its thirteen judges in 1972 were elected to six-year terms through nonpartisan elections. This recruitment mechanism tied the bench to the city's politics, which, beginning in 1961 and extending through 1973, pivoted about the issues of crime, disorder, race, and policy conduct.

Mass arrests by the police in 1960, one year before a mayoral election, played a central part in the incumbent's unexpected defeat. A police raid of an illegal drinking place touched off the 1967 riots. In the spring, shortly before the July Riot, a recall campaign against the mayor was started by homeowner groups charging that he had failed to stem the rise in crime. Both the 1969 and 1973 mayoral contests pitted white, former law enforcement officials against black candidates. A survey in 1971 found that over 50 percent of Detroit's white residents and nearly 45 percent of its black residents felt that crime was the city's most important problem. During 1972, when six of Recorder's Court judges ran for reelection, the city's political divisions shattered its nonpartisan facade. According to one account,

> Although the nonpartisan character of the election blurred lines of cleavage somewhat, the election process reflected many of the basic divisions in the political life of the city—labor versus business, black versus white, liberal versus conservative. According to a newspaper report, one candidate told a white homeowner's group, "It's them against us." "Them" included the UAW, superliberals, and those who wanted more black judges. (Eisenstain and Jacob, 1976, p. 141)

In this setting, where caution would seem the wisest counsel, Recorder's Court nevertheless greatly expanded its use of recognizance release during 1972. For four years the annual proportion of felony defendants freed through personal or recognizance bail had steadily hovered at about 33 percent, but in 1972 the rate jumped to nearly half of all the defendants. The major reason for this change was a civil complaint filed by a group of liberal and radical attorneys in 1971 challenging the legality of overcrowding in the Wayne County Jail. This suit was heard by a three-judge panel of the Wayne County Circuit Court which ultimately imposed a population limit on the jail. The case concluded at a time when Recorder's Court had depleted almost all other solutions to the jail problem and thus was compelled to liberalize its bail policies because it was responsible in large measure for the jail's overcrowded condition. In tracing the evolution of the court's actions it is best to begin with the initial impetus behind these changes.

The Sources of Disequilibrium

Caseloads, the volume of defendants, or docket size figure prominently in many analyses of urban court processes (Blumberg, 1967; Skogan, 1974). Although the model in this study does not rely quite as heavily on this variable, massive increases in Recorder's Court's docket during the late 1960s can be little ignored or lightly dismissed in understanding the factors provoking changes in its policies. The magnitude of these increases can be found in the number of felony warrants issued annually in the city. Figure 7-3 quickly reveals that the period from 1967 through 1973 was far from placid in Recorder's Court.

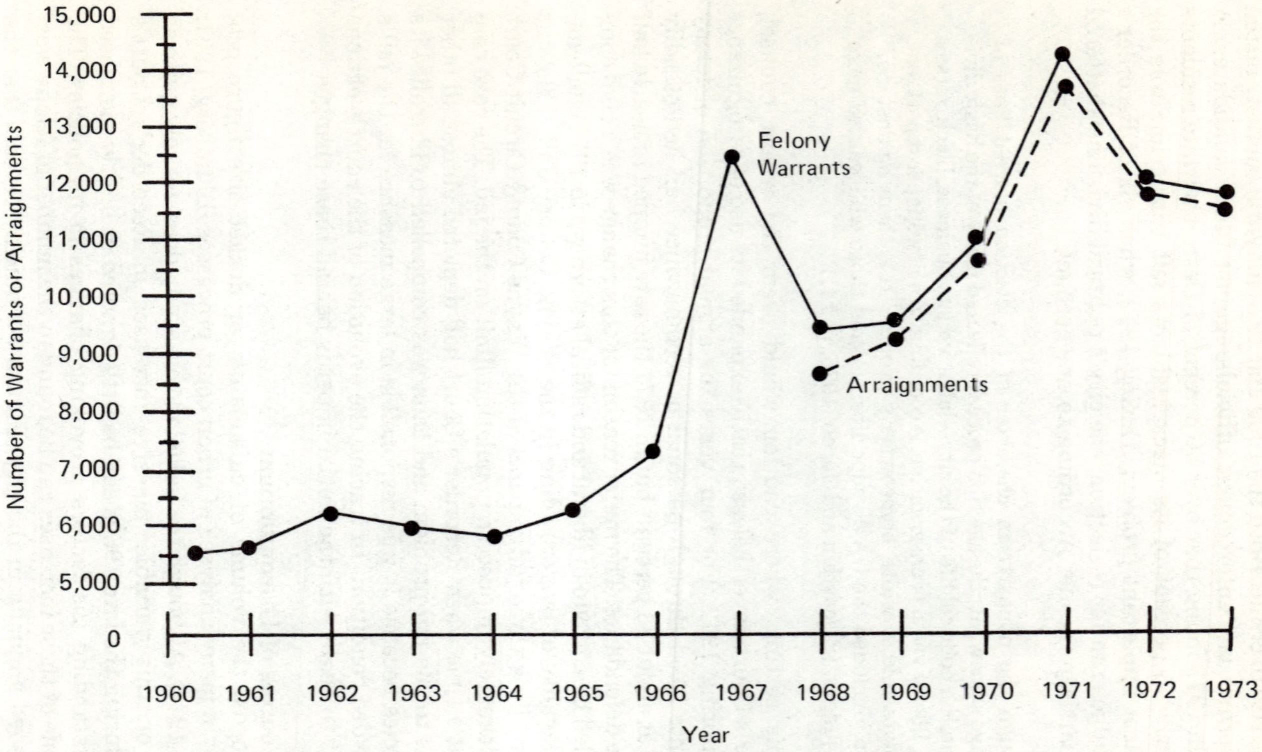

Figure 7-3. Number of Felony Warrants and Defendants Arraigned on Felony Charges in Detroit: 1960-1973

The upheaval of the 1967 riot and the thousands of arrests accompanying it had a sharp impact on the number of felony warrants. Over 12,500 warrants were issued in 1967, about 5,100 more than during the preceding year. While the total for 1968 dropped from this peak, it was still greater than any other year before the riot. The number of warrants then resumed its climb from this plateau until 1971, when it lurched upward once more, reaching an all-time high of nearly 14,300 warrants. Although warrant volumes fell in 1972 and again in 1973, they still remained at levels that were within a few hundred warrants of the 1967 total.

Arraignments, of course, followed the same path as warrants, as shown by the second trend line in Figure 7-3. They are also more accurate and appropriate measures of the court's docket size, since not all warrants result in arrest or subsequent arraignment (for 1968 through 1973 this proportion averaged 3.5 percent of all warrants). Information about arraignment volume only goes back to 1968 and the court's annual reports include pertinent data on the kinds of charges lodged against felony defendants only for the years 1970-1973. Despite these limitations, Table 7-1 breaks down Detroit's bail docket according to arraignments for major offense categories and yields an explanation for the sharp rise in case volume in 1971.

Rioting during the summer of 1967 indisputably lay behind the steep increase in felony arraignments for that year. This was not the case four years later, when the number of arraigned defendants in 1971 leapt by over 3,000 persons compared to the previous year. According to Table 7-1 dramatic changes in the composition of the court's docket lay behind this increase. Between 1970 and 1971 the proportion of charges involving either crimes against persons or property fell from 70.6 percent to 57.5 percent, while narcotics charges rose by nearly 10 percentage points and weapon charges by 3.5 percent. Interestingly the proportion of defendants with other cases pending before the court or with prior arrests dropped during this time. Little change took place in the percentage of felony defendants on probation or parole for other offenses. These background characteristics obviously suggest that defendants in 1971 were somewhat less likely on the whole to be recidivistic—an important consideration in most bail decisions.

Nearly 80 percent of the additional defendants in 1971 were accused of narcotics offenses, most likely possession charges, or carrying a concealed weapon.[3] Compared to most other offenses, these kinds of charges generally involve more vigorous and active use of police discretion in apprehending offenders. They are more often "proactive"

Table 7-1. Composition of Bail Dockets in Detroit: 1970-1973

Charge at Arraignment	*1970*		*1971*		*1972*		*1973*	
	Number of Defendants	*Percent*	*Number of Defendants*	*Percent*	*Number of Defendants*	*Percent*	*Number of Defendants*	*Percent*
Weapon	1,184	11.2	2,050	14.7	2,255	19.0	2,277	19.7
Narcotics	1,274	12.0	3,042	21.9	2,333	19.7	2,256	19.5
Property	4,811	45.5	5,252	37.7	3,634	30.7	3,261	28.2
Personal	2,654	25.1	2,753	19.8	2,616	22.1	2,671	23.1
Other	651	6.1	818	5.9	1,000	8.5	1,099	9.5
Total	10,574	99.9	13,915	100.0	11,838	100.0	11,564	100.0
Proportion of Arraigned Defendants With:								
Other cases pending	16.8		14.5		11.4		13.8	
Prior record	53.8		44.3		45.7		46.9	
On probation/parole	14.8		14.6		17.2		15.9	

rather than "reactive" decisions because officers are acting on their own information, volition, and hunches. On the other hand, proactive decisions are amenable to departmental priorities, and sudden jumps in arrests for such crimes often spring from policy changes and decisions at higher levels (Wilson, 1968). Therefore it appears that some time during 1970-1971 the Detroit Police Department, probably in conjunction with the Wayne County Prosecutor's Office, which handled felony cases in Recorder's Court and had sole responsibility for determining warrant charges, decided to press for greater enforcement of narcotics and weapon laws. The result shows up quite clearly in the rapid rise in the number of persons arraigned on these charges. For the most part this policy remained in force through 1973, although weapon cases increased to the point where they equaled narcotics offenses.

Trends in the Jail

What were the consequences of these changes for the jail? Considering the tidal wave of defendants coursing through Detroit's criminal justice system at this time, overcrowding certainly would come as no surprise. Indeed, if it existed, it would be expected to get worse. But, oddly enough, this did not occur. Figure 7-4 plots the average daily population in the Wayne County Jail, which functioned primarily as a detention facility for Recorder's Court.[4] Unhappily, information for 1968 was not available.

As this figure quickly makes apparent, the daily inmate population remained very nearly the same for 1969 and 1970, about 1,400 prisoners. It is well to recall that during the same period the number of arraignments rose by almost 1,500 cases. The next year, when the number of defendants rocketed to a record high, the jail population dropped. Moreover, this decline continued until the daily average in 1973 was about half that of 1971 and a scant 40 percent of the 1969-1970 average. Before 1972 the jail had been overcrowded; but since its design or rated capacity was 813 prisoners, it could be viewed as actually underutilized afterward.[5]

The reason behind the drop in the jail's population in 1972 is not shrouded in mystery. The civil suit filed the previous year resulted in a judgment mandating that after December 31, 1972, the jail population could not exceed its rated capacity; if it did, the sheriff, who bore administrative responsibility for the facility, would be held in contempt of court. Since Recorder's Court accounted for most of the jail's population, it took certain steps to eliminate overcrowding, and for the most part this meant increasing the use of recognizance release or personal bonds.

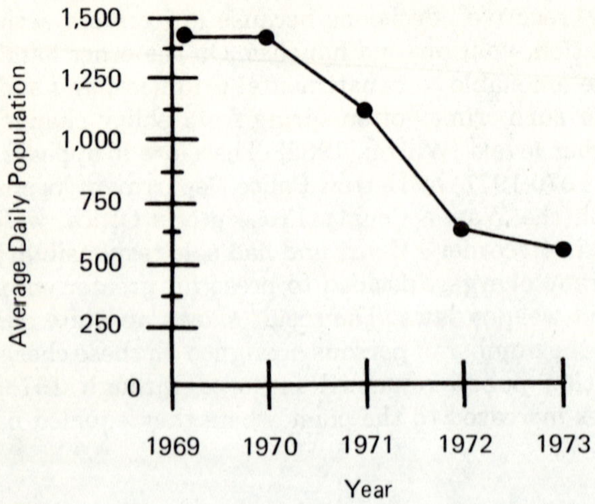

Figure 7-4. Average Daily Population of the Wayne County Jail: 1969-1973

But much more important is the fact that before 1972 Recorder's Court tried to cope with its mounting caseload and the overcrowded jail by quickening its tempo of dispositions. Equally as interesting is the other factor that, until the jail case was concluded, Detroit's court was surprisingly successful in meeting this challenge *without* changing its bail practices. Thus the larger puzzle is not why Recorder's Court eventually revised these practices as much as determining how and why it was able and willing to avoid this decision for so long.

A Policy Anomaly

For four years roughly the same proportion of felony defendants were granted recognizance release each year. Despite a rapidly expanding bail docket, changes in the mix of offenses, an overall decline in the recidivistic backgrounds of defendants, and an overcrowded jail, the percentage stayed at 33 to 34 percent. In 1972, when the population lid was placed on the jail, this proportion shot up to 48 percent and reached 49 percent in 1973. Yet, as Figure 7-5 shows, Recorder's Court's reluctance to use recognizance release more extensively until it was absolutely necessary actually exacerbated its problems, because the overall release rate for defendants fell during 1968-1971.

In 1968 the overall release rate was 85 percent, but by 1971 it had fallen to 71 percent. Behind this decline was the collapse in Detroit's surety bond market. Bondsmen freed about 81 percent of all defend-

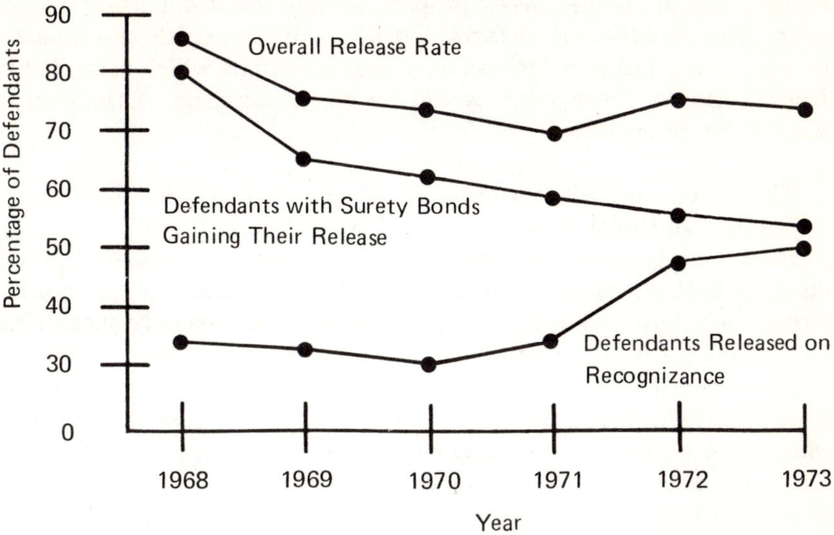

Figure 7-5. Release Rates for Felony Defendants in Detroit: 1968-1973

ants requiring surety bonds for their release during 1968. This was the market's high watermark, for by 1971 the proportion plummeted to 58 percent. Liberalization of Detroit's bail practices, moreover, did not impede the bondsmen's skidding performance as their release rate continued to drop, sinking to nearly 50 percent by 1973. The extent of this change should not be passed over quickly. In six years the release rate for bondsmen fell by 30 percentage points. Regrettably it is unkown whether defendants were less able to afford surety bonds, if bondsmen grew more strict in accepting customers, or whether the surety market as a whole changed in some way (fewer bondsmen, for example).[6] Similarly, data on whether Recorder's Court increased the size of its bails, which also would have had a negative effect on the surety release rate, were unavailable.

This discussion has uncovered some obviously contradictory trends. The volume of felony defendants rose dramatically before 1972, but the jail population, which would be expected to grow accordingly, remained quite stable and then declined. In the meantime, the court's bail policies regarding recognizance releases did not change and therefore the trend in the jail population cannot be attributed to this factor. Furthermore, if Recorder's Court had *reduced* its amounts for surety bonds, so defendants could post them more easily and promptly, this policy was undercut by the behavior of the city's surety market, which steadily freed proportionately fewer defendants every year. The only other major factor left which might explain the anomaly of a declining jail population under the conditions which prevailed in Detroit during these years would be an acceleration of the court's disposition procedures.

The Process of Adaptation: Taking Up Policy Slack

Beginning in 1969, Recorder's Court instituted a number of policy changes that effectively maintained and then altered the balance between the inflow and outflow of jail prisoners. Remarkably successful, these changes were prompted initially by the court's long backlog of untried cases (to some extent a carryover from the 1967 riots), a swiftly growing trial docket, and by conditions in the jail. These changes took place in three stages. During the first phase, encompassing 1969 and 1970, Recorder's Court attempted to quicken the pace at which it disposed of its cases.

Jail problems—overcrowding, physical deterioration, unsanitary conditions—were political issues in Detroit before litigation began early in 1971. Calls for a new jail were voiced by a public official in 1967, by the National Council on Crime and Delinquency in a report released in 1968, and by the Michigan Department of Corrections in 1969. Partly because of these expressions of concern and, as the court itself admitted, its "grossly overcrowded" condition and partly because of its own record backlog and delays in completing its trial dockets, Recorder's Court announced in 1969 that it would participate in a program with the Michigan Supreme Court in which the higher court would temporarily assign "visiting judges" from other jurisdictions to boost Detroit's ability to grapple with these difficulties.

Ultimately lasting four years, the program gave Recorder's Court an infusion of additional personnel to handle the burgeoning number of arraignments, preliminary examinations, and trials. As a further measure the court encouraged more guilty pleas to hasten the movement of cases. The year before this announcement 55 percent of Detroit's felony defendants pleaded guilty. By 1971, guilty pleas had risen to 65 percent. Because of these two changes the average daily population in the jail for 1970 nearly equaled the 1969 figure despite a 15 percent increase in the number of defendants arraigned in the court.

The second stage began the following year when the court reversed its disposition priorities and created a release on recognizance program. During 1971, as the deluge of felony defendants swept through the court, the jail population declined even though the court's caseload had risen sharply and its bail policies remained the same as in earlier years. Although some of this decline undoubtedly stemmed from the court's expanded capacity to dispose of its cases more quickly, an important contribution came from a change in its disposition priorities after the jail suit was filed in January 1971.

Prior to this Recorder's Court put a higher priority on trying defendants who were at liberty and a lower one on jailed defendants. Its rationale rested on the assumption that by trying freed defendants first the chances that they would commit additional crimes while out on bail would be reduced. But the price for this "freed first" rule in the face of a rapidly mounting caseload was that, despite additional personnel on the bench and more guilty pleas, the court still could not reduce the jail's population quickly enough to keep pace with the influx of newly detained defendants.

Recorder's Court, caught between its responsibility for the jail's overcrowding and community expectations that it protect Detroit citizens from crime, was hesitant to increase its use of recognizance to siphon off the flow of defendants into the jail. In its Annual Report for the year, the court explained its dilemma.

> Externally, the court's task during 1971 was complicated by the overcrowded conditions at the Wayne County Jail. The public none-the-less, clamored for protection from recidivistic felons. (Annual Report, Recorders Court of the City of Detroit, 1971 Annual Report, p. 1)

The jail complaint encouraged Recorder's Court to reconsider at least its disposition priorities, but a suicide, several other attempts, and a death from causes related to the jail's poor health facilities during the early part of 1971 added to the political pressure to make these changes. With few choices left, except a revision of its bail policies, the court switched its trial priorities to "jailed first." In its report the court stated:

> New priorities in the assignment of cases for trial were developed. Precedence was given to jail cases to the *virtual exclusion* of cases where the defendant was at liberty pending trial [emphasis added]. (Annual Report, Recorders Court of the City of Detroit, 1971 Annual Report, p. 1)

The nearly 20 percent drop in the jail population betwen 1970 and 1971 reveals the effectiveness of this change. Also the court's new Release on Recognizance Program may have had some impact. It started in February, after receiving federal funding in late 1970. Initially the program interviewed only defendants in the jail detained on cash bails to ascertain whether they could be released on personal bonds or on lower cash bails. No data were available on how many defendants the program released in this way during its first year. But it is important to note that the program's personnel did not participate in the bail hearings held at arraignment—a key point in the proceedings that might have reduced the flow of defendants into the jail. Instead, they were assigned to revising the bails of detained defendants; this could only affect the outflow of prisoners.

By 1972 little slack was left in the court's disposition processes. Guilty pleas accounted for almost two-thirds of its total dispositions and 94 percent of its convictions. (In 1968, 84 percent of the court's convictions were through guilty pleas.) Bench personnel had been bolstered by the assignment of forty visiting judges who, over the course of a year, were rotated through the court and in 1972 handled 21 percent of the court's total dispositions. An ROR program had been established and disposition priorities reversed. Some idea of how these changes improved the speed of Recorder's Court docket process can be found in its 1968 Annual Report, where the court stated:

> In bail cases the average length of time involved from inception to completion is approximately six months. In jail cases the time is approximately three months. (Annual Report, Recorders Court of the City of Detroit, 1968 Annual Report, p. 1)

Contrast these times with the finding by Eisenstein and Jacob (1976, p. 233) that the median number of days from arrest to trial courtroom disposition for their sample of Detroit defendants in 1972 was a mere seventy-one days—about two months and a week from start to finish. A separate calculation based on their data for only those defendants who were detained in the jail during the entire predisposition period resulted in a median of just twenty-seven days (Flemming, 1977, p. 293). Within a span of five years, then, Recorder's Court had slashed perhaps as much as two to four months off the time it took to dispose of its cases.

Finally, as Time Runs Out . . .

By the time circuit court decreed in March 1972 that the jail population had to be reduced, Detroit's criminal court had few other alternatives to changing its recognizance practices. With only about nine months before the ruling took effect, Recorder's Court had little time to find and put into effect further changes in its disposition processes that could be expected to boost the jail's turnover rate to the point where its daily population, which averaged 1,127 in 1971, would be cut to less than 813 by the end of the year. Yet, despite the ruling and limited options, Recorder's Court held back from revising its bail policies until the middle of 1972.

Neither the start of the jail case in January 1971 nor its conclusion in March of 1972 sparked immediate changes in the proportion of defendants released on recognizance. This is rather surprising, since this would have solved the jail problem quite handily, although, of course, there was also some risk attached to this option. Without the need to raise any money or to rely on a bondsman's largesse for their freedom, defendants who might have been detained for whatever length of time could be freed immediately after their arraignments and relieve the population pressure on the jail. But this did not occur, as shown in Figure 7-6, which plots the monthly proportion of felony defendants granted personal bond for the years 1971-1973.

According to the judge who presided over Recorder's Court in 1971, the jail case "brought home the conditions of the jail to the bench." He also felt that the judges had decided personal bonds had to be granted more extensively, since the jail population had to be reduced and Recorder's Court was "responsible for the vast majority" of the jail's inhabitants. While Figure 7-6 indicates that an upward trend in the proportion of felony defendants released on recognizance began in 1971, it was quite irregular, and not until the last six months of 1972 did it level off at about 52 percent. This suggests that, despite the unanimity of concern expressed by Detroit's judges, many still harbored some reluctance to reduce their use of surety bonds and switch to recognizance. Another possibility was that the bench did not fully and immediately appreciate the implications of the jail ruling and it took a while before a consensus emerged as to what the court should do.

Another factor discouraging the court's use of personal bonds was the historically high capias rate for these bonds compared to surety bonds. The proportion of defendants with personal bonds for whom arrest warrants or capiases were issued because of failure to appear in court ranged from three to four times greater than that for defendants released on surety bonds for the years 1968-1971, as Figure 7-7 shows. The Release on Recognizance Program evidently helped reduce the capias rate, since Recorder's Court lacked any means of notifying defendants about their dates and had relied simply on their "signed promise" to appear in court. In September 1971 the program established a "follow-up section" in order to "check on the whereabouts of defendants and to keep defendants informed of their court dates." According to Figure 7-7 the program closed the gap between personal and surety bond capias rates, but the judges' experiences of having trial or hearing dockets delayed or disrupted because

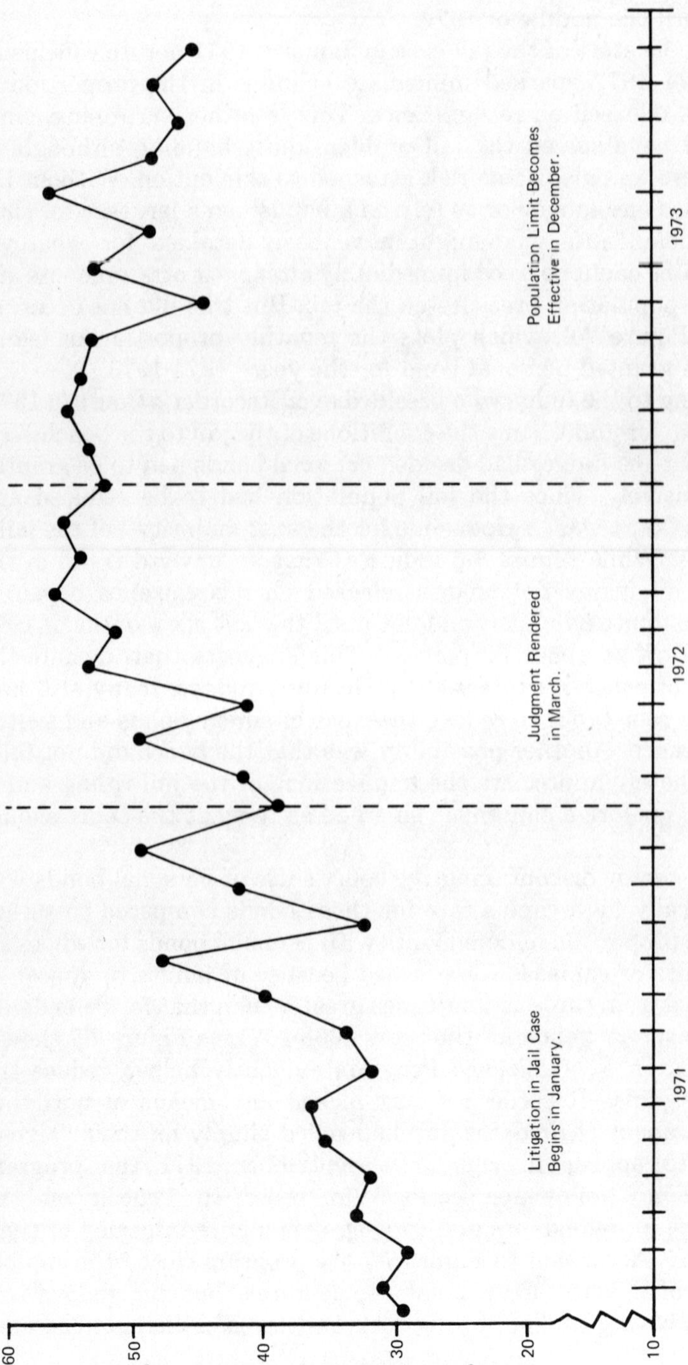

Figure 7-6. Monthly Trends in Percentage of Personal Recognizances Granted to Felony Defendants in Detroit

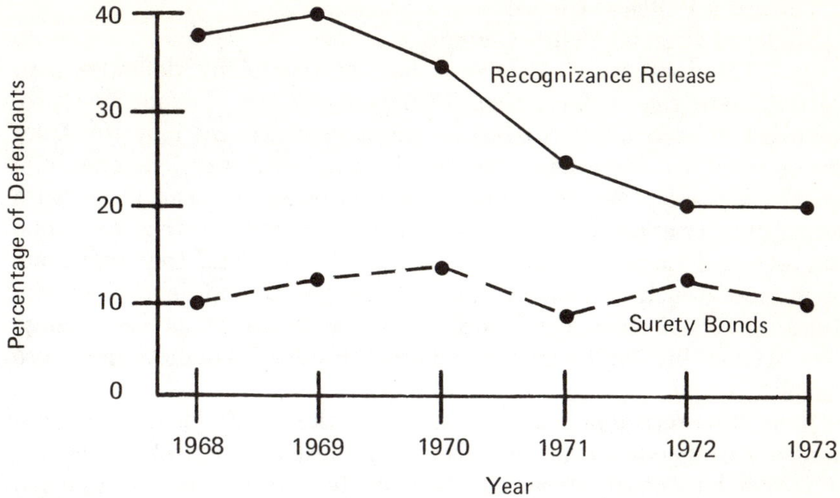

Figure 7-7. Reported Capias Rate by Type of Release: 1968-1973

of absent or tardy defendants probably weakened the credibility of personal bonds as an effective bail option.

Until the middle of 1972, then, Recorder's Court put off major revisions of its bail policies. Instead it focused on quickening the pace of its dispositions. "Speedy trials" have a number of political advantages which the court probably found appealing. Quick and efficient justice simultaneously attracts the support of law-and-order groups and liberal, prodefendant groups. It reduces backlogs, cuts the time spent in jail for defendants who cannot post bail, and lessens the probability of bail crime. Prodefendant groups are placated, since the defendants do not spend months in jail awaiting trial. Those demanding stern law enforcement are appeased because long predisposition periods are thought to reduce the likelihood of conviction as victims and witnesses get discouraged, their memories fade, or they change residences. If Detroit's court had turned immediately to its bail policy to solve the jail population problem, it probably would have ignited conflict. Accordingly, shortening the time between arrest and trial was a more enticing alternative. The jail case eventually compelled Detroit's court to contract the scope of its bail practices and came at a time when it had few alternatives left but to release a substantially greater proportion of defendants on their own recognizance.

Toward a Political Choice Model of Pretrial Policy Change

As 1972 drew to a close, over half of the felony defendants in Detroit were released on their own recognizance. Disposition procedures had been accelerated to the point where the median time from arraignment to disposition for jailed defendants was less than one month. These represented substantial improvements over the court's earlier policies and greatly reduced the breadth of its pretrial sanctions and lessened their severity. The string of events and the conditions surrounding each of Detroit's policy changes provide sufficient empirical material that the simple process model of policy change presented earlier can be elaborated upon. Figure 7-8 depicts this more complex model.

A court's pretrial policies emerge as political demands and expectations are weighed against detention capabilities. Mounting caseloads and other factors can upset this balance, but neither bail nor disposition policies need be changed so long as the jail can readily hold additional prisoners, that is, if there is enough jail slack to soften the impact of these changes. In the event the jail becomes overcrowded (and this appraisal is fundamentally a political judgment reflecting the mood and character of the court's environment), the court may begin to reevaluate its policies. At this point it faces a number of choices, each of which carries political consequences. The argument here has been that courts prefer to revise policies or practices that will placate their environment and minimize the risk of sanctions. Given the existence of disposition slack, measures cutting courtroom delay will be adopted rather than liberalizing bail policies. To some extent this choice may be contingent upon whether the court also sets bail for large numbers of misdemeanants. They are more readily released on recognizance than alleged felons, and the court may prefer to avoid needlessly ruffling its relations with defense attorneys and prosecutors by changing its disposition procedures. In this instance bail reform in the guise of pretrial release agencies may be adopted to help reduce the jail population. When the docket is filled with felony cases, however, the speedy trial option will be an attractive alternative to bail changes.

The original amount of slack in a court's disposition process, the effectiveness of the new program in reducing it, and the persistence of concern over the jail influence whether the court will have to take any further steps. If it finds additional changes are needed, it will continue to look in the neighborhood of those policy areas affecting the outflow of jailed defendants. Disposition priorities may be reversed and bail reviews instituted, as Detroit illustrated, before the court changes its release practices at arraignment.

Finally, if these efforts fail, the court must consider reducing the

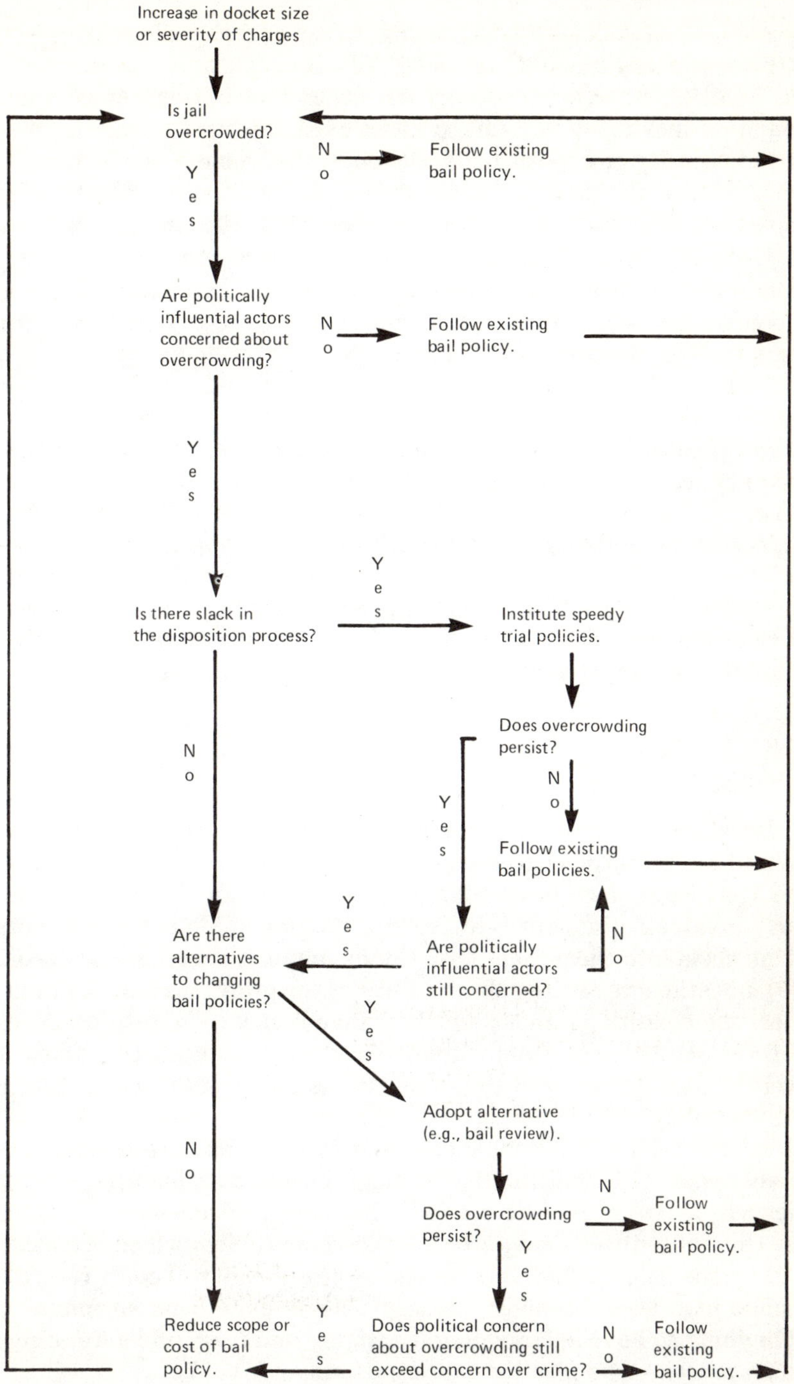

Figure 7-8. A Political Choice Model of Pretrial Policy Changes

scope of its bail policies by decreasing its use of cash bails or by lowering the customary amounts of these bails. Recognizance is a more efficient solution to overcrowding than other bail options since some defendants inevitably will fail to make even the most meager money bail and security or deposit bails, although they remove the bondsman from the scene and do not produce dramatically different release rates compared to sureties (Conklin and Meagher, 1973; Flemming, Kohlfield, and Uhlman, 1978). The court's decision to change its bail policy depends on the balance of concern expressed by important actors in the court's environment regarding continued overcrowding of the jail versus the fear of crime in the city. In Detroit this balance was tipped decisively by the judgment in the jail case. Moreover, by the time this decision was made, the jail had developed a sufficiently notorious image and reputation so that Recorder's Court probably perceived that jail conditions were a paramount issue in Detroit despite the gravity of its crime problem. If overcrowding, however, is seen as less important than the crime problem, the court will continue to follow its existing bail practices. This means that, since overcrowding will be tolerated, the court will be given the slack it needs to support these practices, and that overcrowding will decline only as changes occur in the other variables affecting the inflow and outflow of jail prisoners.

CONCLUSIONS

The dynamics of policy change tend to be slighted as researchers try to map and measure the characteristics shaping the many decision processes that take place in criminal courts. Although these efforts are clearly invaluable in identifying sets of factors and in some instances casting them into theoretical form (for example, Eisenstein and Jacob, 1977), questions regarding the stability of the processes and their outcomes, the conditions under which change is most likely to occur, or the direction of change remain unanswered. In concluding this study it is well to consider some of the implications for future research that a focus on policy change poses.

The need for longitudinal, diachronic, or time series research is obviously apparent if the stability or instability of decision processes or policies in courts is to be determined. In many, perhaps most, jurisdictions this constitutes a major data collection problem which is exacerbated by the poor quality and questionable reliability of court records. In some instances, however, these problems have been surmounted and in doing so have led to valuable insights and fresh understandings of such processes as plea bargaining (Heumann, 1977).

Somewhat less obvious is the possibility that the process through which court policies change may be different from those which occur daily in courtrooms. The manner in which pleas are negotiated, sentences meted out, motions granted or denied, or bails set takes place through various, often different modes of choice (Mohr, 1976). Regardless of their form, however, these processes involve frequent, ongoing decisions; they are customary grist for the court mill. Policy changes tend to be less frequent and more serendipitous. Accordingly, models of choice identified as characteristic of other decision processes may be less applicable when it is the outcomes of these processes or the processes themselves that are the target of change or the bone of contention.

The purpose of this chapter has been to identify a mode of choice employed by courts when altering policies. It does not purport to explain how judges set bail for individual defendants or the manner in which bail setting hearings are conducted; this has been done elsewhere (Flemming, 1977). Policy-changing modes, it has been argued, are likely to be influenced more directly by environmental considerations than policy-implementing modes, since, like other public policies or programs, court policies distribute benefits and attempts to revise them mean an alteration in "who gets what." As a consequence conflict and risk become major characteristics of the process of policy change.

The alacrity with which a court acts and the kinds of revisions adopted reflect not just environmental conditions but the array of options available to it. Particularly in the case of the second factor there is a subtle implication that deserves emphasis. Court policies interact with one another (as in the case of bail and court delay) and the choices available to courts in coping with their problems are structured by these interdependencies. This holds open the possibility that over time changes in one policy may preclude alternatives in another that were viable at an earlier period. In other words, the nature of the court's response when confronted with the need to revise a policy will be shaped by previous decisions regarding other policies. As a result the content of "reforms" may vary not only among courts but over time for individual courts.

NOTES

1. A useful and thorough review of the bail reform literature which questions whether the effects of reform have been satisfactorily established has been done by the National Center for State Courts (1975).

2. The historical account and data indicating the changes in policy for this case study come from a more extended analysis in Flemming (1977). Annual reports published by Recorder's Court and unpublished data from the Wayne County Office of the Sheriff were used in preparing the tables and figures for this analysis.

3. Slightly more than 62 percent of the narcotics cases involved possession of heroin (Flemming, 1977:42).

4. According to records kept by the sheriff's office, 64 percent of the jail inmates were awaiting disposition or sentencing in Recorder's Court.

5. This period of "underutilization" proved shortlived. A full discussion is not possible here, but it is important to note that after 1973 the jail population hovered for a time around its legal limit and then began to climb until it regularly exceeded 1,000 prisoners during the fall of 1975. This set the stage for another major crisis which climaxed with the passage of a bond referendum to build a second jail, with a capacity for 550 prisoners.

6. In Flemming (1977) the reasons for the declining performance of Detroit's bondsmen are analyzed and compared to Baltimore in terms of how court policies expose bondsmen to greater or lesser risks of forfeitures and how the size and competitiveness of the surety market affect their behavior.

REFERENCES

Beeley, Arthur L. (1966). *The Bail System in Chicago*. Chicago: University of Chicago Press.

Blumberg, Abraham (1967). *Criminal Justice*. Chicago: Quadrangle Books.

Conklin, John E., and Meagher, Dermot (1973). "The Percentage Deposit Bail System: An Alternative to the Professional Bondsman." 1 *Journal of Criminal Justice* 299.

Corman, Lois (1974). "The Effect of Publicity on Bail Setting Behavior." Unpublished paper, Department of Political Science, Pennsylvania State University, University Park.

Cyert, Richard M., and March, James G. (1963). *A Behavioral Theory of the Firm*. Englewood Cliffs, N.J.: Prentice-Hall.

Dill, Forrest D. (1972). *Bail and Bail Reform: A Sociological Study*. Ph.D. dissertation, Department of Sociology, University of California, Berkeley.

Eisenstein, James, and Jacob, Herbert (1976). *Felony Justice: An Organizational Analysis of Criminal Courts*. Boston: Little, Brown.

Flemming, Roy B. (1977). *Allocating Freedom and Punishment: Pre-Trial Release Policies in Detroit and Baltimore*. Ph.D. dissertation, Department of Political Science, University of Michigan, Ann Arbor.

———; Kohlfield, Carol; and Uhlman, Thomas M. (1978). "The Limitations of Bail Reform: A Quasi-Experimental Analysis." Unpublished paper.

Foote, Caleb (1954). "Compelling Appearance in Court: Administration of Bail in New York City." 102 *University of Pennsylvania Law Review* 1031.

——— (1958). "A Study of the Administration of Bail in New York City." 106 *University of Pennsylvania Law Review* 693.

——— (1965). "The Coming Constitutional Crisis in Bail." 113 *University of Pennsylvania Law Review* 959.

Friedman, Lee S. (1976). "The Evolution of a Bail Reform." 7 *Policy Science* 281.

Goldfarb, Ronald (1965). *Ransom*. New York: Harper and Row.

________ (1975). *Jails*. Garden City, N.Y.: Anchor Press/Doubleday.

Heumann, Milton (1977). *Plea Bargaining*. Chicago: University of Chicago Press.

Levin, Martin (1977). *Urban Politics and the Criminal Courts*. Chicago: University of Chicago Press.

March, James G., and Simon, Herbert A. (1958). *Organizations*. New York: John Wiley & Sons.

Mohr, Lawrence B. (1976). "Organizations, Decisions, and Courts." 10 *Law & Society Review* 621.

National Center for State Courts (1975). *An Evaluation of Policy Related Research on the Effectiveness of the Pre-Trial Release Programs*. Denver: Center for State Courts.

Skogan, Wesley G. (1974). "Traffic and the Courts: Social Change and Organizational Response." In Herbert Jacob, ed. *The Potential for Reform of Criminal Justice*. Beverly Hills, Calif.: Sage.

Thomas, Wayne H. (1976). *Bail Reform in America*. New York: McGraw-Hill.

________ (1977). *Pre-Trial Release Programs*. Washington, D.C.: National Institute of Law Enforcement and Criminal Justice.

Thompson, James D. (1967). *Organizations in Action*. New York: McGraw-Hill.

Warwick, Donald P. (1975). A Theory of Public Bureaucracy. Cambridge, Mass.: Harvard University Press.

Wilson, James Q. (1968). *Varieties of Police Behavior*. Cambridge, Mass.: Harvard University Press.

Chapter Eight

Thinking about Plea Bargaining

Milton Heumann

The attempt to unravel the processes of case disposition in the local criminal court, with particular emphasis on plea bargaining, has become a major concern of social scientists in the past ten years. A wealth of descriptive, prescriptive, and normative material has been generated and, on the whole, our understanding of what goes on in the criminal courts, and why, has been markedly improved. Tucked away in this literature are some rather intriguing concepts relevant to an understanding of the plea bargaining process. The implications of these concepts, however, have never been fully developed. The aim of this essay is to elaborate upon three such concepts: resource constraints, going rates, and legal culture, broadly defined. After discussing each independently, I will attempt to integrate them and elaborate upon their role in explaining variations in the plea bargaining process across jurisdictions. Then I will discuss their implications for two very important policy-related issues: sentencing reform and deterrence.

In "thinking about plea bargaining" and the plea bargaining literature in these more general terms, I will be less concerned with systematically reviewing the findings of studies of various jurisdictions than I will be with stepping away from the findings and consider-

[a]I would like to thank Jonathan Casper, Thomas Church, Peter Nardulli, Robert Aamoth, and Jane Schacter for their helpful comments on an earlier draft of this chapter. I also would like to thank the Institute for Public Policy Studies and the Office of the Vice President for Research at the University of Michigan for funding the transportation and transcribing costs for a series of interviews in Detroit, the results of which are briefly discussed herein.

ing their implications. This sort of theoretical stocktaking can both clarify what we have learned (much of what I will argue in this chapter is made less than explicit in the literature) and serve to guide future research efforts.

RESOURCE CONSTRAINTS AND PLEA BARGAINING

Much of the earlier academic, journalistic, and legal thought about plea bargaining was clouded by the misperception that plea bargaining was a relatively new phenomenon in criminal courts, a process necessitated by the burden of processing heavy caseloads. A golden age of full-fledged trials was assumed to have existed in the past and was assumed to be present, or possible and desirable, in jurisdictions not burdened with heavy caseloads.

A number of studies have called these notions into question. We have seen that trials have not historically accounted for most dispositions (Heumann, 1978, pp. 27-33, 156-57; Wishingrad, 1974; but see Alschuler, 1978a), that when employed they were abbreviated proceedings, falling far short of our conception of a full-fledged courtroom drama (Friedman, 1978, pp. 17-18), and that a low rate of trials and a high rate of guilty pleas[1] seem generally to have characterized both high- and low-volume jurisdictions (Feeley, 1975; Georgetown University Law Center Institute of Criminal Law and Procedure, 1977, pp. 16-24, Appendix A, 1-64; Heumann, 1978, pp. 27-33; Jacob, 1973, pp. 109-13).

Also relevant here are the various attempts that have been made to abolish plea bargaining. While trial rates have generally gone up in these jurisdictions what is most important to note is that guilty pleas remained the predominant mode of case disposition. New York State attempted to restrict plea bargaining by passing a stringent drug law and providing massive additional resources to courts. Trials rose from 6 percent to 16 percent of all dispositions for drug offenses, but 84 percent of the drug cases were still disposed of by nontrial alternatives (Association of the Bar of the City of New York, 1977, p. 17). Alaska abolished plea bargaining in August 1975. Prior to this action, 6 percent of all felonies in the state (and Alaska only processes about 2,000 felonies a year) were tried; after plea bargaining's abolition, somewhere between 8 percent and 9 percent of the cases were tried. The trial rate for misdemeanors rose from 3.4 percent to 5.6 percent (Gross, 1978, pp. 1, 13).[2] Similarly, jurisdictions which purport to have a low number of guilty pleas and a high number of trials have been found in fact to employ "functional equivalents" of trials. Thus in

Baltimore and Pittsburgh bench trials, which are rather routine procedures equivalent to guilty plea hearings in most jurisdictions, are frequently employed; in Los Angeles trials on preliminary hearing transcripts are, in effect, "slow pleas of guilty."[3]

Finally, findings concerning the centrality of the guilty plea, discussed in two recently published studies of European court systems (Baldwin and McConville, 1977; Goldstein and Marcus, 1977), are also important here. Baldwin and McConville set out to examine jury trial verdicts in Great Britain. They quickly learned that, in many cases where they had thought the defendant would go to trial, the defendant instead pled guilty. Subsequent interviews with defendants uncovered a plea bargaining process that strongly resembles that in the United States. Eighty-five percent of all convictions on indictable offenses in Great Britain result from guilty pleas (1978, p. 1), and though Baldwin and McConville focused on the coercive manner employed by some barristers to induce some of these pleas, their data also demonstrate that a sizable percentage of pleas would be tendered by defendants even if no pressure were brought to bear on them and even if no explicit assurance about sentence were made (1977, p. 28).[4]

Equally significant is Goldstein and Marcus's study of criminal case dispositions in France, Italy, and Germany. In these quasi-inquisitorial systems, defendants are not permitted to plead guilty, prosecutorial discretion is generally proscribed, and decisions about the defendants' guilt on the original charges are supposed to be made at trial. However, in practice, Goldstein and Marcus find that the case disposition processes for many offenders in these three nations are reasonably similar to those in the United States and that analogues to plea bargaining characterize the courts' decisions. Defendants plead by not raising even perfunctory objections in the course of abbreviated trials. As Goldstein and Marcus conclude,

> It is plain from our interviews that prosecutors and defense attorneys rely on a general awareness that cooperation will be rewarded with leniency and that decisions will be made benevolently for the defendant who is helpful to the state. Mutual patterns of acquiescence develop in which the accused and his counsel expect concessions, which are routinely granted by the prosecutor and the court. . . . All that is forbidden is that the arrangements be worked out in advance. Though there are important differences between a system that authorizes or condones plea bargains and one that allows them to operate only through tacit understandings or patterns of reciprocal expectation, the two systems are not as starkly opposed as stereotype would suggest (Goldstein and Marcus, 1977, pp. 278-79).

Collectively, the research on low volume, abolitionist, and European court systems suggests that the trial, rather than being the modal method of case disposition, is the exception. Some variant of plea bargaining or its functional equivalent is employed to dispose of many cases in all of these systems, including those in which plea bargaining was formally proscribed. To appreciate fully why these guilty pleas are so commonly tendered either as a result of explicit or implicit negotiations requires a detailed review of prosecutorial, judicial, defense attorney, and defendant incentives to participate in the plea bargaining process, a review already available in the literature, and one that is far beyond the scope and requirements of this chapter. Suffice it to say for our purposes here that court personnel have a mutual interest in avoiding the uncertainty of trial, that they share a common belief that many defendants have no credible factual and legal claims to make about the circumstances of their case, and that therefore they believe these defendants ought to plead guilty and benefit from the real (or at least perceived) reduction in sentence given the defendant who pleads as compared to the defendant who goes to trial.

We have, in short, moved away from a perspective that viewed trial courts as *trial* courts and that viewed plea bargaining as an aberrant, though necessary, practice in crowded courts. We now share a perspective that recognizes the centrality of negotiated pleas in most courts, and that explains the reliance on these negotiations in terms other than those based on limited resources. Nontrial dispositions are expected in courts independent of the court's case volume; trials, in a sense, are the exceptions and not the norm.

But care must be taken in digesting these findings. To argue that resource constraints[5] do not cause plea bargaining does not mean that such constraints do not influence case disposition patterns in the court. Resource constraints may affect the rate (at least at the margins) of plea bargaining, the use of dispositional alternatives such as the nolle, dismissal, diversion, pretrial screening, and so on, as well as a host of other factors that allow court personnel to process cases. Just as it was naive to believe that plea bargaining was simply an expedient employed to manage heavy caseloads, so too is it naive to ignore the likelihood that beyond certain points resource constraints do in fact affect disposition practices.

A fruitful way to illustrate this point is to imagine—or to construct—a hypothetical court system which, for want of a better term, I will call a "pure system." In this court, personnel have—within reasonable bounds—unlimited resources. Neither judges, defense attorneys, nor prosecutors would complain about an inability to handle their caseload; staffing is more than sufficient for each role incumbent to perform his/her task in the manner that professional norms dictate. Yet, if the plea bargaining literature is correct, if we can explain plea bargaining without reliance on case pressure, we would still expect that a core of cases within these pure systems would be resolved by either implicit or explicit plea bargaining or its analogues. Notwithstanding the ability of court participants to take cases to trial, defendants would still plead because of an expectation that they would fare better if they appear contrite; and court participants would expect pleas because they feel it makes little sense to enact a full-scale courtroom trial drama in a case where the outcome is a foregone conclusion.[6] Though it would be difficult to identify pure systems—we have no good measures of what constitutes "unlimited resources"[7]—in theory at least it seems plausible to construct such a system and to argue that it would still be characterized by a substantial amount of plea bargaining.

The fact that there is a core plea bargaining rate even in pure systems, however, does not mean that resource constraints cannot and do not affect plea bargaining. Many—maybe all—of the courts we have studied in recent years are "mixed" systems, courts in which resource allocations fall short of the unlimited resources level. How short? Again, it is impossible to tell because we do not know what these levels are. But in these mixed systems it is reasonable to expect that beyond some point resource constraints may in fact alter the plea bargaining process and/or other aspects of the case disposition process. For example, as the imbalance between personnel and caseload becomes greater, we would expect more and more changes in the ways cases are processed and possibly in the sentences meted out.

For the purpose of further developing this argument, it is helpful to posit a three-stage transition from a pure to a mixed system and to use caseload as a rough indicator of resource constraints.[8] In the first stage, within a pure system, the caseload begins to increase, but the increase has no effect on any aspect of the plea bargaining process, other than perhaps increasing the amount of work done within regularly scheduled court hours by court personnel. The guiding assumption here (and this is likely to be most true in a pure system) is that court personnel have excess capacity to process cases. In a sense this complements Feeley's argument that "regardless of caseload, there will always be *too many cases* for many of the participants in the system since most of them have a strong interest in being some place other than in court" (1975, p. 36; emphasis his). Viewed from the pure system wherein there were "just enough cases," the addition of more cases may be a burden, but it is well within the bounds of the potential capacity of the system. Or, to borrow Gillespie's (1975, p. 261) conclusion from his study of the relationship between court resources and court delay, there appears to be a "high elasticity of supply of court services.[9] Courts—even those at 'capacity'—retain the ability to process additional demand with existing resources."

The second stage in the transition from a pure to a mixed system begins when the increase in case volume exceeds the alleged and real capacity of court personnel to continue to do things as they had been done. It is at this stage that case pressure may affect plea bargaining practices. Trial rates may drop, dismissals may increase, and so on. But the outer bounds of this stage are set by what we might call "minimally tolerable" personnel/caseload ratios. By this I mean that, although resources are no longer unlimited, they are still sufficient or workable. A case in point might be the caseload limits demanded—under threat of a work stoppage—by several organizations representing indigent defendants in particular courts. Be it in New York City or Ann Arbor, Michigan, these attorneys were arguing that they simply could not accept any more cases, that some outer bound had to be set on their caseloads.[10] In this second stage, then, attorneys, prosecutors, and judges are working in less than ideal conditions but they can muddle through tolerably well. Unlike the first stage, however, case pressure has placed a strain on their resources, and in contrast to the limited core plea bargaining rate in the first stage, additional plea bargaining and/or other adjustments are made because of the case pressure.

In the third stage—a stage not necessarily reached—the imbalance between caseload and personnel becomes even greater, and major adjustments in the court's case processing system must be made. Holding all else constant, I would suspect that in this stage courts are most likely to be disproportionately characterized by the worst aspects of plea bargaining (that is, coerciveness brought to bear on the defendant, laxity in prosecuting serious offenders, a disproportionately high percentage of cases getting lost in the numbers mill of the court, and so on).

Taken alone this three-stage classification suggests certain important questions for further research. We should, for example, begin to think systematically about and estimate unlimited, minimal, and unmanageable resource levels for each role incumbent in the court.[11] These measures in turn would allow us to categorize courts along a resource sufficiency dimension and examine more systematically than we have in the past the effects of different resource levels on case disposition patterns.

But the three-stage classification really should not be "taken alone." By implication it suggests that in the "pure" state communities are equivalent, and that they will adjust to a "mixed" state in similar fashion. Neither assumption is necessarily correct; pure and mixed systems may differ as much among themselves as they do between stages. To clarify this point we must consider two other aspects of local criminal court case processing: the notion of a going rate in a jurisdiction, and the effect of the local legal culture on a court's practices.

GOING RATES

One of the most important themes that runs through the plea bargaining literature is the notion that defendants are sentenced more leniently—or at least expect to be sentenced more leniently—if they plead guilty rather than go to trial. This is a relative statement about sentencing and raises questions such as do defendants really fare better, and, if so, by how much? It is also the issue that prompts much of the debate about the propriety of plea bargaining, for in this reward for the plea are the seeds of a potentially coercive process that can force factually and/or legally innocent defendants to eschew their rights to a jury trial.

These are important questions, and they have received ample attention in the plea bargaining literature. What has received less attention is a consideration of what these sentences for both pleas and trials are, how they are determined, how they differ across jurisdictions, and how appropriate they are.[12] This curious failure is both understandable and vexing. It is understandable because we share no consensus on what constitutes justice, on what the goals of the criminal justice system ought to be, and therefore we are unsure about the appropriate yardsticks to be employed in assessing sentences. It is vexing because sentences are, after all, the bottom line for the criminal justice system. Granting that innocent defendants should not be convicted, and that the integrity of the due process model ought to be maintained, it is still clear that, for most of the cases that come into the court, the single most important question concerns the sentence the defendant ought to receive (Heumann, 1978, pp. 24-43, 69-72, 100-10, 137-43).

Interestingly, plea bargaining is neutral on the problem of arriving at appropriate sentences. Though plea bargaining generates much discussion on the issue of the sentencing differential between pleas and trials, little is said about what the appropriate sentence for an offense and an offender ought to be. Plea bargaining may frequently be criticized by law-and-order advocates alarmed at deals being made with criminals, but there is nothing inherent in plea bargaining that necessarily links it—in absolute terms—to lenient sentences.[13] The sentences given in any jurisdiction are far more dependent on the jurisdiction's going rate than they are on its plea bargaining practices.[14]

Typically, formal statutory sentences exceed by any stretch of the imagination the realistic parameters that court personnel will employ in sentencing defendants. Thus, within courts, norms about realistic sentences evolve, and these norms constitute the jurisdiction's going rates for the "normal crime."[15] They are not necessarily the same across communities;[16] indeed, the literature suggests that going rates are products of the individual courthouse and community, and that they are not primarily shaped by state or national considerations. The following comments, drawn from the literature, are illustrative.

> The features attributed to offenders and offenses are in their content, specific to the community in which the P.D. [public defender] works. In other communities and historical periods the lists would presumably differ. . . . The P.D. refers to the population of defendants in the county as "our defendants" and qualifies his prototypical portrayals and knowledge of the typically operative social structures, "for our county." (Sudnow, 1973, p. 180)

> The courtroom workgroups, through their ongoing interactions among major participants, develop norms and expectations about sentences that constrain all the participants in any individual case. No defendant is sentenced out of context; the sentence he received becomes part of the courtroom's norm. Workgroup members continuously compared defendants and cases with others that had been processed in that courtroom. Thus, the social organization in which courtroom participants operated limited the scope for arbitrary action as much as the law itself. (Eisenstein and Jacob, 1977, p. 286)

> If, for example, a courthouse subculture has established about sixty days in jail as the proper punishment for first offenders who have committed minor burglaries, in that courthouse sixty days in jail is the legal norm, no matter what the statutes might stipulate as a proper punishment for burglary. Any jail term in excess of sixty days, then, is severe punishment, and a prison term of two, five, or ten years—as called for by statutory law—is very severe punishment indeed. In other words, when the law in action sets a certain punishment as usual and just for defendants of certain kinds, invoking the penalities provided by statutory law constitutes severity. (Rosett and Cressy, 1976, p. 156)

In my own research on case disposition processes in Detroit, I have been similarly struck by the existence of these going rates and by the feeling that these rates could—in principle—be set at different levels without doing much damage to the standard operating procedures of the court. Consider the following comments by two judges and three prosecutors, respectively.

> The system operates in terms of defense attorney and defendants' expectations—what is widely known as a rate. The defense attorney has to "get something" for the defendant below the standard operating sentence. It's an expectation model. . . . [judge]
>
> I don't know how I arrived at the first sentence to five years eight years ago. But once you establish yourself however, in a particular mode, a particular way of thinking about a criminal act, it's easy to fit the other cases into that sort of pattern. . . . [judge]
>
> It all depends on what grows up as a practice within a jurisdiction, okay. The common thread though is people will plead if there is any kind of break given them. We gave him a break in terms of charging—charge bargaining. Okay, if we then adopt a policy and we say you have to plead as charged, and assuming there is no sentencing bargaining, when the defendants come through, there is still a consensual operation if you have people who are around your court all the time, they know generally what the going rate is. A going rate, and let's assume the going rate for, I mean that a trial, objectively considered, if the guy went to trial on robbery armed, could be 10-20 based on everything that's there. Attorneys generally recognize that if the guy pleads to robbery armed on the nose that he's going to get some break and he's going to get lower than 10-20, and depending on the judge, he'll have a pretty good idea of what he'll get. . . . [prosecutor]
>
> . . . You judge [when negotiating a case] what's the going rate. It's kind of like the price level. Forty cents for an ice cream cone is shocking to anyone who remembers they used to be a dime. The sentence of course goes the other way. Down. No, but, there is no recognized acceptable scale of how much time people should get. There's a scale of how much cases currently get in this court or that court and so on. . . . [prosecutor]
>
> It's a curious process [that defendants will still plead guilty after mandatory sentences are introduced for certain offenses]. I think, because it's, I don't know, it probably corresponds to some law in economics about the value of silver money or paper money or something. It kind of fluctuates from time to time. But the plea bargaining process, the critical thing is that everyone, the defense attorneys, the defendants, the judges, and the prosecutors, know what the curent value is. I mean as long as you can take a position and make it known and enforce it, then everyone will say, "Well, okay, so it *used* to be I could get probation for armed robbery, now I'm going to have to go to the slammer for two years. So we won't even bargain about that. We'll just bargain in other areas, you know, like my four other pending cases, or the lack of career criminal prosecution, or some other thing." As long as everyone

> understands that, you know, people will still plead, I mean, as I say, it's curious. As long as the limits are known, kind of like laws of negotiation are known to everyone, then everyone really somehow still goes ahead. You still have a tremendous number of pleas like you did in the past. . . . [prosecutor]

These excerpts from the literature and from Detroit judges and prosecutors suggest that within local courts norms evolve regarding appropriate sentences for "typical" defendants. These norms are far afield from the formal statutory terrain and seem to entail some differentiation for a defendant who pleads and one who goes to trial. But they also seem to be—at least within a broad middle range of offenses and sentences—relatively variable with regard to their precise magnitude.[17] In one jurisdiction an armed robber may receive eight years after a trial and five years if he pleads; in another, the comparable figures may be seven and four, or ten and eight, and so on. Plea bargaining may lead to mild dispositions in one jurisdiction and severe ones in another; criminals may be let go in droves because of plea bargaining, but they may also be incarcerated en masse as a result of plea bargaining. Up to a point, at least, it appears that going rates can be set high or low, and that as long as the system is prepared to enforce its expectations, high and low sentences can be compatible with plea bargaining.[18]

In response to these arguments a critic might argue that I have it backwards. If I am saying that going rates are out there, and a system can simply elicit guilty pleas to these, then the major point of plea bargaining has been overlooked. It is the need to plea bargain, the critic might say, that establishes these going rates, and a system's ability to obtain pleas reflects its adjustment of its going rates to levels at which pleas will be forthcoming. This is only partially true. On one hand, plea bargaining can indeed affect a court's going rates. On the other hand, it neither necessarily has such an effect, nor are the going rates, though possibly related to the need to plea bargain, caused or established by plea bargaining. A far better way to appreciate the evolution of going rates—and the differences in these across communities—is to view the courts as being at least in part a product of a local legal culture. It is to a consideration of this issue that we now turn.

LOCAL LEGAL CULTURE, HISTORICAL ACCIDENTS, AND PUBLIC OPINION

An important theme found in the literature on local criminal courts argues that a "political culture" and its derivative, a "legal culture," significantly shape court practices. Herbert Jacob (1973, pp. 7-8) defines a city's culture as "a set of norms which arises from many sources and makes cities distinctive," and argues that "local cultures have an enormous impact on how courts dispense justice." Friedman (1969, p. 34) similarly defines legal culture as "the network of values and attitudes relating to law," and suggests that legal culture may be more important than structural and substantive components in analyzing legal systems. And, in concluding a recent study on the causes of court delay, Thomas Church argues that

> . . . both speed [of disposition] *and* backlog are determined in large part by established expectations, practices and informal rules of behavior of judges and attorneys. For want of a better term, we have called this cluster of related factors the "local legal culture."
>
> . . . The lesson from this discussion is the extent to which the expectations and norms of civil and criminal justice engendered by the legal culture of a community can differ from city to city (Church, 1978, pp. 54, 62).[19]

Closely related to these arguments about the significance of a political and legal culture in shaping local court practices is what we might call the "historical accident" or "tradition in a city" argument. This view suggests that historically certain practices have developed in courts and that these practices have continued to be the norm to the present day. Presumably the implication is that there was something at some time unique about a community's political or legal culture that led it to adopt a particular practice, and that once adopted no one ever sat back and thought that it could be otherwise. A good example of this kind of reasoning is found in McIntyre and Lippman's comparative study of the disposition of felony cases.

> Once a system of criminal justice develops its mode of procesing cases it is unlikely to change. Specific examples can be seen in the Chicago and Baltimore systems. In Chicago the bulk of felony cases are terminated at the preliminary hearing. This practice has changed little over the past fifty years. Changes in the law, including the complete revision of the Illinois Criminal Code in the early 1960's, have had no effect on the basic practice. The Baltimore method of disposing felony cases at the trial level without a jury can be traced to the Colonial period (McIntyre and Lippman, 1970, p. 1158).[20]

In Detroit respondents also seem to resort to a similar "tradition" explanation in accounting for the court's almost exclusive use of charge—and not sentence—bargaining. Sentence bargaining practices that are commonplace in many courts simply were not employed in Detroit (Eisenstein and Jacob, 1977);[21] plea bargaining did not suffer because charge bargaining proved sufficient—in light of the court's tradition—to keep plea rates high. As the following excerpts indicate, the norm in Detroit clearly differed from that of many other jurisdictions; indeed, when Detroit prosecutors and defense attorneys had occasion to travel to these other jurisdictions, they themselves were surprised by what the plea bargaining literature suggests is often the prevailing pattern of negotiation—prosecutorial participation in sentence negotiations and prosecutorial "pitches" on sentencing day.[22]

> . . . Generally speaking people will plead guilty because they do get a break. But all they have to do is get a break. Okay. Our office historically involved itself in what I call charge bargaining. That is to say we substituted, a guy was charged with murder in the first degree, we let him plead to murder in the second degree. What did he get out of that? Murder in the first degree was mandatory life, murder in the second degree was any term up to life, and he could get life imprisonment, but might not get life imprisonment too. He had to receive at least two years, that's the way we always argued it anyway. So, we charge bargained. We lowered the level of the maximum and he took his chances on the sentence from the judge. Our office never engaged in sentence recommendations, and we never engaged in sentence bargaining and almost no judge on the bench involved himself in sentence bargaining.
>
> THAT'S QUITE SURPRISING. IN CONNECTICUT THEY USE SENTENCE BARGAINING. . . .
>
> Oh, sure. It's, in fact all around the country people couldn't believe it when I'd go to other areas of the country and I'd say we do model pretrial negotiations and I would tell them our way, and people couldn't believe what was going on. They'd say why do defendants plead in Detroit? . . . So that's what they always said, but, see, it all depends on what grows up as practice within a jurisdiction, okay. The common thread though is people will plead if there is any kind of break given them. We give them a break in terms of charging. . . . [prosecutor]

> . . . The other thing is that in this county, I don't know historically how it developed, is the prosecutor's lack of role in sentencing which is very unique in this state and especially in Wayne County. I know for example in Washington, D.C., the prosecutors make speeches like, you know, and they really sort of represent the interest of the victim, and in fact I know that, I was down there doing a case and listened to this guy rap, it was great. I mean it was very eloquent thing about this poor prostitute who had been murdered. And it added a few years to this guy's sentence. The public defender who I was in the court with told me that sometimes it's part of the plea bargain, that they will bargain for the government to give up their right of elocution as it's called. Here the prosecutors usually even aren't in on the sentencing. . . . [defense attorney]

A more specific variant on the culture and tradition themes is the argument that public opinion affects court practices and dispositions. Public opinion is considered a better specified variable than the generalized "legal culture" of a community, but one that may function in a comparable way; that is, differences across courts can be explained by differential public attitudes toward procedures and outcomes.

If legal culture and tradition shape basic court practices, the role assigned to public opinion is frequently a narrower one. Typically it is argued that the public is generally unaware of and uninterested in what goes on in the court, and that it is only with regard to the highly visible case (for that community) that the public makes its voice heard.[23] And when its voice is heard, some of the literature suggests that the probability of trial rather than a plea bargain, and a harsh rather than a lenient sentence, increases. For example, Jacob (1973, p. 107) calls our attention to "many prominent cases where the prosecutor is unwilling to accept a guilty plea to a lesser offense because the crime attracted considerable public notice, and he is afraid of public criticism if he reduces the charges." Friedman characterizes the cases that do go to trial in the modern court system as the "exceptional, lurid, politically charged, unusual cases";[24] in France "some *crimes* are not 'correctionalized' [essentially a charge reduction of the 'crime' to the equivalent of a misdemeanor] because they are complicated, or serious or controversial . . . [or] because the case has been widely publicized or because political considerations are involved" (Goldstein and Marcus, 1977, p. 252; underlining theirs). Perhaps the best example of an explicit recognition of the role public opinion can play in plea bargaining is found in a series of nonbinding guidelines that then Attorney General Levi prepared for U.S. attorneys. In deciding upon whether to make a plea bargaining offer, Levi instructed the attorneys to consider, among other things,

> . . . what the public attitude is toward prosecution under the circumstances of the case. It may be that there is public indifference, or even antipathy, toward enforcement of the controlling statute, whether on substantive grounds, or because of a history of non-enforcement, or because the offense is essentially a matter of private concern and the victim does not wish to have it pursued. On the other hand, the nature and circumstances of the offense may be such as to create strong public sentiment in favor of prosecution. While public interest, or lack thereof, deserves the prosecutor's careful attention, it should not be used to justify a decision to prosecute, or to decline to prosecute, that cannot be supported on other grounds. . . . There may be situations in which the public interest might better be served by having a case tried rather than by being disposed of by means of a guilty plea—including situations in

which it is particularly important to permit a clear public understanding that "justice is done" or in which a plea agreement might be misconstrued to the detriment of public confidence in the criminal justice system. For this reason, the prosecutor should be careful not to place undue emphasis on factors which favor disposition of a case pursuant to a plea agreement (Levi, 1978, pp. 6-7, 18).

One must, however, be cautious about postulating too direct a link between public opinion (even on highly visible cases) and a prosecutor's decision to go to trial. Certainly cases can be found in which this dynamic seemed to be operative, and Levi's memo suggests that public opinion can be properly considered as at least one factor in a prosecutor's decision not to plea bargain. But we can also point to a number of recent highly publicized cases in which prosecutors chose not to insist on trial and instead to negotiate a plea. The fact that a vice president, various Watergate luminaries, and a well-known nursing home exploiter—to mention just a few—could, in spite of a tremendous amount of publicity, still "cop a plea" while some seemingly mundane cases were being tried daily in these same courts suggests that public opinion alone is neither necessary nor sufficient to explain either the choice of disposition process or the sentence in any particular case.[25] Public opinion no doubt affects some decisions by some courts at some time, but it would be naive to believe that there is any general and necessary one-to-one correspondence even on highly visible cases between the public's attitudes and the court's action. For our purposes, it is sufficient to preserve this notion of a possible effect—albeit if it is only for certain types of cases—of public opinion.

Similarly, one should recognize that there is a risk attendant on placing too much credence in the political culture and tradition explanations. Given the difficulty of operationalizing these concepts, it is all too easy to use them as a residual explanation without much direct empirical support to account for processes that are in fact products of complex organizational dynamics. Despite this dilemma, and in light of the various suggestions in the literature and my own findings in several courts, I believe that these concepts have some explanatory viability and are useful. Perhaps our tools are still too crude to capture the contribution of culture and to measure traditions, but, like pornography, I think we can still "know it when we see it."

PLEA BARGAINING, GOING RATES, AND LEGAL CULTURES: SOME INTEGRATIVE THEORETICAL COMMENTS

Thus far I have introduced and discussed several important concepts in the literature on local criminal courts. My concern has been less with viewing the detailed findings of sundry studies than with distilling several significant theoretical implications of the literature. The hope is that these might bear in a helpful way on the comparative analysis of courts. It now seems worthwhile to carry the theoretical discussion one step further and suggest more explicitly how these concepts can help increase our understanding of the plea bargaining process and the role it plays in the criminal process.

The most fruitful way to attempt this integrative task is to return to our hypothetical pure plea bargaining system. Recall that this is the system in which there exists a core of plea bargained cases. Borrowing from Wilson's discussion of police behavior (1970, p. 233) I would argue that in these communities (and indeed in all communities) there is a "zone of indifference" surrounding local court practices, an area within which the community is relatively indifferent to how outcomes are arrived at and, in fact, to what these outcomes are. Cases outside the zone are more visible and thus more subject to the general constraints imposed by the community's political and legal culture. But even within the zone the community has some effect, for it was its decision-making processes that selected the court personnel, and presumably these court officials represent in a rough way community values.[26] The difference, then, between actions taken within and without the zone is more a matter of degree than kind.

No necessarily perfect correspondence exists between those cases in the plea bargaining core and those falling in the zone of indifference. Though I would expect a large overlap between the zone and the core, the zone would probably also extend into some of the cases that are tried and would not cover some of the plea bargained cases. As indicated earlier, it is too simplistic to assume that plea bargaining is always incompatible with the political culture or public opinion and that trials are always highly visible events in which community values or dictates are preeminent.

In our pure system, then, we expect a core of plea bargained cases, a zone of indifference covering some of these plea bargained cases and some trials, and—through both the direct and indirect effects of the political culture—some translation of community values into court decision-making. These values will affect processes (for example, preference for negotiated, rather than adversarial, dispositions) and outcomes (for example, sentence). Though I have argued that in every community (independent of resource constraints) a core of plea bargained cases will be found, this core will vary with community preferences; similarly, the going rate for crimes will also vary. This variation is a product of the legal culture and, perhaps, historical happenstances; some procedure was used, and some rate was set and became the norm. Since communities vary, and since historical accident is, by its very nature, accidental, we would expect variations among courts even in the "natural state of things."

When resource constraints begin to exact their effects, and courts move to one of the two mixed states, there is not a necessarily predictable equivalent change in court practices and outcomes. This is true both because pure systems are different to begin with and because there is enough latitude, or slack, left in the system to allow for a variety of responses to these constraints. One court, for example, might choose simply to widen the difference between sentences after trial and those after a plea. The going rate for a plea would remain constant, but the cost of trial would increase. Such a response would presumably increase the willingness of defendants to plead without decreasing the sanctions distributed by the court. In another court, the going rate for pleas might drop; in this court, more lenient dispositions would be associated with an increase in case pressure. However, because going rates differ in absolute amounts across communities, the resultant going rate need not—in absolute terms—be "lenient."

Adjusting plea/trial ratios and going rates are only two of the possible reactions of a court in a mixed state. Various other techniques are at its disposal (for example, an increase in dismissals or nolles; greater use of diversion programs; increased use of charge reduction without any effect on sentence). It is not necessary for our present purposes to consider all of these possible adaptive mechanisms; suffice it to say that, as resource constraints increase, these may directly affect plea and going rates, or they may have other, more involved, consequences, some of which alter substantially the overall criminal justice process, and others of which change the name of the game (for example, charge reduction) but leave the court's dynamics and outcomes essentially untouched.

Although it seems conceptually useful to examine the effects of resource constraints on plea bargaining by beginning with a pure system, such an approach takes its toll on reality. In point of fact, many courts may start out in a mixed state; that is, they are established with a built-in resource problem. These courts never enjoyed the pleasures of a pure state in which social scientists could easily discern the variables, other than resource constraints, that shaped plea bargaining and sentencing practices. Instead, the problem of insufficient resources, like political culture, intraorganizational dynamics, and so on, played a constant role from the very beginning. The parameters of a tolerable plea bargaining/trial ratio and of the going rates were shaped not just by political culture, happenstance, and so on, but by the interactive effect of these phenomena with resource constraints. The worse the imbalance between cases and personnel, for example, presumably the greater the effect.[27] But, again, the point of the pure system argument is that even without this imbalance, even without case pressure, "core" plea bargaining would take place, and going rates that are substantially lower than the maximum set by law would probably be established.

By examining these differences in resources, going rates, and legal cultures across communities, we can begin to map systematically differences in disposition patterns. These efforts in turn will clarify the relative impact of each of these variables, will further elaborate on alternate dispositional modes in communities, and will suggest additional variables to be included in our continuing search for a comparative theory of local courts.[28]

No pretense at developing a comparative theory of the plea bargaining process was made in this paper. Instead, our goal was more modest—namely, to tease out some of the elements of such a theory, point to some of the measurement problems that await consideration, and urge further comparative research. The set of ideas presented in this section, then, is only suggestive. It indicates how several themes that emerge from the literature can be integrated. While it does not purport to be a definitive statement on these matters, however, it does urge that we move beyond mere descriptions of similarities in plea bargaining systems to a more sophisticated theory building effort. Such a theory would recognize similarities and also explain the significant differences in the variables that affect plea bargaining rates and dispositional modes.

POLICY IMPLICATIONS: SENTENCING REFORM AND DETERRENCE

At the outset of this chapter I indicated that, in addition to suggesting directions for a comparative theory of courts, "thinking about plea bargaining" in more theoretical terms could also generate several important insights about local courts for scholars and policymakers who have recently given their attention to related criminal justice concerns. Specifically, I was referring to the movement—perhaps crusade is the better term—to alter sentencing schemes, to move from open-ended, indeterminate sentencing plans to some form of fixed—or at least presumptive—sentences, and to the increased attention being given to the problem of the efficacy of criminal sanctions, to the relationship between certainty and severity of sanctions and crime deterrence.

Curiously the work on sentencing reform and deterrence has not benefited as much as it could and should have from the plea bargaining research. Indirect evidence for this assertion can be gleaned from some recent work in which several authors have pointed out the naivete of many of the sentencing reform proposals and the inadequacies of the deterrence literature when both of these bodies of literature are scrutinized from the perspective of the actual operation of the criminal justice system. For example, Daniel Freed (1978), testifying before a House Subcommittee considering the presumptive sentencing provisions of the proposed new Federal Criminal Code, noted that the legislation simply enhanced the prosecutor's plea bargaining powers at the expense of judicial discretion. Alschuler (1978b, pp. 570-77) reached a similar conclusion about the widely touted California sentencing reforms. Comparable "plea bargaining related considerations" may also bedevil the findings of deterrence scholars. Nagin (1978, pp. 97-98), for example, raises the possibility that the asserted inverse relationship between sanctions and crime rates may not reflect any deterrent effect of sanctions, but instead may simply be an artifact of the way records are maintained in jurisdictions that frequently bargain over charge.

The point to be stressed here is that even a cursory sojourn into the plea bargaining literature leads one to raise quite serious questions about the efficacy of sentencing reform and about the utility of the findings of deterrence scholars. A failure to merge what we have learned about criminal court case processing with these newer areas has led to work whose conclusions are founded on a more naive model of the court than is warranted by the state of the art in local court research.[29]

The themes that we have developed about plea bargaining would seem to intersect at several points the work that is being done on sentencing reform and deterrence. It is beyond the scope of this chapter to attempt any sort of detailed, systematic review of these points, but it is worth our while at least to point out a few general considerations.

First, sentencing reforms aim to impose either statewide or nationwide (for the federal courts) presumptive or mandatory sentences for particular crimes and criminals. To the extent that these reforms fail to consider the current differences in going rates across communities, and the flexibility that prosecutors have to manipulate charges to preserve "old going rates," blanket rules will rapidly unravel and turn into patchwork quilts in which the jurisdiction's sentences more closely resemble the old going rates than the new presumptive or mandatory sentences.

Second, an ongoing controversy in deterrence literature involves the problem of the simultaneous effects of sanctions on crime and crime on sanctions. Apparently, some who have examined this problem have been all too quick to conclude that sanctions deter and have given too short shrift to the possibility that the causal arrow might run predominantly in the other direction, that is, that increases in crime lead to decreases in sanctions (Nagin, 1978, pp. 117-24). The discussion in this chapter of the possible effects of increases in caseload on plea bargaining lends some support to the notion that, with increases in crime, sanctions may be lowered, but it also cautions against assuming that they must be lowered. In this regard, it is encouraging to learn that a recently concluded major national study of the literature on deterrence urges, as one of its priorities, further inquiry into the relationship between heavy workloads and the imposition of sanctions (Blumstein and others, 1978, pp. 10, 47-49).

Third, we all strive for—indeed, science dictates—the most parsimonious explanation for the phenomenon under consideration; but parsimony does not justify ignoring complexity. It would be convenient to assume that criminal justice systems are essentially the same, that plea bargaining operates in the same fashion in each of these systems, that deterrence will work for all crimes in all communities, and that explicit sentencing rules, once promulgated, will be implemented in identical fashion across jurisdictions. These would be convenient assumptions, and we could proffer parsimonious explanations of plea bargaining, crime, and sentencing disparity that would justify them. They would also, however, be incorrect assumptions, for they would be built on a naive understanding of the complexity of criminal justice systems. The task that lies ahead for all of us concerned with these problems is to develop realistically parsimonious explanations for the complex problems of crime and for its processing through the complex environments of local criminal courts.

NOTES

1. The assumption made here, and throughout the paper, is that guilty pleas are either the product of implicit or explicit plea bargaining. See Heumann (1978:158).

2. For similar findings from other jurisdictions which have attempted to "abolish" plea bargaining, see Church (1976); *Iowa Law Review* (1975); and Heumann and Loftin (1978).

3. On Baltimore's trials see Eisenstein and Jacob (1977:250-51); for a discussion of bench trials in Pittsburgh see Levin (1977:80-81); and for the argument that trials on transcripts in Los Angeles are "slow pleas of guilty" see Mather (1973).

4. Their data probably understate the percentage of "non-coerced" plea bargaining because their sample was drawn from those defendants who had not pled guilty earlier in the proceedings, and who had thus advanced to the

trial stage. It is also of more than passing interest to note the controversy that surrounded the publication of Baldwin and McConville's research. Apparently the British legal establishment is even less comfortable with coming to grips with the centrality of plea bargaining than is ours. Baldwin and McConville (1978:15) describe the furor that preceded publication:

> A campaign has been conducted, both privately and publicly, by the legal profession to suppress publication of the book. This campaign—which is unprecedented even in England where there has always been a thoroughly uneasy relationship between researchers and the legal profession—culminated in the Chairman of the Bar writing to the Home Secretary, urging him to intervene to prevent publication of the report which would be, he said, "directly contrary to the public interest." The Home Secretary's response to this letter was as swift as it was unpleasant. First a letter was sent to the Vice-Chancellor of our University seeking his support in discouraging publication of the report; secondly, three months before publication, the Home Secretary gave a lengthy comment about our report in Parliament stating that, whilst he did not wish to suppress publication of the book, he nevertheless regarded the conclusions as "questionable." Our Vice-Chancellor, Sir Robert Hunter, mindful of the long-term interests and reputation of the University, was greatly disturbed by the public furor and press speculation about the findings of the research. He decided to carry out his own assessment of whether the methods we had adopted were those that others in the discipline would regard as sufficiently sound to support the conclusions we had drawn. In the end, our approach was vindicated and the Vice-Chancellor offered to contribute a Foreword to the book making this point explicit.

5. I prefer "resource constraints" to case pressure because the latter does not include variables such as skill, the number of part-time employees (that is, two half-time prosecutors may not "equal" a full-time prosecutor), the responsibility of judges on the court for a civil docket, the size of this docket, and so on. Though case pressure may be the best measure we have at hand, and I will occasionally use it interchangeably with resource constraints, it is plain that more robust measures of resource levels need to be developed, and I suspect that a significant effort will be made in this regard as part of a recently funded L.E.A.A. study on performance measures in the criminal justice system. For a discussion of this project see National Institute of Law Enforcement and Criminal Justice (1978).

6.For a more extensive discussion of why prosecutors, defense attorneys and judges develop these views see Heumann (1978:57-89, 100-26, 137-52).

7. One approach to measuring relative resource levels would be to employ an attitudinal scale. Respondents could be asked to estimate the extent to which the resources at their disposal affect their job performance. Though such a measure would be less satisfactory than objective indicators of resource sufficiency, imbalance, and so on, it nonetheless could prove useful for a preliminary sorting of courts along a resource continuum.

8. See note 5 above.

9. Unlike Gillespie, however, I assume that for the second and third stages the court's "capacity" is exceeded, and that some alteration in the court's routine is required.

10. On the actions of the Legal Aid Society in New York, see *New York Times* (May 2, 5, 7, 1970). In the fall of 1974 Ann Arbor's public defender refused to accept any more misdemeanor cases, claiming that assistant public defenders simply could not handle any additional cases. The county commissioners capitulated and provided funding for new assistant public defenders. Interestingly, the Wayne County (Detroit) Prosecutor's Office recently raised similar arguments, and indeed filed suit, in objecting to a planned reduction by the county in the number of authorized assistant prosecutors. See *Detroit Free Press* (January 10, 1979).

11. For the sake of keeping the three-stage argument as uncluttered as possible, I did not introduce the possibility that one of the role incumbents might be at a particular resource level while one or more of the others was at a different level. Thrashing out the implications of this sort of mixed system will shed further light on the effects of resources on disposition modes.

12. An important exception is Eisenstein and Jacob (1977). They undertook a systematic comparison of the organizational dynamics *and* sentencing outcomes of three courts, and generated a number of hypotheses that speak to these issues.

13. I am indebted to Professor Sam Krislov of the University of Minnesota for aptly and succinctly summarizing this point in a telephone conversation. He noted that, contrary to the views of many observers of the criminal courts, plea bargaining does not necessarily mean that the defendant receives a plea *bargain*.

14. This is not to say that plea bargaining does not affect going rates. I will consider this problem of the "direction of the causal arrows" in a subsequent section.

15. Normal crime was a term originally developed by Sudnow (1973:174-85).

16. For a discussion of an ongoing effort at developing measures of jurisdictions' going rates see Wilkens and others (1976).

17. I am not referring here to those offenses which are obviously so trivial that a prison sentence is unimaginable or to those which are so serious that anything other than an extremely lengthy sentence would be unthinkable. Instead, I am arguing that there is a broad middle range of offenses and offenders for whom there is no automatically obvious sentence, and thus a substantial amount of variation in sentence is possible. For a more detailed discussion of the factors that prosecutors employ in sorting these cases, see Heumann (1978:102-10).

18. In *Bordenkircher* v. *Hayes*, 46 LW 4089 (1978), the United States Supreme Court agreed that it was constitutional for a prosecutor to file an habitual offender charge against a defendant who refused a plea bargaining offer and was convicted at trial. The availability of such tools to the prosecutor increases his ability to set the "going rate" at a high level. For example, in *Bordenkircher*, the defendant refused to plead to five years on the charge of forging an $88.00 check. However, upon conviction after trial on this charge, and the filing of the habitual charge (proof only requires showing that the defendant had two prior felony convictions), he received a sentence of mandatory life imprisonment. Presumably, subsequent defendants will hesitate

more than a bit before refusing what seems like an extraordinarily high "rate" on a relatively minor crime. However, it should also be noted that, under the forgery statute in Kentucky, the defendant could have received up to ten years for his offense. Though to many an outside observer (myself included), a far milder disposition than five years would have seemed fairer, formally the prosecutor was under no obligation to make any such offer, and, in light of the Court's ruling, he apparently can employ potent tools to encourage pleas that comport with his sense of where within this ten-year range the defendant ought to plead. Relatedly, I suppose one's judgment as to whether a sentence is high or low, fair or unfair, depends in part on who is going "to do the time." As Daniel Freed (1978:6-7) notes, "Federal plea bargains in recent years involving a vice-president, an attorney general and a CIA director, were variously considered unfair to the defendants, or inadequate to the public, or inappropriate."

19. On the relationship between political/legal culture and court practices, see also Klonoski and Mendelsohn (1970:3-19) and Mather (1976); on civil courts, see Jacob (1969); and on the police, Wilson (1970).

20. For the argument that an "organizational approach" explains these practices more successfully than does one that relies on "tradition," see Eisenstein and Jacob (1977:299).

21. Recently, however, there have been some indicators that suggest greater prosecutorial involvement in sentence recommendations in Detroit. See Heumann and Loftin (1978:74).

22. On prosecutorial participation in sentencing negotiations and on the issue of "pitches" on sentencing day, see Heumann (1978:41-45). Rosett and Cressey (1976:92) also found that court personnel are simply not aware of major differences in practices even in neighboring jurisdictions: "[The prosecutor] knows the customs of the courthouse in which he works, but he does not know if these ways of doing business and moving cases are used elsewhere. It is likely that he would be surprised at the variations in procedure and outcome that persist, even in nearby counties."

23. For example, McIntyre and Lippman (1970:1154) observe that "[t]he decisions of the prosecutor are ones of low visibility and, in the absence of highly publicized cases, are seldom brought to the attention of law reformers, much less the public." Similarly, Eisenstein and Jacob (1977:47) discuss "a certain number of 'important' cases [which] always surface—cases involving heinous crimes, large sums of money, or prominent members of the community—and they must be handled with visible competence."

24. Friedman's remarks can be found in the informal transcript of the discussions held during the Special National Workshop on Plea Bargaining, French Lick, Indiana, June 15-17, 1978.

25. There has been little systematic academic research on plea bargaining in these highly visible cases. Watergate—and its progeny—however, certainly contributed to greater public debate about the propriety of negotiating dispositions. For example, Leon Jaworski, former special Watergate prosecutor, observed: "There is nothing wrong with upright plea bargaining. My predecessor, Archibald Cox, believed in plea discussions; I believe in them; my

successor, Henry Ruth, believes in them, and I am not aware of an instance in which the practice was abused in the special prosecutor's office during my time" (*New York Times*, April 23, 1975).

26. According to Eisenstein and Jacob (1977:59), "The persons who hold key posts and their attitudes reflect roughly the distribution of power and opinion in the community."

27. Friedman (1978b:37) reaches a similar conclusion based on a preliminary examination of some fascinating historical data:

> Plea bargaining, then, really cannot be explained as a response to pressure on the docket; in big cities . . . of course, crowded urban courts come to use plea bargaining very heavily; they come to depend on it. Once the system is established, it affects the way resources are allocated, and it is not easy to dispense with. Plea bargaining and crowded urban courts became locked in a kind of holy embrace.

28. Eisenstein's and Jacob's *Felony Justice* is an important step in this direction. Their discussion of organizational variables and various attributes of the court's setting (indigent representation plans, case and personnel assignment practices, and so on) suggest that these variables will loom large in a broader, more inclusive comparative theory.

29. It is difficult to proffer any single definitive explanation for the failure to benefit from the plea bargaining research, though several possibilities come readily to mind. Academic discipline boundaries within the broader legal process area may be tightly drawn, and there may be less cross-fertilization than one might desire. Perhaps the sort of merging of research findings that we are discussing really falls within the interstices of desciplines, a sort of "no-person's land" from which scholars depart with their own models in mind, and with their own narrowly drawn problems to guide them. Or perhaps an interest in parsimony dictates a narrowly drawn approach initially, with an expectation that eventually a return to the "broader picture" will be essayed. A final possibility is that the plea bargaining literature has been so dominated by efforts to detail the actual day-in, day-out operations of various court systems that it leaves the "outsider" no easy way to distill the central findings of this body of research. Though I believe that there is more than a modicum of merit to each of these explanations, it is with the last that this chapter was concerned. As indicated ealier, it may be that in our efforts to describe and explain particular court systems, we have failed to step away from these courts and think more generally about "what it all means," and thus have precluded easy access to our findings for the "outsider."

REFERENCES

Alschuler, Albert (1978a). "Plea Bargaining and Its History." Presented at the Special National Workshop on Plea Bargaining, French Lick, Indiana, June 15-17.

——— (1978b). "Sentencing Reform and Prosecutorial Power: A Critique of Recent Proposals for 'Fixed' and 'Presumptive' Sentencing." 126 *University of Pennsylvania Law Review* 550.

Association of the Bar of the City of New York (1977). *The Nation's Toughest Drug Law: Evaluating the New York Experience.* Washington, D.C.: Drug Abuse Council, Inc.

Baldwin, John, and McConville, Michael (1977). *Negotiated Justice.* London: Martin Robinson and Co.

_______ (1978). "Plea Bargaining and Plea Negotiating in England." Presented at the Special National Workshop on Plea Bargaining, French Lick, Indiana, June 15-17.

Blumstein, Alfred; Cohen, Jacqueline; and Nagin, Daniel, eds. (1978). *Deterrence and Incapacitation: Estimating the Effects of Criminal Sanctions on Crime Rates.* Washington, D.C.: National Academy of Sciences.

Church, Thomas, Jr. (1976). "Plea Bargains, Concessions and the Courts: Analysis of a Quasi Experiment." 10 *Law & Society Review* 377.

_______ (1978). *Justice Delayed: The Pace of Litigation in Urban Trial Courts.* Williamsburg, Virginia: National Center for State Courts.

Eisenstein, James, and Jacob, Herbert (1977). *Felony Justice.* Boston: Little, Brown.

Feeley, Malcolm (1975). "The Effects of Heavy Caseloads." Presented at the Annual Meeting of the American Political Science Association, San Francisco, California, September 15.

Freed, Daniel (1978). "Flaws in the Federal Criminal Code Reform Act," Statement Presented before the Sub-Committee on Criminal Justice, House Judiciary Committee, on S. 1437, H.R. 2311 and H.R. 6869 (April 19).

Friedman, Lawrence (1969). "Legal Culture and Social Development." 4 *Law & Society Review* 29.

_______ (1978a). "Plea Bargaining in Historical Perspective." Presented at the Special National Workshop on Plea Bargaining, French Lick, Indiana, June 15-17.

_______ (1978b). "Plea Bargaining in the Light of Archival Data: A Study of Alameda County, California." Report to the L.E.A.A.

Georgetown University Law Center Institute of Criminal Law and Procedure (1977). *Plea Bargaining in the United States: Phase I. Report.*

Gillespie, Robert (1976). "The Production of Court Services." 5 *Journal of Legal Studies* 243.

Goldstein, Abraham, and Marcus, Martin (1977). "The Myth of Judicial Supervision in Three 'Inquisitorial' Systems: France, Italy, and Germany." 87 *Yale Law Journal* 240.

Gross, Avrum (1978). "Plea Bargaining—The Alaska Experience." Presented at the Special National Workshop on Plea Bargaining, French Lick, Indiana, June 15-17.

Heumann, Milton (1978). *Plea Bargaining.* Chicago: University of Chicago Press.

_______, and Loftin, Colin (1978). "Mandatory Sentencing and the Abolition of Plea Bargaining: The Michigan Felony Firearms Statute." Presented at the Special National Workshop on Plea Bargaining, French Lick, Indiana, June 15-17.

Iowa Law Review (1975). "Note: The Elimination of Plea Bargaining in Black Hawk, Iowa: A Case Study." 61 *Iowa Law Review* 1053.

Jacob, Herbert (1969). *Debtors in Court*. Chicago: Rand McNally.

_______ (1973). *Urban Justice*. Englewood Cliffs, N.J.: Prentice-Hall.

Klonoski, James, and Mendelsohn, Robert, eds. (1970). *The Politics of Local Justice*. Boston: Little, Brown.

Levi, Edward (1978). "Memorandum—Materials Relating to Prosecutorial Discretion." (January 18) Washington, D.C.

Levin, Martin (1977). *Urban Politics and the Criminal Courts*. Chicago: University of Chicago Press.

Mather, Lynn (1973). "Some Determinants of the Method of Case Dispositon: Decision-making by Public Defenders in Los Angeles." 8 *Law & Society Review* 187.

_______ (1976). "Ethnography and the Study of Trial Courts." Presented at the Annual Meeting of the Midwest Political Science Association, Chicago, April 29-May 1.

McIntyre, Donald, and Lippman, David (1970). "Prosecutors and Early Dispositon of Felony Cases." 56 *American Bar Association Journal* 1154.

Nagin, Daniel (1978). "General Deterrence: A Review of the Empirical Evidence." In A. Blumstein, J. Cohen, and D. Nagin, eds. *Deterrence and Incapacitation: Estimating the Effects of Criminal Sanctions on Crime Rates*. Washington, D.C.: National Academy of Sciences.

National Institute of Law Enforcement and Criminal Justice (1978). *Research Bulletin*, December 1978. Washington: Law Enforcement Assistance Administration.

Rosett, Arthur, and Cressy, Donald (1976). *Justice by Consent*. Philadelphia: J.B. Lippincott.

Sudnow, David (1973). "Normal Crimes." In E. Rubington and M. Weiberg, eds. *Deviance* (Second Edition). New York: MacMillan.

Wilkens, Leslie; Kress, Jack; Gottfredson, Don; Calpin, Joseph; and Gelman, Arthur (1976). *Sentencing Guidelines: Structuring Judicial Discretion*. Washington: NILECJ, LEAA.

Wilson, James Q. (1970). *Varieties of Police Behavior*. New York: Atheneum.

Wishingrad, Jay (1974). "The Plea Bargain In Historical Perspective," 23 *Buffalo Law Review* 499.

Chapter Nine

Sentencing Problems and Internal Court Reform

Beverly Blair Cook

How can trial judges improve their performance in sentencing offenders? This question is important to judges because their authority to sentence depends upon the confidence of the public and politicians. Although criminal court judges resist the erosion of their sentencing power, many judges have never felt comfortable exercising sentencing discretion. Judges admit that sentencing is an art or craft unconfined by clear legal or cultural standards (Kaufman, 1962). Their training in criminal law and rules of evidence and their experience in managing trials make them expert in finding guilt but not in predicting behavior, which is essential to effective sentencing. Caught between critics of tough and soft penalties and between complaints of mechanical and of disparate sentences, judges are disturbed and frustrated. One federal judge epitomizes the feeling of never knowing

> whether the purposes of his sentence are appropriate, let alone whether the purposes will be achieved. The erosion of many of our assumptions about wise penal policy has created a crisis of confidence in the administration of justice, which no one feels more keenly than a sentencing judge (Renfrew, 1977, p. 590).

The fact that judges do not function within a structure that facilitates their setting of sentence goals which the public and politicians will accept further compounds their problem. Trial judges work in decentralized court organizations, make sentence decisions on a case-by-case basis, and lack formal linkages to trial judges in other courts or to laypersons not associated with a case.

Two basic values are the focus of most complaints about sentencing: effectiveness and fairness. Effective sentencing involves two aspects: (1) whether the sentence is appropriate for the goal, and (2) if so, whether the sentence achieves its goal. There are also two aspects to fair sentencing: (1) the legitimacy of the factors used in selecting a sentence, and (2) the consistent use of the same goal and factors for similar offenses and offenders. Judges have limited authority and resources to define the goals and to monitor the impact of their sentences; they do, however, have wide discretion in choosing factors. They can be held acountable for the legitimacy of the factors they employ. But, with no clear mandate from the legislators on goals, judges have no standard for the appropriateness of the factors.

In order to respond to the external pressures for goal-oriented and uniform sentences, judges have developed modest reforms—sentencing seminars, councils, and guidelines. These efforts to derail incursions upon their sentence authority have educated fellow judges to the problems but have not produced successful voluntary solutions. A basic aim of this chapter is to describe the three internal reform efforts and to point out their shortcomings. In addition, some alternatives to the traditional sentencing process will be considered.

To discuss these basic issues within a theoretical framework, three perspectives will be utilized consecutively. First, to highlight the uniqueness of criminal sentencing as a social endeavor, the sentencing process will be conceptualized as a societal assignment and compared with other compulsory assignment procedures. Second, to demonstrate the inherent intellectual complexities and contradictions involved in calculating sentences, sentencing goals will be reviewed and compared. Finally, in an attempt to illustrate the processual complexities, competing forces, and alternative considerations involved in the sentencing decision, a political model of sentencing will be proposed and discussed. Such a model will permit a more meaningful assessment of internal reform efforts and alternatives to conventional sentencing practices.

SENTENCING AS COMPULSORY ASSIGNMENT

The compulsory assignment of individuals to socializing institutions is part of a selection process that exists in all societies. In the United States political authorities distribute persons involuntarily only to prisons, schools, and mental institutions and, during periods of national emergency, to the armed forces or concentration camps. A sentence is a postconviction assignment of an individual to a supervised role inside or outside a correctional institution. The power to assign an individual to his "place" in or out of society is the most significant power wielded by an authority, with larger personal consequences than a decision to redistribute resources. The significance of the "in-out" assignment should be reflected in the factors that go into making this decision, distinguishing it from decisions on fines or length of supervision.

A sentence, then, is one example of a complex process used to select persons for various institutional roles by identifying, classifying, and assigning. The basis for eligibility may be an ascribed or achieved characteristic of the individual (or both). The qualifications required of those who process the candidates may, but need not, be highly specialized and professional. The quality of decisions at the identification and classification stage affects the equity of the assignment, while the quality of the treatment after assignment reflects the appropriateness of the assignment. How the individual is actually treated in his new role may be outside the authority of the assigner.

Sentencing and Other Assignment Processes

A better understanding of the problems associated with the sentencing function can be gained by comparing the process of selecting members for different involuntary roles (Table 9-1). Who does the selection—and on what basis—depends upon the positive or negative valence of the organization. Assignment to a criminal or mental institution connotes the incompatibility of the individual with free social groups; the process classifies as deviant and excludes the individual from society for storage and/or treatment. In contrast, assignment to school or military forces connotes expectations for contributions to the public good after or during membership. The classification offers good labels—student (graduate) and soldier (veteran)—which will qualify the individual for social rewards. The identification of new members for a socially respected role can be based on attributes such as age and health, but the identification of new members for a socially despised role, in a political system which values equality and fairness, should be based upon behavior. Table 9-1 shows examples of attributes which have been used, properly or not.

Classification by attribute allows accuracy and efficiency. Classification by behavior involves difficult problems of precise description in law and accurate recognition in fact. Identifying, classifying, and assigning on the basis of behavior is necessarily time-consuming and expensive. The costs of the process of assigning persons to prison and mental institutions are high in comparison to the costs of assigning to public schools and the armed forces. The criminal

Table 9-1. Model of Process of Selecting Involuntary Members for Organizations

Organization	*Prison*	*Asylum*	*Army*	*School*
Membership Basis:				
Attribute	Sex Race Health Age	Sex Indigency Health	Sex Age Health	Age Health Residency
Behavior as described in	Criminal code	Psychiatric textbook	–	–
Identification:				
Private	Informer	Family	Self	Family
Public	Police	Police	Clerk	Social worker
Classification:				
Technical			Clerk	Clerk
Professional	Prosecutor	Doctor	Counsel	
Judicial	Judge	Judge		
Amateur	Jury		Lay Board	
Assignment:				
Technical			Clerk	Clerk
Professional			Officer	Principal
Judicial	Judge	Judge		
Treatment:				
Technical	Guard	Orderly	Sergeant	
Professional		Nurse	Lieutenant	Teacher

process decision-makers who screen candidates on the basis of behavior are well-trained and well-paid professional and/or independent actors to insure the most competent and objective classification. The decision-makers for attribute-based screening can be technicians.

For valued social roles, a self-identification process is available. Individuals may present themselves for admission, or a parent or peer recognizes the attribute which signals eligibility. For negative social roles, informers or public officials usually identify the candidates. At the classification stage, clerks or even part-time volunteers ("friends and neighbors") check birth and health certificates for students and draftees. But for labeling as deviant, specialized professional (district attorneys, defense counsel, psychiatrists, and judges) and sometimes specially instructed laypersons (jurors) examine and weigh the evidence. The major function of the judge after a guilty plea or trial is to certify that the classification as a criminal is correct.

The criminal court judge with structural independence from other social actors supervises the entire process of identification and classification and then takes responsibility for the assignment or sentencing of the deviant. Judges face hard choices among many alternatives for the place and the timing of each disposition (Vasoli, 1965). The place and the length of the assignment are not as neatly tied to the behavior of the criminal as age is to the entry and exit of the student from school. The first assignment choice of the judge is the role and place of the offender, for example, as a probationer returned to society, as a resident of a local jail, or as a prisoner in a maximum-security facility. The next decision, on the length of the assignment, is also difficult.

In most assignment processes, the assigner does not carry out the treatment of the individual. A partial exception is the school, where the roles of identifier, classifier, assigner, and processor are closely integrated, often within hierarchies of workers located in the same building. More typical is the criminal justice system in which the police as the primary identifier and public and private attorneys and trial judges as classifiers interact across the boundaries of different organizations. Moreover, the court group is physically remote and lacks regular communications with the correctional officers who treat the assigned offender inside the institutions.

Compounding the problem of separation is the fact that, after assignment, the treatment of members of involuntary organizations depends upon the social expectations attached to their labels. The processing of students and soldiers is handled by well-paid and well-trained professionals, teachers, or officers; the processing of prisoners and mental patients is by poorly paid and poorly educated custodians. (The prison employment of doctors and teachers is token.) Thus, where the assignment process is relatively cheap, the treatment is expensive; where the assignment process is expensive, the treatment is cheap (although the facilities for security may be costly). Moreover, the socially valued organizations have a relatively clear purpose, which informs the choice of programs, while the negative institutions with inchoate purposes and/or no scientifically established treatments have no obvious basis for investing in specific programs.

When viewed from certain perspectives this can be justifiable. The socialization of prisoners is not even relevant to some goals of sentencing, such as incapacitation, "just deserts," or general deterrence, where the prisoner is simply stored for punishment or public safety. For these goals inexpensive caretakers are appropriate. However, complaints about the costs of custodial care of large numbers of inmates, about violence and corruption in prisons, and about recidivism suggest that the public also wants some training of prisoners before their return to society. To achieve individual-centered goals, prisons need expensive professionals. The judge with an individual goal in mind will feel tremendous frustration in making an assignment to places which do not provide appropriate personnel and programs. Short of taking over the prisons and jails (which judges can do at second hand, as in Alabama and Texas), judges make their assignments without any guarantee of treatment for the individual. Judges, then, are not accountable for sentence effectiveness.

Sentencing and Assigners

The quintessential function of the judge is classification; assignment was a routine task, rationally and automatically attached to classification, until the late nineteenth century. As sentence alternatives proliferated, legislatures experimented with the location of the assignment function, sometimes giving it to administrative boards through an indeterminate sentence policy, sometimes keeping it for themselves through a mandatory sentence policy. Prosecutors are now trying to take over the function without formal authority.

It should be emphasized that the official designated to make the formal assignment is not necessarily the official who controls the sentence served. Decisions made about identification and classification will affect the sentence unobtrusively (Ross, 1976); and decisions made subsequently by other trial and appellate judges, probation, parole, pardon, and prison officials will revise the sentence openly. Thus formal authority to sentence conceals "a low-visibility, busy, and pragmatic system of informal decisions regulating the actual sentence . . ." (Clear and associates, 1978, p. 443). In this situation, attention focused on the judge's sentence is misplaced and the judge's responsibility for equity, as well as effectiveness, is questionable. There is no clearcut locus of responsibility for sentencing because decisions by prosecutors before formal sentencing and by parole boards afterwards significantly affect it.

As the power of parole boards declines, one official is currently challenging the judge for control of the assignment function; this is the prosecutor. The prosecutor has quietly used the resource of information to exert influence over the judge's sentence decisions, particularly in guilty plea cases. Two contemporary innovations bring the prosecutor's bid for assignment power out of the closet: diversion and guidelines. Diversion is a preconviction version of probation in which the prosecutor offers conditional release to offenders who confess, with a promise of dropping the charge if the offender plays a straight social role. The prosecutor assigns offenders back to society and turns the risky cases over to the court for classification and assignment. Many judges recognize diversion as an open threat to their authority and credibility as assigners (Orland and Tyler, 1974).

Prosecutor guidelines are formulas for sentencing in case categories which replace the usual case-by-case recommendations. The prosecutor adopts a set of factors with which he can produce consistent sentences to fill the gap of missing legislative or judicial standards. The Antitrust Division of the Department of Justice, for example, recommends a baseline sentence with specific adjustments for aggravating and mitigating circumstances. By accepting the prosecutor's schema the judge reduces decisional cost. But the official with responsibility at the identification and classification stages has expanded into the assignment stage, destroying boundaries and bringing with it some due process significance.

Parole boards also have guidelines for their decisions to keep or reduce sentence length. They reexamine the same factors used by the judge for the original sentence choice. The federal court staff warn the judges that "once you have sentenced a man to prison, you lose control of him, and employees of these agencies make judgments that you might not have made if you'd been in their shoes" (Partridge, 1977, p. 290). To keep control of the assignment, judges now take account of the parole board guidelines in order to manipulate these officials in the same fashion that prosecutors anticipate judicial decisions.

SENTENCING GOALS

Although "rationality" is valued in the legal system, the sentencing judge cannot act as a "rational" decision-maker. A subjectively rational decision-maker maximizes the opportunities to achieve a goal within the limitations of available information and resources. Judges, however, do not have clearly specified goals imposed by external authorities (legislative or appellate) and do not have extensive information about specific criminals or crimes. This situation is particularly frustrating for judges who are supposed to be "consciously" rational decision-makers, that is, whose role is culturally defined as rational (Simon, 1959). The only alternative for judges without externally defined goals is to produce and work toward personal goals. The existence of a variety of personal or local workgroup goals results in disparity. With no legislative definition of the purpose of sentencing and few criteria for locating a case within a broad range of choices, judges not unpredictably put their own values, their "character, bias, neurosis, and daily vagary," and the bureaucratic needs of their associates into the vacuum left by the legislature (Frankel, 1972, p. 21; Eisenstein and Jacob, 1977).

Without a clearly defined goal, sentences chosen by judges cannot be criticized as inappropriate or disparate. An appropriate sentence to achieve an offender-centered goal might be entirely inappropriate for a society-centered goal. Sentences chosen for the same type of crime and criminal may be disparate but fair in relation to different sentence goals. There are five traditional sentence goals with conflicting assumptions about human nature and about social values. Two goals are oriented to the interests of society in public safety and crime reduction: incapacitation and general deterrence. Two other goals are oriented toward the interests of the individual in reassignment to the free society: rehabilitation and specific deterrence. For three goals—rehabilitation, specific deterrence, and incapacitation—disparity is difficult to recognize because of the diverse personal histories and needs of the offenders. The fifth goal—"just deserts"—serves community values and individual spiritual needs but expects neither social betterment nor personal improvement.

Table 9-2 lists the goals with their expected effects. The last column shows that the effectiveness of sentences for social goals can be measured by crime statistics and for individual goals by case histories. For the unique "just desserts" goal, the efficacy of sentencing can best be estimated by degree of public satisfaction reported in polls.

Like legislators, judges find political security in claiming to pursue all goals at once. However, in practice, judges adopt different goals for different crimes. For example, specific deterrence instead of general deterrence is applied to white-collar crimes, and incapacitation instead of "just deserts" to blue-collar crimes. Judges generally follow the fashion in legal philosophy. During the progressive period of great optimism concerning the resocialization of deviants, judges introduced a new kind of sentence, probation, which expanded their own sentencing alternatives and fit the rehabilitation goal. Judges have not settled on a practice which would achieve the latest fashion in goals, "just

Table 9-2. Traditional Sentence Goals

	Expected Effect On				
Goal	*Offender*	*Society*	*Require Information On*	*Judge Capability*	*Measure of Effect*
Specific deterrence	Adjust to law	Order	Individual resources	Good	Case history
General deterrence	Punish	Crime reduction	Motives of population subset	Poor	Crime statistics
Rehabilitation	Reorganize personality	Social consensus	Individual psychology	Poor	Case history
Incapacitation	Impotence	Community safety	Individual threat	Average average	Crime statistics
"Just deserts"	Absolution	Sense of justice	Crime seriousness	Excellent	Public opinion

deserts." Instead, judges seem receptive to the guidelines reform, discussed later, which specifies factors but not goals.

The legitimacy of certain kinds of personal information is a significant question in selecting sentences to meet these goals. Some personal data, such as race or sex, should not enter into the consideration for any goals. Other facts may pertain to one goal but not another (Sutton, 1978a). For incapacitation, the "dangerousness" of the offender is the primary consideration, while job history relates directly to specific deterrence. For incapacitation and rehabilitation, those who commit the same crime receive terms which are not a standard price, but fit their personal likelihood of recidivism. Although courts have precise rules for the admission of evidence during the classification stage, at the assignment stage few rules restrict information about the offender.

For the goals of general deterrence and "just deserts," disparity is a very serious criticism. Achieving general deterrence requires that potential offenders know exactly what the punishment will be for a crime (as well as the probability of identification and classification). "Just deserts" means that the punishment suits the crime and not the individual, so that the same appropriate penalty must be repeated for the same offense. Judges must agree upon the "seriousness" of crimes and of the significance of aggravating and mitigating circumstances before they can begin to achieve these goals. Criminal codes usually provide judges with vague guidelines about the "seriousness" of offenses, but some new criminal codes include specific directives for the use of aggravating and mitigating circumstances to revise the base sentence (Lagoy and associates, 1978; Oppenheim, 1976).

The problems involved in pursuing a rational, widely acceptable sentencing policy are obvious from the above discussion. The different goals reflect different values, emphasize different factors, and require different types of information. This divergence of goals also makes it difficult to evaluate and understand sentencing. Evaluation is difficult because it requires that one know the individual judge's underlying philosophy. Understanding becomes more difficult because the existence of this diversity of views, with its concomitant confusion, permits other factors (for example, conformance to accepted courtroom norms, requirements of ongoing relationships) to influence the sentencing decision as well. The nature of these other factors has received a good deal of attention recently, especially by political scientists. In the view of these researchers, the impact of traditional goals upon sentencing has been mitigated by judges' attempts to accommodate the interests and demands of their immediate coworkers and the sociopolitical environment within which they operate.

The work of these researchers can be incorporated into what might be labeled a political model of sentencing. This model will be discussed in some detail here because it is consistent with many of the observed disparities in sentencing and can shed some light on various attempts at sentencing reform.

A POLITICAL MODEL OF SENTENCING

As may be seen in Figure 9-1, the political model of sentencing suggests that sentencing takes place within a politico-legal jurisdiction or geographically defined environment which can be described by its social, economic, and political characteristics. The law and culture of the jurisdiction provide the outer limits for the judge's sentence choices. Unlike a mechanistic model in which law directly explains and predicts the decision, in the political model criminal law allows the judge large scope for discretion. Culture, which has a close interactive relationship to law, provides additional limits upon sentencing. The demands of the political elite and the public further narrow the options of the judge by specifying the sentence goals and factors that suit their interests. Legislatures through hearings, executives in speeches, and party leaders in campaign documents normally exert pressure toward law and order goals (unless their own peers are the miscreants). The local D.A.s and private attorneys with whom the judge works regularly, called the "workgroup," also develop sentencing expectations based upon their mutual interests. In addition, the public, albeit sporadically, develops an opinion on how to deal with a criminal or a type of offense or expresses a preference for a goal. At the next level, the judge perceives the expectations of law, culture, and the political system through his own cognitive and affective processes. Moreover, the judge's own values, role definitions, and needs serve to reinforce or to reject the external norms and demands. The judge's response to demands takes place within a situation or context, for example, during a competitive local election, after a riot, or in a dirty, noisy courtroom.

All of these concepts—environment, law, culture, situation, political demands, and judge's attitudes—have a relationship in the model to the judge's selection of goals and factors and upon the sentence choices. Given this view one would not expect two independent variables, describing the offense and the offender, to explain all the variation in sentences. Moreover, unless most of the variables associated with the concepts in the model are included, it is not possible to measure disparity or to identify impropriety. To elaborate upon the utility of the model in this regard, it is necessary to discuss its component parts in some detail, beginning with the decision-

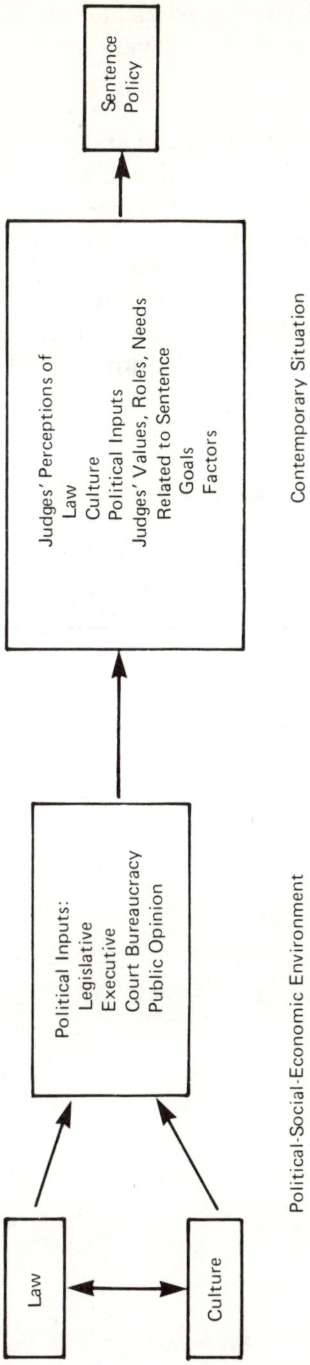

Figure 9-1. Political Model of Sentencing or "Assigning" Criminal Offenders

maker's inputs. In this discussion particular emphasis will be placed upon reviewing empirical evidence relevant to the model.

Decision-maker Inputs

The idea that the attitudes, roles, and ambitions of a judge or other decision-maker contribute to the explanation of decisions is conventional in the political model, if not in the legal models. Various studies have shown that the identity of the judge—after controlling for the offense—explains 29 percent of sentence variation in Philadelphia (Uhlman, 1978) and 44 percent in Iowa (Gibson, 1978b). In Baltimore, Chicago, and Detroit the identity of the courtroom, which could indicate either the judge alone or the "workgroup" of the court elite, explains up to 18 percent of sentence length differences (See Table 9-3).

Table 9-3. Patterns of Explanation for Sentence Decisions: Case Analyses by Regression Programs

		Variable Contribution to Explanation of							
State Courts			*In-Out*		*Length*		*Both*		
Baltimore[a]	R^2	.37		.66					
Offense			.13		.33				
Offender			.09		.13				
Case process			.04		.03				
Decision-maker			.11		.18				
Chicago[a]	R^2	.19		.66		.60[b]		.51[c]	
Offense			.10		.47		.46		.36
Offender			.02		.04		.00		.04
Case process			.02		.06		.10		.11
Decision-maker			.05		.09		.04		—
Detroit[a]	R^2	.43		.50				.81[c]	
Offense			.11		.32				.68
Offender			.19		.08				.13
Case Process			.04		.04				.00
Decision-maker			.09		.06				.00
Denver[d]	R^2					.50			
Offense							.33		
Offender							.18		
Federal Courts									
Eight Offenses[e]	R^2	.26		.50		.58			
Offense			.06		.48		.49		
Offender			.18		.00		.06		
Case process			.03		.02		.04		
Auto Theft[e]	R^2	.20		.10		.24			
Offender			.18		.07		.19		
Case process			.00		.03		.03		
Political: court			.02		.00		.02		

Table 9-3 continued

Robbery[e]	R^2	.20		.14		.25	
Offender			.13		.08		
Case process			.07		.04		
Political: court			.00		.02		
Counterfeiting[e]	R^2	.17		.22		.22	
Offender			.14		.08		
Case process			.03		.06		
Political: court			.00		.08		
Narcotics[e]	R^2	.20		.26		.42	
Offender			.07		.04		
Case process			.14		.22		
Marijuana[e]	R^2	.15		.29		.31	
Offender			.07		.03		
Case process			.08		.25		
Political: court			.00		.01		
Draft[e]	R^2	.09		.15		.36[f]	
Offender			.00		.00		–
Case process			.09		.07		–
Political: court			.00		.08		.04
Decision-maker			–		–		.07
Environment			–		–		.25

Code: In-Out = dichotomous decision to incarcerate or not.
Length = length of incarceration for prison cases only.
Both = scale of all cases, with in-out measured zero.

[a]Eisenstein and Jacob, 1977, Tables 10.1, 10.2, 1972 cases.

[b]Nardulli, 1978, Table 8.1, 1972 guilty plea cases.

[c]Sutton, 1978b, Tables 21, 22; cases decided in federal district courts in Chicago and Detroit.

[d]Wilkins and associates, 1978, Tables 2, 3.

[e]Sutton, 1978a, Tables 2, 3, 4, 6, 9, 10, 12, 13, 14, 17, 18, 23-26.

[f]Cook, 1973.

Judges have their own idiosyncratic reactions to some crimes. The offense "seriousness" variable would not help to predict the sentence of a judge with a special aversion to a particular crime such as rape, drunk driving, or draft violations (Cook, 1973; Kaufman, 1960; Galanter, 1977). Some judges may take on the role of creative policymaker and opinion leader with respect to a particular crime and other judges will be seeking attention for their own personal satisfaction or political interests (Masters, 1978). In either case their behavior will fit the political model better than the legal model.

The different perceptions and values of judges explain the disparity of sentence among judges working within the same environment, law, culture, and political pressures. In order to control for the confounding variables in different cases, a simulation technique was employed to study federal sentencing. Fifty trial judges in the 2nd Circuit indicated their sentence preferences in thirty identical, fabricated cases (Partridge and Eldridge, 1974). Judges disagreed strongly on type of sentence in all but four cases. Experienced judges varied as much from the average as new judges. Judges had different responses to different kinds of cases; only two judges were severe across all cases, and one was lenient. A similar simulation of misdemeanor sentencing by Virginia state judges also revealed disagreement, but there was less disparity for low-cost nonprison offenses than for high-cost prison offenses (Austin and Williams, 1977).

The complexity of the judge's decision-making process can be illustrated with reference to Table 9-3. It shows the results of regression analyses of sentence choices employing variables relating to three basic factors: the offense, offender characteristics, and process factors. The results show that these factors explain such a small portion of the variation that the existence of disparity can hardly be denied.[1] The squared multiple correlation (R^2) specifies the amount of the total variation in sentences explained by the factors, and it can be taken as a measure of the consistency of sentences, under the assumption that no important factor which judges should include has been excluded from the study. Variables which describe the offense, the offender, and the case process explain less than one-half of the decisions to incarcerate or not. Up to two-thirds of the variation in length of jail terms can be explained in Baltimore and Chicago and half in Detroit and all in federal trial courts. For specific offenses, offender and case variables explain up to 20 percent of sentence type and up to 30 percent of the sentence length. Judges evidently use many other factors or weigh the three basic factors differently. A more in-depth analysis will clarify the role of each in the sentencing process.

Offense Seriousness. Judges generally indicate that offense seriousness is the most important factor they take into account in sentencing (Yale Project, 1975). There is a cultural expectation that the severity of punishment will be commensurate with the seriousness of the crime. Crime seriousness, however, is not a constant, but changes over time in the same culture and varies by population subgroups within a jurisdiction (Sebba, 1978). Since criminal codes grow by piecemeal addition, "the scheme of maximum penalties laid down by the penal code as an indicator of the severity of the offense is generally somewhat anomalous, remote from current public opinion, and barely paid lip service by the courts" (Sebba, 1978, p. 252). In California the popular ranking of crimes, the punishments provided by the penal code, and the actual sentences served by offenders show no relationship (Rose and Prell, 1955).

Neither judges nor social scientists have an accurate yardstick for seriousness. Studies which include an offense variable use several types of measures. The simplest approach in studying a universe of cases involving different crimes is to use a dummy variable to describe each case, for example, bank robbery or not, forgery or not, and so on (Sutton 1978a; Eisenstein and Jacob, 1977; Tiffany and associates, 1975). This device avoids the subjective rank ordering of crimes. A dummy offense variable does not predict severity, but instead seriousness is defined by severity. When the sentences of crimes of widely different "seriousness" are examined together, then the offense factor appears to be very significant (Tiffany and associates, 1975). However, the correlation only means that judges treat most robbers differently from most embezzlers, but either could have the more severe punishment.

Scholars use state criminal codes, despite their inadequacies, to prepare indicators of seriousness from the minimum (Scott, 1974) or the maximum (Gibson, 1978b; Wilkins and associates, 1978; Hagan, 1975) available penalty in prison months. Nardulli (1978) follows a more complex regression procedure to develop an index of *case* seriousness which takes account of several offenses in the same case. However, by including the sex of the defendant in the score, his findings cannot be compared to other studies that employ a separate offender variable. His measure is more realistic in its ranges than the code penalty measures, which assign the same seriousness score to every case in the same statutory category.

The penalties for some offenses have been routinized by judges to clear their docket expeditiously. The tacit policy adopted for auto theft offenses by federal judges is shown by the low coefficient of variation (.75; Sutton, 1978a, Table 8) and by the stable percentage receiving imprisonment over time (less than 10 percent variation in 1960-1976; Federal Offenders, 1972; AO Report, 1973-1976). Although sentences for auto theft have little disparity across judges and jurisdictions they may still be out of line with the sentences for other crimes. The mean sentence for auto theft is three times higher than for embezzlement and half the mean sentence for narcotics (Sutton, 1978a, Table 8). Those sentenced to prison for auto theft in 1976 received 65 percent of the maximum, but, for income tax evasion, 26 percent. A rank order of offense seriousness is absolutely necessary to reveal this kind of unfairness.

A measure of offense can be used to examine variation of sentences for one type of crime, as Tiffany and associates (1975) do with federal bank robbery. Circumstances in mitigation and aggravation can be introduced, such as defendant sobriety, victim vulnerability, use of weapon, or extent of injury to victim (Wilkins and associates, 1978).

Using indicators that describe the crime rather than the legal charge also takes account of the suspicion that judges often sentence for the "real" offense (Johnson, 1972; Eisenstein and Jacob, 1977; Wilkins and associates, 1978). In fact, by introducing indicators for both the formal charge and the actual behavior into the analysis, it would be possible to compare their relative influence upon the sentence.

The offense factor contributes heavily to the explanation of the length of the sentence in federal courts and in state courts located in Baltimore, Chicago, and Detroit (Table 9-3). However, offense does not explain the "assignment" of thc criminal to a place in or out of society. Those convicted of very serious offenses are only somewhat less likely to escape institutionalization. The goals of incapacitation or special deterrence must, therefore, be influencing the decision on length.

Offender. The personal characteristics of the offender which judges consider in sentencing can be described under the headings of behavioral, attitudinal, and opportunity cost. The behavioral characteristic includes the prior criminal record of the offender and his current legal and social status. The attitudinal characteristic covers general respect for the court. Opportunity cost involves the resources of the offender which would be lost to himself or to society if he were imprisoned. Under each of these headings the indicators of offender capacity to rejoin society may be more or less proper to different sentence goals.

Behavioral. The visible characteristics of offenders—race, ethnicity, class, and sex—provide the judge with cues to their worth and their "threat" to the community. Whether or not judges use particular cues depends upon contemporary cultural norms. Only a few judges let race trigger personal prejudices (Gibson, 1978a); and aggregate sentence patterns no longer correlate with race (Chiricos and Waldo, 1975; Burke and Turk, 1975; Clarke and Koch, 1976; but see Adams, 1977; Castberg, 1971). However, judges still employ sexual stereotyeps of female weakness and "place" in the home to give less severe sentences (Alabama Project, 1975; Pope, 1975; Crites, 1978). For bank robbery the sex of the offender accounts for 10 percent of the sentence variations (Sutton, 1978a).

Prior record is a behavioral measure generally accepted by judges and social scientists as a legitimate criterion for sentence severity. The practice measure of previous criminal activity which can properly be used as a cue to sentence is not so clear. Some of the problems are: Should arrests be counted? (Johnson, 1972). Should trivial convictions be included? Should convictions for an entirely different type of crime be noted? Should the period of time elapsed since the last criminal behavior be considered? (Wilkins and associates, 1978). Empirical studies show that offender record explains a minor portion of the sentence variation. Prior record of convictions explains from 4 to 8 percent of sentence choice in the federal circuits (Sutton, 1978b, Tables 3-7). But in a few cities the federal judges are very much influenced by prior record (Detroit, .13; Dallas, .28; Sutton, 1978b, Tables 18-23). Record is more important in certain offense categories in certain geographical areas, for example for robbery in the 9th Circuit (.19, Table 11); for auto theft in the 5th Circuit (.19, Table 13); and for eight focal offenses in the 6th Circuit (.17, Table 14) and the 9th Circuit (.28, Table 15). Prior record almost entirely explains the sentence choice of Detroit federal judges for bank robbers (.69, Table 27).

Attitudinal. Although the attitude of the offender may be plain to the judge, such a variable is difficult to operationalize without direct observation. Two measures of "respect for the court" were used in a study of the sentencing of traffic offenders: appropriate dress and deferential demeanor (Jaros and Mendelsohn, 1967). The symbolic indicator (dress) affected the sentence of recidivists but not of first offenders, suggesting the importance of interactive effects. This seminal article has not been replicated in felony court, although there is evidence that judges who have discretion react to defendant attitude. Frankel (1972) reports that one federal judge adds a year for criticism of the court.

The attitude of the defendant toward government and society also influences the sentence. Showing repentance for hurting the social fabric, often by an early guilty plea, brings a lighter penalty than resisting the legitimacy of law and the judicial process. Judicial and other public authorities want deviants to approve and accept the rules—and, in fact, most offenders do prefer to belong (Casper, 1978, Tables V-1, VII).

Opportunity cost. Persons worth more to society because of ability, training, money, family support, or productivity receive less punitive treatment. For society as a whole, there is a greater loss in committing one educated and productive person to prison than one untrained and unemployed person (Aranson, 1973). Judges balance their past and predicted contributions to sicety against the debit of their offense. Indicators of opportunity cost are in common use in the guidelines for bail, diversion, and probation decisions. Collecting accurate information about offenders' intelligence, education, family life, work history, and social behavior is expensive; most probation reports provide little more detail than the prosecutor obtains from standard record sources. As a result judges rely on crude cues to ascertain the offender's value and threat to society. For the "just deserts" goal, opportunity cost would be irrelevant and personal data would not be required to make the sentence decision.

Process Factors. Time is the most important resource that court personnel can distribute, and important indicators of the case process factor relate to the conservation of time. In the federal courts ". . . the persistent emergence of process-related factors as significant predictors of sentence outcome across offenses, jurisdictions, and time is persuasive evidence of the cost to the defendant for invoking the elements of due process" (Sutton, 1978a, p. 10). Casper (1978) reports the view of adult males charged with felonies in Detroit, Baltimore, and Phoenix that judges had little time for their cases and showed more interest in getting finished with the procedures than "doing justice." Only half (52 percent) thought the judge tried to find out if the individual was innocent. The basic assumption of the court elite about the defendant explains their attitude toward time. Every offender not screened out of the criminal process is considered guilty despite the constitutional injunction to the contrary (Nardulli, 1978). Therefore, the time defendants require to present evidence of their innocence at bench or jury trial is considered wasted (Mileski, 1974). The minutes used by offenders in misdemeanor court cost as much proportionately in penalty as the hours used by felony defendants.

Offender Resistance: not guilty plea. One federal judge explains his policy for pricing time: "I follow the rule of thumb that where a man pleads guilty, and saves the government the expense of a lengthy trial, he deserves consideration. . . ." His formula for computation was one-half the maximum for a guilty plea (Gaylin, 1970, p. 106). An example of the meaning to the offender of opting for a trial can be found in the sentencing for drug crimes in the federal courts. For marijuana offenses 18.5 percent and for narcotics offenses 16.4 percent of the national variation in length of prison term can be explained by the exercise of the trial right (Sutton, 1978a, Tables 24, 26). The contribution of the not guilty plea to narcotics sentence weight by circuit is startling: 25.5 percent in the 2nd Circuit, 16.2 percent in the 5th, and 30.6 percent in the 9th (Sutton, 1978b, Table 16). Of the federal districts examined, only Detroit sentences could be explained without reference to waiver of trial rights (Sutton, 1978b, Table 27).

In so-called political trials the offender resists the system by refusing to plead guilty to a criminal act openly performed and by using the courtroom as a public forum. Occasionally defendants and their lawyers find ways of disrupting the normal trial routines and literally wasting court time; judges and prosecutors sometimes incite the defense behavior. Defendants in notorious political trials, such as the Communist trials in the 1950s and the pacifist trials of the 1920s, 1940s, and 1960s, usually receive the maximum sentence. The court elite cannot be unaware that their immediate personal rewards for harsh treatment of political offenders will be trial and appellate judgeships. In such cases a good predictor would be interactive between offender attitude (disrespect to court) and case process (trial time).

Offender resistance: right to jury. The jury trial uses more time and money than other procedures, and the cost of the due process right to the defendant is high (Newman, 1966; Dawson, 1969; Downie, 1971; Casper, 1972). In Baltimore, Chicago, and Detroit state courts the average sentence after jury trial is longer than after bench trial or guilty plea (Eisenstein and Jacob, 1977, Table 10.1). In federal courts the average sentence for all offenses following a jury trial is more than twice as severe as a bench trial and almost three times as severe as waiver of trial (Federal Offender, 1971, Exhibit VII; see also Tiffany and associates, 1975, Tables 7, 10). The price of jury trial differs among judges and courts. For eight federal offenses the use of jury contributes 3.5 percent of the explanation of varying sentence weights nationally (Sutton, 1978a, Table 2), but ranges up to 9 percent in the 9th Circuit (Sutton, 1978b, Tables 5, 6, 7). In the Chicago state courts the jury variable contributes 17 percent to the explanation of the sentence of those who go to trial (Nardulli, 1978).

Those who commit a more serious offense pay a higher price for demanding a jury trial. Nardulli (1978) found that the interactive effect of offense and jury added another 14 percent to the explanation of the sentence variation. Since convictions for serious offenses are more important to protect the community and more difficult to prove, the judge has a special incentive to discourage the defendant from using a process which is less predictable and could make the court elite appear ineffective.

The jury right affects the judge's decisions on type of sentence and on length of sentence. In California state courts, where the adult authority until recently set length, jury use was the major correlate of the judge's choice of prison over probation, controlling for offense seriousness and prior record (Greenwood and associates, 1973). In federal courts the jury variable is a more powerful predictor of sentence length than type (Sutton, 1978a, p. 10), particularly for the blue-collar offenses of robbery, auto theft, larceny, and counterfeiting (Sutton, 1978a, Tables 10, 13, 16, 17; 1978b, Table 14). An interactive variable for jury use and type of crime could check the hypothesis that white-collar offenders, who have a greater social value, are not similarly penalized for protecting their interests. In other words, a variable which includes both the costs to the court elite and the opportunity costs based on offender characteristics would be more useful than either alone.

Cooperation in case solution. An important factor in sentence disparity which has not been used as a variable in empirical research is the contribution made by the offender to the solution of other crimes, either his own previous crimes, his partner's, or persons in his circle of acquaintances (but see Forst and Lucianovic, 1977). Federal judges who responded to a *Yale Law Journal* survey (1956) indicated that shorter sentences were an appropriate reward for aiding in the administration of criminal justice. The U.S. Supreme Court has authoritatively approved the "plea bargain"; however, the Court will have to approve or disapprove the specific exchanges of goods on a case-by-case basis.

Where the arrangement with a stool-pigeon is sub rosa to protect his usefulness, hidden disparity will occur through police or prosecutor decisions to dismiss or reduce charges for his continuing petty crimes. Where the offender turns state's evidence on the stand, disposition will reflect a plea bargain, an agreement to drop charges or sentence lightly, which creates visible disparity among cooperative and uncooperative offenders. The judge plays little part in this exchange, except to approve the rules of the game by passive formal behavior. The game of cooperation creates disparity largely among blue-collar criminals. But in 1978 a white-collar criminal, a lawyer who embezzled over a million dollars, complained of his prison sentence in comparison to the probation received by another lawyer-embezzler who helped the prosecution in its investigation (Goldstein, 1978). The offender had "no information to give up," the resource he needed to buy leniency.

The amount of time spent on a case has a relationship to the sentence goal. For society-centered goals of general deterrence and "just deserts" the processing of offenders in open court followed by condemnation and punishment is an important ritual. For incapacitation or individual-centered goals, adjudication can be abbreviated and invisible. Drug cases in federal courts fit this pattern (Table 9-3). The exchange of goods between court elite and offenders which the case process variable describes does not fit conventional sentence goals, but implies a political goal: the security and satisfaction of the court elite.

Political Inputs

The judges (or workgroup) make their sentence decisions within a political environment which includes the expectations and specific demands of an elected elite, appellate judges, the trial court bureaucracy, and the public. Although the demands for "law and order" by executives and legislators—from the president and Congress to local mayors and city council members—belong in a political model of sentencing, their demands have seldom been operationalized for empirical studies. One exception is the Sutton study (1978a, b) which includes a juror utilization variable, a measure of the response of the court bureaucracy to the pressure from Congress to save on jury administration costs. Some hypotheses about the relationship of political demands and sentencing which have been tested will be discussed.

Court Bureaucracy. Judges on multi-judge courts generally follow the standard operating practices of their courts (Orland and Tyler, 1974, p. 67). These practices fit the needs of those with regular jobs in the courts, from clerks to professionals. Court regulars, for example, may support the policy of discouraging jury use, since they waste time which could be spent on more rewarding tasks (Nardulli, 1978). Counsel must prepare more carefully for jury trial, doing research on the backgrounds of the jurors for voir dire and translating the cross examination and arguments into language understandable to laypersons. The judge is under more stress in handling motions, risking error, and managing a group of amateurs as partners in the decision-making process. Except in unusual cases with some payoff in political or professional publicity, the costs of jury trial are too high to support a pro-jury policy. In courts with strong administrative judges and central calendars, the practice is often to send jury cases to judges with tough reputations.

What is the impact of the "cheap jury" policy on federal sentencing? Sutton (1978a) employs a juror usage index, an indicator of district efficiency in delivery jurors, as a predictor. The index contributed a small amount (1.7 percent) to the explanation of the length of robbery and larceny sentences (Tables 10, 15). Where the court minimized juror availability, sentences were lower. On the other hand, where a court had a history of great jury use, there were longer sentences in counterfeiting, auto theft, embezzlement, and draft cases (Table 10). The interactive effect of the offender's choice of jury in the case process and the court policy on juror utilization needs to be tested, since a conflict would suggest a higher sentence.

Probation officers, like the lawyers in the court bureaucracy, have an investment in their own routines and decisional cues. Although probation officers may spend one-fourth or more of their time in preparation of presentence reports (Stanley, 1976), the documents are often boiler-plate, providing the judge with little fresh insight into the offender's character and no specific recommendations for the use of community resources (Eisenstein and Jacob, 1977; Orland and Tyler,

1974). Probation officers, like judges, measure their work-product by quantity of cases processed. The probation officer generally anticipates the sentencing tendencies of the judge being served (Cook, 1977; Carter and Wilkins, 1967). When there is disagreement, the judge inclines toward probation more than the adviser, except in the case of violent crimes (Federal Offenders, 1965-69). In white-collar sentencing, judges reject advice against probation in a large percentage of cases. Since probation officers disagree among themselves on good risks for probation, they exacerbate rather than ameliorate sentence disparity (Carter and Wilkins, 1967).

Public Opinion. Public opinion is a variable that is seldom introduced into a judicial behavior study because of the deeply ingrained norm of judicial independence. Judges, perhaps more than social scientists, recognize the legitimacy of public opinion as a sentence factor. At the first California Sentencing Institute a judge made this statement:

> I think that judges have to take into consideration the feelings of the general public as one factor but not as the sole governing factor. You cannot set aside public reaction completely in deciding your sentences because if judges get too far out front of the popular conception of punishment, it will cause ultimate disrespect for the law (45 Cal Rptr Appendix, 1967).

Public opinion has two uses in a political model. For sentences in different geographical areas at the same point in time, opinion focusing on a particular case may explain an outlying data point in an empirical analysis. Some comparative disparity may be due to short-term public reactions of outrage over a crime or series of similar cases. Generally culture is more important than opinion in a comparative analysis (Levin, 1977).

On the other hand, to understand changing sentence policy over time, public opinion about a type of crime is an important predictor (Cook, 1979). Public opinion on the Vietnam War explains 84 percent of the variation in national aggregate sentences from 1967 to 1975 (Cook, 1977, Table 5). The diverse sentencing policies of federal judges for Prohibition violations in the 1930s (Boldt, 1963) reflect the same intense public feelings as for draft offenses during wartime. The reduction over time of imprisonment for marijuana offenses indicates the adjustment of the judges to the changing public posture toward smoking pot. Sentence policy change over time of politically salient crimes is understandable within the political model, but not in legal models.

Environment, Law, and Culture

Environmental variables have not been as popular in studies of judicial policy as in studies of legislative policy (but see Cook, 1973). Law has been taken as a constant in examining sentences in the same legal system; only in comparing sentences across jurisdictions, such as federal and state sentences, is some control for law necessary. The same law may be binding within different environments and cultures. Culture is not perfectly correlated with environment or with legal boundaries. The geographical disparity of sentences is a clue to the importance of culture (Harries and Brunn, 1978); Levin (1977) and Eisenstein and Jacob (1977), in their respective studies of criminal courts in Minneapolis and Pittsburgh, and in Baltimore, Chicago, and Detroit, show that distinctive urban political cultures affect the type of judges and their decision-making practices and outputs.

A test of the relationship of culture to sentence is a comparison of aggregate sentences of federal and state courts located in the same city. These courts administer different criminal codes and perform with different structures and selection procedures. But the hypothesis is that despite these differences, judges socialized and working within the same local culture would have similar patterns of sentencing. The test of the hypothesis is the correlation of the rank order of federal and state decisions on length of sentences for ordinary crimes. The available data cover the five cities only, so the results simply suggest the utility of a broader study.

The correlation between the rank order of prison length averages between the two court systems is very high (.87 < .01). Federal courts are harsher for all five types of crime (Table 9-4). The state courts range in prison length from six months average in Detroit for possession to 105 months in Baltimore for robbery, while the federal courts have a wider range, from thirty-one for possession in Detroit to 189 for robbery in Baltimore. The column showing state sentences as a percentage of the federal sentences reveals that the Pittsburgh and Detroit courts are less similar across legal systems than the Baltimore, Chicago, and Minneapolis courts. Evidently the differences in law and structure exert an impact upon court output, but within the confines of the cultural pattern. In the absence of any alternative hypotheses to explain the congruent ordering of federal and state sentences, it appears that culture is indeed a powerful element in establishing the basic sentence policy.

The disparity of sentences and the questionable considerations provoking sentencing are not surprising in the light of the conflicting or vague requirements of law and culture in the same jurisdiction and of the political demands upon the judge. The different views of judges

Table 9-4. Local Culture and Length of Prison Sentence

	Average Months in Prison		
Area/Crime	*State*	*% of Federal*	*Federal*[a]
Pittsburgh			
Robbery	35	.241	145
Larceny	11	.290	38[a]
Baltimore			
Robbery	105	.556	189
Hard drugs	80	.930	86
Detroit			
Robbery	46	.447	103
Hard drugs	11	.275	40
Weapons	9	.273	33[a]
Possession	6	.194	31[a]
Chicago			
Robbery	57	.460	124
Hard drugs	32	.711	45
Weapons	21	.568	37[a]
Possession	26	.667	39[a]
Minneapolis			
Robbery	75	.573	131
Larceny	18	.487	37

Sources: Levin (1977), Tables 10-13, 74-77; Eisenstein and Jacob (1977), Table 10.4; Federal Offenders (1972-1974), Appendix Table x-4.

[a]Where 1974 has less than ten cases, added to 1972 and 1973.

simply contribute to the irrationality which has already been set. Since there are no indications that the American culture will dispense with contradictory values and norms or that the legislative bodies will clarify their goals, the judges themselves are in a situation in which they must necessarily clean their own house or give up the assignment function. Over the last twenty years judges have made real efforts to develop policies on a courtwide or systemwide basis to deal with the sentence problems. The reform structures created for this purpose will be examined in the next section.

INTERNAL COURT REFORMS

Trial judges have met the general dissatisfaction with sentencing by introducing their own reforms. They have created schools for judges to learn sentence techniques and discuss sentence philosophies, set up decision-making councils for consultation on specific cases, and cooperated with social scientists to create sentence guidelines. The major purpose of the court reforms is to reach agreement upon sentence factors in order to reduce disparity. Efforts to establish a judicial philosophy of sentencing, which would simplify the identification of appropriate factors, have failed. Reform efforts have been strongly motivated by the desire to avoid the imposition of a rigid sentence policy by the legislature or the removal of the assignment function to some new sentencing commission.

Education for Sentencing

In recognition of their lack of preparation for the sentencing function, court systems have developed judicial education programs. Traditional law school courses provide prospective judges with minimal preparation for criminal trial practice or for judging. Judge Walter Hoffman (1976, p. 199), a former director of the Federal Judicial Center, reports that the "vast majority of district judges have little or no experience in the field of criminal law and procedure prior to their appointment." Participation in plea bargaining by prosecutors and defense attorneys is the prebench experience closest to taking formal responsibility for a sentence. But new judges on lower trial courts have less experience to bring to the sentencing role than new judges on major trial and appellate courts. Table 9-5 shows the level of preparation of California judges serving during the ten-year period 1968-1977. Preparation for sentencing is measured by positions held in law enforcement, in private criminal practice, in public prosecution or defender roles, and in trial courts with a criminal docket. Judges on the lowest courts needed in-service training more than general jurisdiction or appellate judges. Less than half the California judges on municipal court had prior experience with criminal matters, while over two-thirds of the superior court judges and over 85 percent of the appellate judges had some relevant experiences.

Trial judge seminars and conferences serve two purposes: to instruct judges on the mechanics of sentencing to improve their effectiveness and to develop policy on goals and factors to reduce disparity (Parker, 1965). Since the pilot institute of 1959 the federal court system has offered trial judges in every circuit several opportunities to participate in a sentencing conference (Proceedings, FRD 1960, 1961, 1969; Devitt, 1967; Orland and Tyler, 1974). The seminars that indoctrinate every new federal judge into the ways of the system now include sentencing in the curriculum (Hoffman, 1977; Partridge, 1977). State trial judges enjoy the same opportunity to discuss sentence goals and disparity at state and national seminars (NCTJ Proc. 1965; Phila. Comm., 1969). The National College of State Trial Judges, founded in 1963, offers a two-week course on criminal law and sentencing, a one-week course on misdemeanor sentencing, and a one-week graduate course on sentencing. The California courts offered annual sentencing institutes from 1965 through 1973; then the new Center for

Table 9-5. California Judges: Preparation for Sentencing[a]

Experience Measure	*Appellate*[b]	*Superior*	*Municipal*
0	11 (.126)	247 (.317)	312 (.491)
1	42 (.483)	364 (.467)	264 (.416)
2	28 (.322)	143 (.184)	57 (.090)
3/4	6 (.069)	25 (.032)	2 (.003)

Index for experience:
criminal law private practice = 1
prosecutor or public defender = 1
FBI, police, probation, or parole officer = 1
trial judge with criminal jurisdiction = 1
(maximum of two points)

Source: Arnold (1973, 1977).

[a]All judges serving 1968-1977; judges elevated counted more than once.

[b]Appellate includes Supreme and Court of Appeal judges.

Judicial Education and Research took over the program (Proceedings, Cal Rptr, 1965-1973). This on-the-job training has covered almost the entire state trial judiciary above the justice of the peace level.

The federal judges paid special attention at their institutes to the ethics of giving light sentences to white-collar criminals, particularly income tax offenders. Although the judges reached an abstract consensus that general deterrence was the correct goal in such cases, they were not willing to give the appropriate prison terms. In their simulated exercises half the judges persisted in giving probation both before and after the seminar discussions (Thomsen, 1962). In real cases the percentage assigned to prison exceeded 40 percent only once in the twenty-year period since the first seminar (Federal Offenders, 1972, Tables H3, H9, H11, H13; Annual Report, AO, 1973-76, Table D5). Neither were the judges able to agree on a standard sentence which would offer general deterrence to other white collar crimes. Federal judges give more predictable sentences for burglars and thieves (see Table 9-3), for which the appropriate goals of specific deterrence and rehabilitation indicate individualization. White-collar criminals run the least risk of prison but the most uncertainty as to length of prison term. The greatest disparity remains in the crime types where predictability is most important to the goal.

The federal seminars also offer practical information and advice to judges. Senior judges and lecturers invited from the probation and prison staffs review statutory provisions, explain complicated alternatives for offender treatment, describe services which the probation officer can perform for the judge, and even chaperon visits to correctional institutions. The California institutes included dialogues between judges and prisoners, as well as between judges and parolees. Emphasis is placed upon accurate information about the codes and the facilities. However, judges do not receive information about population subgroups which would help them decide upon general deterrence sentences, the goal which receives the most emphasis at the sessions.

Despite the many positive aspects of these schools and seminars, there were a number of problems connected with them. Since the judges did not develop any rank order of crime "seriousness" at their schools or receive any information on public opinion on crime, they did not get any assistance in achieving the "just deserts" goal. The statistics on crime and recidivism which were circulated did not help the judges reach any conclusions about the relevant factors. The sentencing schools raised the consciousness of the judges about the sentencing problem and provided essential factual information to avoid illegal sentences. Since the structure was ad hoc, providing lectures and opportunities for discussion, and had no authority to make policy for the respective court systems, no policy on goals or factors emerged which could have reduced disparity.

Judge Devitt (1967) admitted that "... regardless of how many sentencing institutes we have and how often we get together to discuss consensus among ourselves, the facts, supported by dependable statistics, continue to reflect unjustified disparity between the sentences imposed for the same crime upon persons in like circumstances and with similar histories and backgrounds." Judge Frankel (1972) evaluates the schools as "trivial and sometime things" from which the judges leave "as miscellaneous and unpredictable as ... when they arrived." Judge Hoffman's hopes that a federal sentencing philosophy would evolve from the free exchange of views at meetings was dead by 1977. He admitted that "there is no such thing as a standardized sentencing philosophy ..." (Hoffman, 1968, 1977).

Sentence Consultation

At the time the sentencing schools offered general information and abstract discussion, the sentencing council was introduced as a structural reform at the federal district level to deal with actual cases. The purposes of the council were more ambitious: to assist judges in making a particular decision in line with colleagues and to develop a district sentencing standard. The first council began in Detroit (EDMich) in 1960; Brooklyn judges (EDNY) established a council in 1962; Chicago (NDI11), in 1963; and Portland (DOre), in 1974. The majority of federal district courts did not copy their model.

The particular form of the council is unique to each district, but the basic arrangement is the same: the sentencing judge presents his case problem to several other judges for their recommendations before making a final decision. In Detroit and Brooklyn the judges consult in panels of three; in Chicago one panel of fluctuating size includes over half of the judges; and in Portland all judges belong to the council (Smith, 1963; Doyle, 1961; Diamond and Zeisel, 1975). In Detroit the panel usually meets at 8:30 A.M. for coffee and doughnuts and discussion of the cases. The judges have prepared summary sheets, organizing their evaluations of the gravity of the offense, and the attitude, prior record, and personal situation of the offender; they also make a recommendation for sentence. The sentencing judge briefly presents the essentials of the case, and the judges try to estimate the offender's adjustment, danger to society, and need for training. They explicitly consider the relation of a possible sentence to general deterrence and the congruence of possible sentences with decisions in similar cases. The other two established councils in Brooklyn and Chicago are not as well organized around sentence goals, factors, and relationship to disparity. The new Oregon council uses the most modern statistical tools: a prediction score of the offender's danger to the community, the salient factor score of the parole commission, and historical data on district and national sentencing of the offense from the national court bureaucracy.

Since one of the changes anticipated from the council reform was the development of a common approach, the extent of disparity in council and noncouncil districts will give some indication of the achievement of that goal. The impact of the Brooklyn council on disparity has been examined in three studies using different methods: simulation, analysis of council recommendations, and analysis of data on district sentences.

The Second Circuit Sentencing Study (Partridge and Eldridge, 1974), which generated data from simulations, showed enough disparity within Brooklyn to indicate that no consistent sentence policy had developed. In Brooklyn only 9 percent of the judges selected sentences equal to the median sentence for the Circuit, in comparison to 15 percent in New York City and 16 percent in the smaller districts. The council did not succeed in reducing the proportion of severe sentences; Brooklyn gave 57 percent severe sentences in contrast to 42 percent in New York City and 34 percent in the smaller districts. Of twenty simulated cases the Brooklyn judges disagreed on the "in-out" decision in thirteen cases, and their choice of sentence length varied up to ten years in six cases.

Cases processed through the Brooklyn council showed an average sentence disparity for proposed sentences before council deliberation of 45.5 percent (Diamond and Zeisel, 1975). The reduction in disparity attributable to council deliberation was only four points. There was no more predictability of sentence decision in the Brooklyn court on eight major offenses in 1971 (R^2 = .51) than in New York City (R^2 = .51, Sutton, 1978b, Tables 18, 19). Only 12 percent of the robbery sentences in Brooklyn could be explained, but 32 percent in New York City. The Brooklyn judges had a policy only for the disposition of narcotics offenders (R^2 = .68, Table 24). The Brooklyn sentences in 1971 were 35 percent less predictable than in 1964, soon after the council was established.

Cases handled by the Chicago council showed an initial average disparity among proposed sentences of 36.7 percent (Diamond and Zeisel, 1975). The Chicago judges reduced their differences with their colleagues upon final disposition in 57 percent of the cases, but the impact upon disparity was only four points. In sentence decisions in 1971, the unexplained variation in Chicago (R^2 = .49) was larger than in Los Angeles (R^2 = .59), a much larger court without a council. The predictability of Chicago sentences declined from 1964 to 1971 by 9 percent (Sutton, 1978b, Tables 22, 23).

Only the statistics for Detroit support the claim that the council device reduces disparity. For all offenses, 81 percent of the variation can be explained by the two "legal" factors of seriousness and record (Sutton, 1978b, Table 21). Detroit reveals considerably more consensus than any other district in the study. Sixty-nine percent of variation in the single offense of robbery in Detroit could be understood by the single factor of prior record, while the offender factor explained none of the variation in robbery sentences in Brooklyn, only 9 percent in New York City, and 13 percent in Los Angeles (Table 24). The consensus in Detroit increased from 1964 to 1971 by 27 percent.

The introduction of a new structure for consultation does not solve the disparity problem. It is illogical to expect that case-by-case discussion would produce consistency without other kinds of inputs, such as historical statistical data used by the new Oregon council. Other factors of personality and environment probably interact in Detroit with the council device to create a district approach to sentencing. What may be unique about the Detroit council, which accounts for its success, is a special combination of humility, compatibility, and willingness to spend time on the sentence decision (Doyle, 1961).

Contemporary Reform: Sentencing Guidelines

The guidelines reform is the contemporary judicial response to external threats to restrict sentencing discretion. Although the Criminal Justice Research Center at Albany, New York, developed the latest approach under a federal LEAA grant, judges participate in the discussion and formulation of the sentencing standard, just as they did in sentencing institutes and councils. The difference is that judges and social scientists in partnership produce a written document adopting a precise formula for sentence choice instead of oral commitments to vague understandings. The guidelines derive from a description of past sentencing factors plus a prescription in preferred factors.

A guideline appears in a simple bureaucratic form, which directs the user (who has certain facts about the case) to a recommended punishment. The device for presenting the recommendation is a two-dimensional matrix, such as the one for felony offenses developed for the Denver court shown in Table 9-6. Such a matrix could cover all offenses in a jurisdiction, a category of offenses as in Table 9-6, or a single offense. One dimension of the matrix shows the scores for seriousness of offense and the second dimension shows the scores for the dangerousness of the offender. In each cell at the intersection of the dimensions on the grid is the recommended range of sentence. Cells contain recommendations of "out," which means no jail, or various lengths of time in jail or prison.

The pragmatic basis for the guidelines approach is that judges use indicators or "cues" about the offense, offender, and other factors to cut down the time cost of decision-making. Agreement on simple cues is a compromise which allows decision-makers working in isolation from each other to reach fairly consistent conclusions. The adoption of any standard set of indicators assures uniformity; the quality of the resulting decisions depends upon the relevance and the propriety of the indicators in relation to a common goal.

In the Denver experimental guidelines, the offense seriousness

Table 9-6. Typical Guideline Matrix for a Felony Category

Offense Seriousness Score	*Offender Prediction Score*				
	−7 to −1	*0 to 2*	*3 to 8*	*9 to 12*	*13+*
10-12	4-5 years	8-10	8-10	8-10	8-10
8-9	Out	Work project	3-4	8-10	8-10
6-7	Out	Out	3-4	6-8	8-10
3-5	Out	Out	Out	4-5	4-5
1-2	Out	Out	Out	Out	3-4

Source: adapted from Wilkins and associates (1978, Table 14), which includes manslaughter, second-degree burglary, theft, and other crimes; only recommendations for maximum prison shown.

score is calculated by assigning a weight to statutory crimes and adding a weight for the degree of harm to the victim (0 to 5). The range of the seriousness score is 1 to 12. The offender prediction score is computed by subtracting "social stability" weights from criminal record weights. The indicators of dangerousness are prior convictions, prior imprisonment (more than thirty days), prior revocation of adult probation or parole, and current legal status as probationer on adult conviction. Social stability indicators are current employment or school attendance and their duration. The range of the offender score is from −7 for those with no record and good social stability to an indefinite maximum of 20 or more. The total calculation requires only seven pieces of information.

In Table 9-6 the cell at the intersection of the lowest scores shows "out," which means no incarceration; the cell at the intersection of the highest scores shows eight to ten years in prison. Judges have more discretion for the most serious crimes and risky offenders. The guidelines narrow but do not eliminate judicial discretion. When a judge decides to sentence outside the guidelines, the project suggests that a sentence council might be triggered. The extra judge-power of a panel would only be directed toward hard or unusual cases.

The Wilkins group predicts positive consequences from the adoption of written guidelines, "the potential to revolutionize the sentencing process" (Wilkins, 1978, p. 27). The reduction of disparity would be the major accomplishment of this reform. The new mechanism is so simple that judicial energy could be conserved for the more difficult cases. Using fewer criteria judges could handle a larger caseload. The incentive for judge-shopping would be reduced as judges fit their sentences into the "cells." Appellate judges could use the guidelines to recognize and review idiosyncratic sentences. Offenders who complain of sentence severity would be able to focus their arguments on the relationships between the criteria and the actual sentence.

Development and Use of the Guidelines Matrix. The precursor to the guidelines format is the scoring table of offender characteristics devised by the Vera Institute of Justice as a basis for "out" recommendations to judges (Lieberman and associates, 1972, Appendix H). A few criminal courts have worked out their own point system for sentencing (Alschuler, 1978). The exact model for the sentencing guidelines is the parole guidelines, also a two-dimensional grid developed by Wilkins and his associates with federal support (Gottfredson and associates, 1975). All of these experiments owe an intellectual debt to the prediction tables developed by the Gluecks (1936, 1940) from records of postrelease offender behavior to help judges recognize likely recidivists. Unlike those of the Gluecks, the modern guidelines build their offender dimension on data about previous *judicial* sentencing behavior, not on data about previous *offender* behavior.

Guidelines are created from the findings of a computer analysis of sentences decided in prior terms of the court and from subjective preferences expressed during the discussion among the judges and consultants. The Wilkins (1978) research group collected data on 205 factors, describing the offense, the offender, and processing of each case in their Denver sample. They were able to explain one-half of the variation in sentences in Denver (see Table 9-3) by six variables; the most important were seriousness of offense (measured by maximum statutory penalty), number of offenses, and prior incarcerations. The larger contribution of offense to the solution is not reflected in the guidelines, in which the offender dimension has equal weight. The amount of variance not explained by the variables entered into the regression means that the guidelines can only be loosely founded upon the analysis.

The project assumed that the collection of data and calculation of the scores would be done by a court staffer and reported to the judge prior to the sentencing hearing. After the judges had used the guidelines for a period of time, perhaps six months, they would meet to discuss their utility, to find out why some sentences fell outside, and to consider revisions. A regression analysis of sentences decided under the guidelines would show whether the guidelines or other factors explained more or less variation than in the original study. For such a simple model the data on a "small number of key variables" could be collected with more assurance of accuracy. However, if information about factors not used in the scoring is not collected, it will be impossible to do an empirical analysis to evaluate the model.

The guidelines approach is a method to develop standards. The same process of data analysis, consultation, and experiment could produce different factors in different regions and court systems. Moreover, the unarticulated and perhaps improper factors which enter into sentences can inform the sentence in an unobtrusive way. If, for example, jury use is an important factor in sentence severity, judges can select the top of the cell range for offenders who insist on jury trial. Or, if judges need to meet environmental pressures for "law and order," the dimension scoring can remain unchanged but the cell entries can be revised upwards; or the scoring can be changed to include arrests and juvenile contacts.

Whether or not guidelines reduce disparity will depend upon how disparity is defined. Disparity between courts with clearly defined but different guidelines would become larger and more visible as the judges on each court moved toward their mean sentence. Although the construction of guidelines might well begin as a local affair with individual participation, the pressure to resolve intercourt disparity within the same system would probably result in a systemwide program. The centralization of guidelines development would be accelerated by prisoner lawsuits claiming a denial of equal protection on the basis of a unique factor adopted by the court where sentencing took place but not employed by other courts in the state for the same code violation and for similar offenders. What is now beginning as a local effort to establish voluntary benchmarks will probably end as a systemwide imposition of an indicator list and weights.

Projected Judicial Reactions to Guidelines. The Pavlovian response of trial judges to the development of any standards to contain their discretion is resistance. Guidelines formulated collegially would no doubt be more acceptable than those imposed by appellate judges or by external executive or legislative bodies. Judges have expressed very strongly, however, their distaste for rigid use of prediction tables (Herlands, 1964) and for treating an offender as a "composite type" or a statistical average (Kaufman, 1962, p. 4). A possible reaction of judges to the cells on the matrix is the following comment: "I have never found a pigeonhole into which I could put . . . any two offenders" (Goodman, 1958, p. 498). Judges have strenuously objected to subordinating their own judgment to conform to other judges' (Renfrew, 1975, p. 617), exactly what the guidelines require in generating an average court practice from the regression solution. An admission of the need for guidelines is most unusual (Devitt, 1967, p. 255).

Judges who join a bench after the advent of guidelines will not object as much as their seniors, who have worked out their personal sentencing philosophies by trial and error. Judges who have never experienced the lonely frustration of balancing the factors which go into a sentence will probably accept guidelines as a matter of course, just as judges who join a court with an administrative judge do not question his authority (Cook, 1972). With judicial turnover, the particular indicators which define seriousness and dangerousness on the guidelines will be accepted as part of court tradition.

Aspects of the guidelines with which judges would feel comfortable are the paperwork and the simplified instructions. Judges have learned to rely upon deskbooks and jury instruction patterns, quickly available for the right occasion. With the increasing bureaucratization of the courts, form-filling is an unavoidable part of the daily routine. Sentencing may become as routinized as explaining law and evidence to juries or describing a workday by fifteen-minute intervals. Many areas of discretion which trial judges enjoyed before the Pound era of reform have disappeared, and sentencing may be their last stand.

Guidelines and Sentencing Goals. Which goals are implicit in the guidelines model? An offense seriousness dimension alone would suggest a "just deserts" goal, if the weighting of offense indicators fit the contemporary public rank-ordering of crimes; or a general deterrence goal, if the weighting fit the expected response of potential offenders to the punishment. However, the statutes and consultants did the ranking from the code and their own values. The offender dimension alone would suggest rehabilitation, if there were indicators for offender needs; or specific deterrence, if there were indicators for offender resources. By considering the social threat of the offender within each offense category, the Denver guidelines seem to fit the incapacitation goal. Although the judges did not agree on a goal, they implicitly adopted through their selection and weighting of indicators the goal with the least modern support. This approach to decision-making is the antithesis of Frankel's demand (1972) for a clearly stated rule backed by principle.

The guidelines translate into a simple formula the prior practice of the judges, although in the light of continuous criticism about effectiveness and equity it can hardly be assumed that current practices are desirable or justifiable (Singer, 1978). The guidelines use indicators that only explain half of the sentences but use them to choose all future sentences. The computer analyses are expensive window dressing for a product which is simple, traditional, and acceptable to the judges. The simplicity and unprincipled nature of the guidelines are virtues in a reform proposal. At least in the first stage the guidelines are voluntary, free of the coercion of appellate or legislative authority. The reform is beginning to spread; Denver, Newark, Chicago, and Phoenix are developing guidelines by contract with a service that grew out of the Wilkins project (Gelman and Kress, 1978). The National Center for State Courts has a grant to evaluate sentencing in the courts that have adopted guidelines. The major benefit flowing from the reform may be the growth of a new professional consultant industry to serve the more affluent court systems. Like its predecessors, this particular reform with its scientific gloss fails to deal effectively with the serious and complex issues faced by the sentencing judge.

CONCLUSION

Despite their real distress about the sentencing function, judges are political animals who have shown little inclination either to allot more time to sentencing or to relinquish their power to other officials. Although judges save time and resources by sharing their power informally with prosecutors in the courtroom "workgroup," they can be expected to resist the open assertion of authority by prosecutors through diversion. Judges have tried to improve their own competence through minor reforms—educational programs, consultation with peers, and local guidelines—which demanded only participation but no involuntary change in their own sentencing behavior. Judges have answered external criticisms at the least cost to judicial resources, patterns of operation, and power.

The training of judges prepares them to handle the procedures and evidence to decide upon "classification," that is, guilt, but the skills needed to "assign" an offender are not taught in their law school curriculum. Judges have tried to fill the gap with in-service training at institutes and seminars. Despite their own inadequacies in the behavioral sciences, judges feel that no other public authority has the prestige and confidence of the public to make a decision to exclude an individual from society.

Is it possible for judges to render effective and fair sentences? If not, what are the alternatives?

Effectiveness

The effectiveness of sentences cannot be measured without a standard or goal. Currently American society is between goals. Rehabilitation is outmoded and "just deserts" not yet widely accepted. The sentencing goals embody fundamental and conflicting American beliefs and norms about human behavior: that human beings can change for the better (rehabilitation); that people are rational and want to avoid trouble (special deterrence); that people feel better if they pay for their mistakes ("just deserts"); that people fear public obloquy and banishment (general deterrence). Incapacitation is the only goal without cultural support; it implies the opposite of the four sayings. Yet the factors which correlate with sentence as well as the proposed guidelines suggest that judicial practice serves incapacitation. The popularity of "guidelines" among prosecutors, parole boards, and now judges is evidence that officials find safety in using cues to their decisions and in hiding the goal against which their performance could be measured.

The training of judges provides them with the skills to select sentences which fit some but not all of the traditional goals. Judges have the capability for excellent performance when the standard is "just deserts," since they only need a crime seriousness to apply to the classification of the offender and can adjust their performance to the feedback from public opinion. Judges understand from their civil work the "rational man" of the specific deterrence goal, although the empirical evidence suggests that they put greater confidence in the rationality of white-collar than blue-collar offenders. With advice from their probation staff, experienced criminal judges can make a fair prediction of "dangerousness" for incapacitation. However, the goal of rehabilitation requires a psychological, not a legal, diagnosis, and general deterrence assumes sociological knowledge about the behavioral propensities of subsets of the population. Judges are unlikely to improve their skills in respect to the last four goals, because they receive little feedback about the subsequent behavior of offenders.

The effectiveness of the "just deserts" and general deterrence goals is contingent upon the recognition of a standard offense seriousness scale. But the weighing of offense seriousness is almost as touchy an undertaking as specifying goals. The regression analyses which use a dummy variable for an offense show quite clearly that judges do make crude distinctions between major and minor crimes. But the difficulty is not in separating crimes which involve assaultive behavior from others, but in ordering crimes which involve different amounts of money, different victims, different provocations, and different kinds of social costs. Seriousness is not important for some goals: specific deterrence and incapacitation may require lesser penalties for very serious crimes (murder) than for minor crimes (checkwriting). The "just deserts" goal solves the moral problem of treating minor offenders more harshly than major offenders by punishing for past behavior instead of trying to predict future behavior.

"Just deserts" is the only goal which rests upon the information available at the trial rather than information collected about the offender's life history, family, and prospects. From this perspective it is the goal that allows the intelligent combination of the functions of classification and assignment in the judicial role. Assuming the adoption of a seriousness scale, the goal also allows judges to control disparity. The beauty of "just deserts" is that its anticipated consequence is in the area of moral satisfaction and equity and not of social or individual improvement.

Fairness

Fair sentencing means that judges will only consider legitimate factors. Judges who spend little time on the decision and accept the recommendations of their workgroup may be oblivious to the factors actually entering a sentence choice. Offenders who insist on trial or on jury receive longer sentences; and offenders who are of greater value to society receive lighter sentences. Taking account of the use of due process rights and of class status in sentencing is generally, if not unanimously, approved of by judges. There are few limits on the kinds of information a judge who espouses the rehabilitation goal can consider. The "just deserts" goal sidesteps the problem of legitimate offender and case process factors by concentrating entirely on the nature of the offense. The tests of effectiveness and of fairness for the "just deserts" goal are identical. Establishing the legitimacy of factors for the other goals in order to achieve fairness is much more difficult.

Consistency is the new standard for sentences, diverting attention from the problem of specifying goals. The issue of disparity is not simple; some kind of disparity can be discovered in any set of sentences. The criticism has no meaning apart from a list of all relevant and legitimate factors. If offense seriousness is a factor, then an ordering of offenses must be established before consistency can be evaluated.

To expect isolated and independent judges to distribute a negative resource uniformly without precise standards is irrational. Even personal consistency is difficult when every sentence decision is reached separately. Except for traffic and small misdemeanor courts which occasionally approximate group sentencing, cases with similar charges or defendants appear randomly over time and space. Except for incidents of rioting or protest when similar people commit the same act together, judges on felony courts have little opportunity to think through the implications of a sentence. An alternative approach to the contemporary management of the sentence task is for urban courts to store up the burglary (or rape or fraud) cases for a certain week of the calendar and process them all together. Disparity would become more apparent to court elite and to attentive publics. Judges would have a motive for consultation and could discuss those factors affecting the sentence choice for a specific offense. The irrational impact of "queuing," or using the last case as a baseline for sentence regardless of offense, could be avoided (Green, 1968). The manipulation of the flow of cases by private attorneys for their clients or personal ends would also be impeded. Since courts historically had "terms" devoted to a specific place and/or type of case, such a modification would not be innovative. The arrangement would also draw the attention of the court to crime patterns and to the degree of social harm and expense of particular crimes. This proposal is a compromise between two extreme practices: the complete routinization of sentencing, as in traffic courts, and the complete individualization of sentencing in felony courts. A rationalization of the handling of cases might improve the quality of the sentences.

Major Alternatives

There are three alternatives to the traditional sentencing process:

(1) to emphasize the significance of the assignment of individuals to negatively valenced institutions by investing large public resources in a new independent agency (Nardulli, 1978); (2) to simplify the assignment process by reducing the criteria for selection of a sentence to the minimum and saving the judge's time for other work by allowing staff to compute the sentence and the judge to provide ritual legitimacy (Wilkins and associates, 1978); (3) to consider the incarceration of criminals as punishment and not as assignment for resocialization and therefore to choose sentences entirely on the basis of "seriousness" (von Hirsch, 1976).

The first alternative would involve a major structural innovation and the loss of authority for judges, unless the function were assigned to a specialized court inside the system. This compromise would not provide the separation needed to prevent the exchange of favors among court elite. It is doubtful that officials in a new sentencing unit would have different attitudes and interests than judges; the experience with parole boards, which review sentences remote in time and space from prosecutors and judges, is not encouraging. With a heavy caseload the decision-makers would be seeking "cues" to expedite their work. Moreover, there might be a real danger in turning sentencing into a specialty, since the task carries a heavy psychic burden. Generalists in the long run may bring a more balanced perspective to the assignment choice. The introduction of a new structure would not eliminate the perennial problems of specifying goals, ranking seriousness of offenses, eliminating illegitimate factors, or reducing disparity across jurisdictional lines.

The second alternative concerns the use of guidelines. Here social scientists with LEAA grants are "intervening" to help judges solve their sentence problems, much as social workers intervene to help individuals solve personal problems. Neither intervenor has a scientific foundation for direct advice, but instead helps the responsible individual to work things out by bringing to light what has been done in the past and proposing a plan for future behavior.

The methodological tool for this sentence reform is linear regression, and the guidelines rest upon the best predictor variables uncovered. There are a number of difficulties with this approach. First, sentencing is operationalized as a single decision, instead of two separate steps: "in-out" and how long. Research results (Table 9-3) show quite clearly that judges use different factors for each decisional stage. They weigh offender characteristics heavily in an effort to keep the offender "out" if possible. The significant factors suggest that judges are not concerned at this point with "just deserts" or with general deterrence but with some unarticulated broader goal to avoid coercive assignment if possible. For the length decision the judges rely upon the details of the offense and the case process. Quite clearly judges are not sentencing to achieve rehabilitation but are using goals of retribution, general deterrence, and protection of their own time and resources to distinguish among those who will be incarcerated for longer or shorter periods. Two different guidelines seem absolutely essential to suit the past practices of judges.

The groundwork for future proposals for federal guidelines exists in the analyses of federal sentences discussed in some detail earlier (Sutton, 1978a, b, c). The wisdom and feasibility of insisting upon a uniform, simple formula for sentencing across the diverse cultures covered by federal criminal law need to be thoroughly explored. Sutton (1978c) argues that the national regression model fits the current practices within federal subdivisions, because factors which explain national sentence policy also explain from 50 to 65 percent of district and circuit sentencing (Tables 2, 7). Guidelines formulated from the national model would impose consistency upon the 35 to 50 percent of the cases not explained, ignoring their salient features. The cost of treating disparity as the single critical sentencing issue could be very high.

A final problem with the guidelines solutions is that they rest upon analyses which assume that predictive factors do not interact. Recent sentence research shows plainly that the presence of some factors blocks or accelerates the impact of others (Gibson, 1978b; Nardulli, 1978; Tiffany and associates, 1975). Throughout the section on the political model, the likelihood of the interaction of variables, such as court costs and opportunity costs, was noted. A more realistic model might be generated by dropping the assumption of linearity; the guidelines produced would then lose the characteristic of simplicity which is their chief virtue.

The simplicity of the guidelines is appealing to time-conscious judges and administrators. In fact, the LEAA report gives the task of calculating guidelines to a clerk. The guidelines make consistency possible by providing simple criteria and ignoring other aspects of the case. The simple facts are no more difficult to use than the attributes used for involuntary assignment and certainly could rely upon the capabilities of a clerk. The public, however, probably expects professionals to balance many more criteria in reaching such a significant decision as separating an individual from a role in the community and still to achieve consistency. Otherwise, the assignment function could be transferred permanently to clerks, leaving the delicate matter of classification as a deviant with the judge.

The third alternative—to change the meaning of the sentence from assignment to punishment—is perhaps too easy. Justice has never been the value with highest priority in the culture. The values of freedom and individualism which supported the rehabilitation goals did not die with the faith in prison programs. Although "just deserts" may become the predominant goal, judges are unlikely to follow its requirements rigidly to the exclusion of other human and social interests. A new philosophy of sentencing would provide the stimulus for rethinking old programs and policies; with the introduction of a new myth some small adjustments and innovations, like the calendaring together of similar offenses, may improve the quality of sentencing incrementally. The easy answers to actualizing effective and fair sentencing are deceptive.

NOTE

1. A stepwise, multiple linear regression program measures the independent contributions of each factor to the sentence choice. Such a computer program selects the most powerful variable, controls for its effects, and then enters the best predictor of the remaining variation. The assumptions of this model are that the factors are additive, not interactive, and related linearly to the dependent variable. The model is simple and possibly not the most accurate representation of the relationship.

REFERENCES

Adams, Stuart N. (1977). "The 'Black-Shift' Phenomenon in Criminal Justice." 3 *Justice System Journal*, pp. 185-94.

Administrative Office of the U.S. Courts (1965-1975). *Federal Offenders*. Washington, D.C.: Government Printing Office.

Alabama Law Review Summer Project (1975). "A Study of Differential Treatment Accorded Female Defendants in Alabama Criminal Courts." 27 *Alabama Law Review*.

Alschuler, Albert W. (1978). "Sentencing Reform and Prosecutorial Power: A Critique of Recent Proposals for 'Fixed' and 'Presumptive' Sentencing." 126 *University of Pennsylvania Law Review*, pp. 550-76.

Aranson, Peter H. (1973). "The Optimal Length of Prison Sentences." Paper delivered at American Political Science Association meeting, New Orleans, September 1978.

Arnold, Kenneth James (1973). *California Courts and Judges Handbook*, 2nd Edition. San Francisco: Law Book Service Co.

_____ (1977). Cumulative Supplement.

Beha, James Kenneth Carlson, and Rosenblum, Robert H. (1977). *Sentencing to Community Service*. Washington, D.C.: National Institute of Law Enforcement and Criminal Justice.

Boldt, George H. (1963). "Recent Trends in Criminal Sentencing." 27 *Federal Probation* (March), pp. 3-6.

Burke, Peter, and Turk, Austin (1975). "Factors Affecting Post-Arrest Dispositions." 22 *Social Problems.*

California. *Proceedings of the Sentencing Institutes for Superior Court Judges.* First through Ninth, 1965-1973. 45, 52, 62, 77, 85, 93, 100, 112 Cal Rptr Appendixes.

Carter, Robert, and Wilkins, Leslie (1970). "Some Factors in Sentencing Policy." In *Probation and Parole.* New York: John Wiley.

Casper, Jonathon D. (1978). "Criminal Courts: The Defendant's Perspective." National Institute of Law Enforcement and Criminal Justice.

Castberg, A. Didrick (1971). "The Ethnic Factor in Criminal Sentencing." 24 *Western Political Quarterly* (September), pp. 425-37.

Chiricos, Theodore G., and Waldo, Gordon P. (1975). "Socioeconomic Status and Criminal Sentencing: An Empirical Assessment of a Conflict Proposition." 40 *American Sociological Review.*

Clarke, Stevens A., and Koch, Gary G. (1976). "The Influence of Income and Other Factors on Whether Criminal Defendants Go to Prison." 11 *Law and Society Review* (Fall), pp. 57-92.

Clear, Todd R.; Hewitt, John D.; and Regoli, Robert M. (1978). "Discretion and the Determinate Sentence: Its Distribution, Control, and Effect on Time Served." 24 *Crime and Delinquency* (October), pp. 428-45.

Cook, Beverly B. (1972). "Role Lag in the Trial Courts." 25 *Western Political Quarterly* (June), pp. 234-48.

_____ (1973). "Sentencing Behavior on Federal Judges: Draft Cases—1972." 42 *University of Cincinnati Law Review*, pp. 597-634.

_____ (1977). "Public Opinion and Federal Judicial Policy." 21 *American Journal of Political Science* (August), pp. 567-600.

_____ (1979). "Judicial Policy: Change Over Time." 23 *American Journal of Political Science* (February).

Crites, Laura (1978). "Women in the Criminal Court." Chapter 8 in *Women in the Courts*, Winifred L. Hepperle and Laura Crites, National Center for State Courts.

Dawson, Robert O. (1969). *Sentencing: The Decision as to Type, Length and Conditions of Sentence.* Boston: Little, Brown.

Devitt, Edward J. (1967). "How Can We Effectively Minimize Unjustified Disparity in Federal Criminal Sentences?" Joint Institute on Sentencing, 8th & 10th Circuits, Denver, July 1966. 41 FRD 249.

Diamond, Shari Seidman, and Zeisel, Hans (1975). "Sentencing Councils: A Study of Sentencing Disparity and Its Reduction." 43 *University of Chicago Law Review* (Fall), pp. 109-49.

Downie, Leonard (1972). *Justice Denied.* Baltimore: Penguin.

Doyle, Richard F. (1961). "A Sentencing Council in Operation." 25 *Federal Probation* (September), pp. 27-30.

Eaglin, James, and Partridge, Anthony (1977). "An Evaluation of the Probable Impact of Selected Proposals for Imposing Mandatory Minimum Sentences in the Federal Courts." Federal Judicial Center Research report 77-3.

Eisenstein, James, and Jacob, Herbert (1977). *Felony Justice.* Boston: Little, Brown.

Forst, Brian, and Lucianovic, Judith (1977). "The Prisoner's Dilemma: Theory and Reality." 5 *Journal of Criminal Justice*, pp. 55-64.

Frankel, Marvin (1972). *Criminal Sentences: Law Without Order*. New York: Hill & Wang.

Galanter, Marc; Palen, Frank S.; and Thomas, John M. (1977). "The Crusading Judge: Judicial Activism in Urban Trial Courts." Unpublished paper.

Gaudet, F.J.; Harris, G.S.; and St. John, G.W. (1933). "Individual Differences in the Sentencing Tendencies of Judges." 23 *Journal of Criminal Law and Criminology* (January-February), pp. 811-18.

Gaylin, Willard (1970). *In the Service of Their Country: War Resisters in Prison*. New York: Viking.

Gelman, Arthur M., and Kress, Jack M. (1978). "How Chaotic Is Sentencing in Your Jurisdiction?" 17 *Judges' Journal* (Spring).

Gibson, James L. (1978a). "Race as a Determinant of Criminal Sentences: A Methodological Critique and a Case Study." 12 *Law and Society Review* (Spring), pp. 455-578.

_____ (1978b). "Judges' Role Orientations, Attitudes, and Decisions: An Interactive Model." 72 *American Political Science Review* (September), pp. 911-24.

Glueck, Sheldon (1936). *Crime and Justice*. Boston: Little, Brown.

_____, and Glueck, Eleanor (1940). *Criminal Careers in Retrospect*. New York: The Commonwealth Fund.

Goldstein, Tom (1978). "Closing the Ring around White-Collar Criminals." *New York Times* (January 29).

Goodman, Louis E. (1958). "In Defense of Federal Sentencing." 46 *California Law Review* (October), pp. 497-507.

Gottfredson, Don; Hoffman, Peter B.; Sigler, Maurice H.; and Wilkins, Leslie T. (1975). "Making Paroling Policy Explicit." 21 *Crime and Delinquency* (January).

Green, Edward (1968). "The Effect of Stimulus Arrangements on Normative Judgment in the Award of Penal Sanctions." 31 *Sociometry* (June), pp. 125-37.

Greenwood, Peter (1973). "Prosecution of Adult Felony Defendants in Los Angeles County: A Policy Perspective." Santa Monica, Calif.: Rand Corporation.

Hagan, John (1974). "Extra-Legal Attributes and Criminal Sentencing: An Assessment of Sociological Viewpoint." 8 *Law and Society Review* (Spring), pp. 357-81.

Harries, Keith D., and Brunn, S.D. (1978). *The Geography of Law and Justice: Spatial Perspectives on the Criminal Justice System*. New York: Praeger.

Heumann, Milton (1975). "A Note on Plea Bargaining and Case Pressure." 9 *Law and Society Review*, pp. 515-28.

Hoffman, Walter E. (1968). "A Sentencing Philosophy." 32 *Federal Probation* (December), pp. 3-8.

_____ (1977). "Purposes and Philosophy of Sentencing." Seminar for Newly Appointed U.S. District Judges, 1976, pp. 199-241. St. Paul: West Publishing.

Jaros, Dean, and Mendelsohn, Robert (1967). "The Judicial Role and Sentencing Behavior." 11 *Midwest Journal of Political Science* (November), pp. 471-88.

Johnson, James N. (1972). "Sentencing in the Criminal District Courts." 9 *Houston Law Review* (May), pp. 944-97.

Kaufman, Irving R. (1960). "Sentencing: The Judge's Problem." *Atlantic Monthly* (January).

_____ (1962). "Enlightened Sentences through Improved Techniques." 26 *Federal Probation* (September), pp. 3-10.

Lagoy, Stephen P.; Hussey, Frederick A.; and Kramer, John H. (1978). 24 *Crime and Delinquency* (October), pp. 385-400.

Levin, Martin (1977). *Urban Politics and the Criminal Courts*. Chicago: University of Chicago Press.

Lieberman, Joel B.; Schaffer, S. Andrew; and Martin, John M. (1972). "The Bronx Sentencing Project of the Vera Institute of Justice." Washington, D.C.: LEAA, Department of Justice (October).

Masters, Roger (1978). "Attention Structures and Presidential Campaigns." Paper presented at American Political Science Association, Annual Meeting, New York City, August.

Mileski, Maureen (1972). "Courtroom Encounters: An Observation of a Lower Criminal Court. 5 *Law and Society Review* 473-538.

Morris, Norval (1978). "Conceptual Overview and Commentary on the Movement Toward Determinacy." *Proceedings, Conference on Determinant Sentencing* (March). Washington, D.C.: LEAA, Government Printing Office.

Nardulli, Peter F. (1978). *The Courtroom Elite: An Organizational Perspective on Criminal Justice*. Cambridge, Mass.: Ballinger Publishing Company.

National Conference for State Trial Judges (NCSTJ) (1965). *Proceedings of the Eighth Annual National Conference for State Trial Judges* (August 6-8).

Newman, Donald J. (1966). *Conviction: The Determination of Guilt or Innocence without Trial*. Boston, Mass.: Little, Brown.

Oppenheim, Maurice H. (1976). "Computing a Determinate Sentence . . . New Math Hits the Courts." *California State Bar Journal* (November-December), pp. 604-59.

Orland, Leonard, and Tyler, Harold R., Jr. (1974). *Justice in Sentencing*. Papers and Proceedings of the Sentencing Institute for the First and Second U.S. Judicial Circuits. Mineola, N.Y.: The Foundation Press.

Parker, Graham E. (1965). "The Education of the Sentencing Judge." 14 *International and Comparative Law Quarterly* (January), pp. 206-51.

Partridge, Anthony, and Eldridge, William (1974). *The Second Circuit Sentencing Study: A Report to the Judges of the Second Circuit*. Washington, D.C.: Federal Judicial Center, August.

Partridge, Anthony J. (1977). "The Consequences of Alternative Sentences." Seminars for Newly Appointed U.S. District Judges, September 13-18, 1976, Federal Judicial Center. St. Paul: West Publishing.

Philadelphia Crime Commission (1969). *Proceedings of the Fourth Judicial Sentencing Institute*. June 1968. 46 FRD 497.

Pope, Carl E. (1975). "Sentencing of California Felony Offenders." Utilization of Criminal Justice Statistics Project, Report #6. Washington, D.C.: LEAA, Department of Justice.

Renfrew, Charles B. (1977). "The Paper Label Sentences: An Evaluation." 86 *Yale Law Journal* (March), pp. 590-618.

Robertson, John A., ed. (1975). *Rough Justice*. Boston: Little, Brown.

Rose, Arnold M., and Prell, Arthur E. (1955). "Does the Punishment Fit the Crime?: A Study in Social Valuation." 61 *American Journal of Sociology* (November), pp. 247-59.

Ross, H. Laurence (1976). "The Neutralization of Severe Penalties, Some Traffic Law Studies." 10 *Law and Society Review* (Spring), pp. 403-13.

Scott, Joseph E. (1974). "The Use of Discretion in Determining the Severity of Punishment for Incarcerated Offenders." 65 *Journal of Criminal Law and Criminology*, pp. 2-17.

Sebba, Leslie (1978). "Some Explorations in the Scaling of Penalties." 15 *Journal of Research in Crime and Delinquency* (July), pp. 247-65.

Sheldon, Charles H. (1974). *The American Judicial Process: Models and Approaches*. New York: Dodd, Mead.

Simon, Herbert (1948). *Administrative Behavior*. New York: Macmillan.

Singer, Richard (1978). "In Favor of 'Presumptive Sentences' Set by a Sentencing Commission." 24 *Crime and Delinquency* (October), pp. 401-27.

Smith, Talbolt (1963). "The Sentencing Council and the Problem of Disproportionate Sentences." 27 *Federal Probation* (June), pp. 5-9.

Stanley, David T. (1976). *Prisoners among Us: The Problem of Parole*. Washington, D.C.: Brookings Institution.

Sutton, L. Paul (1978a). "Variations in Federal Criminal Sentences: A Statistical Assessment at the National Level." Utilization of Criminal Justice Statistics Project, Report #17. Washington, D.C.: LEAA, Department of Justice.

——— (1978b). "Federal Sentencing Patterns: A Study of Geographical Variations." Report #18.

——— (1978c). "Predicting Sentences in Federal Courts: The Feasibility of a National Sentencing Policy." Report #19.

Thomsen, Roszel C. (1962). "Sentencing in Income Tax Cases." 26 *Federal Probation* (March), pp. 10-13.

Tiffany, Lawrence P.; Avichai, Yakov; and Peters, Geoffrey W. (1975). "A Statistical Analysis of Sentencing in Federal Courts: Defendants Convicted after Trial, 1967-1968." 4 *Journal of Legal Studies*, pp. 369-80.

Uhlman, Thomas (1978). "Black Elite Decision-Making: The Case of Trial Judges." 22 *American Journal of Political Science* (November), pp. 884-95.

U.S. *Proceedings of the Institute on Sentencing, D.C. Circuit*. November 1968. 54 FRD 285 (1969).

U.S. *Proceedings of the Pilot Institute on Sentencing*. Boulder, Colo. July 1959. 26 FRD 231 (1960).

U.S. *Proceedings of the Seminar and Institute on Disparity of Sentences*. Highland Park, Ill. October 1961. 30 FRD 401 (1962).

Vasoli, Robert (1965). "Growth and Consequences of Judicial Discretion in Sentencing." Reprinted in *The Invisible Justice System*. Burton Atkins and Mark Pogrebin, eds. (1978). Cincinnati: Anderson Publishing Company.

VonHirsch, Andrew (1976). *Doing Justice: The Choice of Punishments*. New York: Hill & Wang.

Wilkins, Leslie; Kress, Jack; Gottfredson, Don; Calpin, Joseph; and Gelman, Arthur (1976). *Sentencing Guidelines: Structuring Judicial Discretion, Final Report of the Feasibility Study*. Washington, D.C.: National Institute of Law Enforcement and Criminal Justice, LEAA (October).

Wilson, James Q. (1975). *Thinking about Crime*. New York: Basic Books.

Yale Project. "Parole Release Decision-making and the Sentencing Process." 84 *Yale Law Journal* (March), pp. 810-902.

Index

About the Authors

Beverly Blair Cook has taught at Iowa State University, California State University-Fullerton, and since 1967 at the University of Wisconsin-Milwaukee. Her research on judicial behavior of federal and state judges has been published in the *American Journal of Political Science; Law & Society Review; American Politics Quarterly; Western Political Quarterly;* and various law reviews. Research support has come from the Social Science Research Council; Ford Foundation Fellowship for Political Science; and most recently from Eagleton-National Center for the Study of Women and Politics for research on the selection and behavior of women judges. During sabbatical year 1979-80 she will give a paper at a roundtable at the University of Essex based on a national survey of women trial judges.

Roy B. Flemming is assistant professor of Political Science at Wayne State University, Detroit, Michigan, and received his Ph.D. (1977) from the University of Michigan. His general interests in organization theory, citizen encounters with bureaucracies, and the allocative and regulatory role of bureaucracies in society have guided his research concerns in the past. His current focus is on urban justice and policing.

James L. Gibson is assistant professor of Political Science at the University of Wisconsin-Milwaukee. His primary research interest is in the politics of decision-making, and his published work has appeared in the *American Political Science Review*, the *Journal of Politics,* and *Law & Society Review*. In addition he is currently conducting research on the conditions of elite commitment to civil liberties, focusing on the American Civil Liberties Union and the rights of American Nazis.

Milton Heumann is associate professor of Political Science at the University of Michigan at Ann Arbor. His principal research interests are in the areas of criminal justice and civil liberties. He is the author of *Plea Bargaining* (University of Chicago Press, 1978), and is currently engaged in a study of the effects of sentencing and plea bargaining reforms in Detroit.

Herbert Jacob is professor of Political Science at Northwestern University. He previously taught at Tulane University and the University of Wisconsin-Madison. His previous publications in the area of criminal justice have included his book with James Eisenstein, *Felony Justice* (1977), and articles in *Social Science Quarterly, Political Science Quarterly,* and *Law & Society Review*. His *Crime & Justice in American Cities* will appear in 1979. He is presently principal investigator of the Governmental Responses to Crime Project, which examines the policy responses of ten major American cities and their suburbs to the problem of crime during the period 1948-1978.

Herbert M. Kritzer is assistant professor of Political Science at the University of Wisconsin-Madison. He is a regular contributor to scholarly journals with publications in the areas of public law, political elites, voting behavior, and research methodology. He is currently working on the Civil Litigation Research Project.

Peter F. Nardulli is assistant professor of Political Science at the University of Illinois. He has contributed to several scholarly journals and is the author of *The Courtroom Elite*. He is currently engaged in research on the delivery of police service. In addition he is currently collaborating on a comparative study of criminal courts in three states.

Austin Sarat is an associate professor of Political Science at Amhert College. He has also been on the faculties of Yale University and Johns Hopkins University. He has published articles in numerous professional journals including the *American Political Science Review, Law & Society Review,* and the *Journal of Politics,* and he is the author of forthcoming books on the rule of law in America and on the implementation of the Safe Streets Act. He is currently working on a manuscript entitled *Thinking about Courts* and is on the senior staff of the Civil Litigation Research Project.

Frances Kahn Zemans is assistant professor of Political Science and Education at the University of Chicago. Currently on leave, she is spending this year as a Visiting Scholar at the American Bar Foundation. Having recently completed a study of the legal profession (*The Making of a Profession: Legal Education and the Professional Development of Lawyers*, coauthored with Victor G. Rosenblum, forthcoming), her current research focuses on citizen participation in the American legal system.